The
Magical Writings
of
Thomas Vaughan

(Eugenius Philalethes)

<u>A VERBATIM REPRINT OF HIS FIRST FOUR TREATISES:</u>

ANTHROPOSOPHIA THEOMAGICA, ANIMA MAGICA ABSCONDITA,

MAGIA ADAMICA, AND THE TRUE CŒLUM TERRÆ

WITH THE LATIN PASSAGES TRANSLATED INTO ENGLISH, AND WITH A BIOGRAPHICAL
PREFACE AND ESSAY ON THE ESOTERIC LITERATURE OF WESTERN CHRISTENDOM BY

ARTHUR EDWARD WAITE

ISBN 1-56459-241-3

Kessinger Publishing Company
Montana, U.S.A.

CONTENTS.

BIOGRAPHICAL PREFACE.

HE long confusion of Eugenius Philalethes—otherwise Thomas Vaughan—with the anonymous cosmopolite adept, Eirenæus Philalethes, who is said to have accomplished the *Magnum Opus* at the age of twenty-two, and to have subsequently wandered over a large portion of the habitable globe, performing astounding transmutations under various names and disguises, has cast so much doubt upon the history and identity of the Welsh initiate, that it will be best to present the reader with certain verbatim citations from the chief authority concerning him, which is the *Athenæ* of Anthony à Wood.

"Thomas Vaughan, who stiles himself in all or most of his writings which he published, Eugenius Philalethes, was the son of Thomas Vaughan of Llansomfreid, but born at Newton, in the parish of S. Bridget, near Brecknock in Brecknockshire, an. 1621, educated in grammar learning under one Matthew Herbert, entred in Jesus Coll. in Mich. term, 1638, and was put under the tuition of a noted tutor; by whose lectures profiting much, he took one degree in arts, was made fellow of the said house, and afterwards taking holy orders from Dr Manwaring, bishop of St. David's, had about that time the rectory of S. Bridget before-mentioned conferred upon him by his kinsman Sir George Vaughan. But the unsetledness of the time hindring him a quiet possession of the place, he left it, retired to Oxon, and in a sedate repose prosecuted his medicinal geny (in a manner natural to him), and at length became eminent in the chymical part thereof at Oxon, and afterwards at London under the protection and patronage of that noted chymist, Sir Rob. Murrey or Moray, knight, secretary of state for the kingdom of Scotland. . . . He was a great chymist, a noted son of the fire, an experimental philosopher, a zealous brother of the Rosie-

Crucian fraternity,* an understander of some of the Oriental lan-
guages, and a tolerable good English and Latin poet. He was neither
papist nor sectary, but a true, resolute protestant in the best sense of
the Church of England. . . . He did accompany Sir Rob. Murrey
before-mentioned to Oxon, at what time the great plague at London
drove their majesties and their respective courts to that place, where
he continued for a time. Soon after taking up his quarters in the
house of Sam Kem, rector of Albury, near to Thame and Ricot in
Oxfordshire, [he] died there as it were suddenly, when he was
operating strong mercury, some of which by chance getting up into
his nose, killed him,† on the 27th of Feb. in sixteen hundred sixty
and five, and was buried on the first of March following in the
church belonging to the said village of Albury alias Oldbury (about
8 miles distant from Oxon), by the care and charge of the said Sir
Robert Murrey."‡

The history of Brecknockshire, written by Theophilus Jones in
the year 1809, speaks of a farm-house at Newton which was once of
some celebrity, being "occupied by two brothers of the name of
Vaughan, of very eccentric characters," but for the facts in the life
of Eugenius, this work is mainly indebted to Wood. It enumerates,
however, the alleged reasons for the expulsion of Thomas Vaughan
from his ecclesiastical position. "He was ousted by the propa-
gators of the gospel in Wales, for drunkenness, swearing, incontin-
ency, and carrying arms for the king."§

This information, together with a few scraps which may be gleaned
from Elias Ashmole, has been the sum total of our knowledge concerning the Welsh Royalist, who is now counted among the first of
British mystics and Hermetic adepts. After much research, I am
fortunately able to supplement it from an unexpected quarter. I
have discovered a genuine autograph manuscript, which bears on its
fly leaf the inscription, " *Ex Libris Thomas et Rebecca Vaughan,*
1651, Sept. 28. *Quos Deus conjunxit quis separabit?*" It is entitled
"Aqua Vitæ non Vitis, or the Radical Humiditie of Nature
Mechanically and Magically Dissected by the conduct of Fire

---

* This statement is twice expressly contradicted by Vaughan himself, who says
in his Preface to the "Fame and Confession of the Fraternity of R. C.": "As
for that Fraternity, whose History and Confession I have here adventured to
publish, I have, for my own part, no relation to them, neither do I much desire
their acquaintance." And again, "I have no acquaintance with this Fraternity
as to their persons."
† So Mr Harris of Jesus Coll. Wood, MS. note in Ashmole.
‡ *Athenæ Oxoniens.*, Ed. Philip Bliss, 4to, 1817, iii. 722.
§ "History of the County of Brecknock," ii. pt. ii. p. 540.

and Ferment;" but it is not a consecutive treatise. It is an occasional diary, and a note book of personal experiments in several classes of mystic physics. The diurnal memoranda are in English, and the thaumaturgic recipes in Latin somewhat hard to understand. The latter, being sufficiently numerous to form a small volume, and presenting many obvious difficulties of interpretation, are necessarily withheld for the present, but the fragmentary memorials are sufficiently curious to demand their entire transcription, and I shall give them as far as possible in their chronological order, without any further preface. The manuscript is ostensibly written on one side of the paper only, but the reverse pages are covered with notes, additions, and with the memoranda which I am about to reproduce.

MEMORIÆ SACRUM.

On the same day my dear wife sickened, being a Friday, and at the same time of the day, namely in the evening, my gracious God did put into my heart the Secret of extracting the oyle of Halcali, which I had once accidentally found att the Pinner of Wakefield, in the dayes of my most deare wife. But it was again taken from mee by a most wonderfull judgment of God, for I could never remember how I did it, but made a hundred attempts in vain. And now my glorious God (whose name bee praysed for ever) hath brought it again into my mind, and on the same day my dear wife sickened; and on the Saturday following, which was the day shee dyed on, I extracted it by the former practice: soe that on the same dayes, which proved the most sorrowfull to mee, whatever can bee: God was pleased to conferre upon mee ye greatest joy I can ever have in this world, after her death.

The Lord giveth, and the Lord taketh away: blessed bee the name of the Lord. Amen! T. R. V.

N. B.—N. B.—N. B.

When my dear wife and I lived at the Pinner of Wakefield, I remember I melted doune æquall parts of Talc, and ye Eagle, with Brimstone, repeating the fusion twice. And after that, going to draw Spirit of Salt with Oyle of Glass, I chanced (as I think) to mingle some Bay-Salt, or that of Colla Maris, with the former Composition, and I had an oyle with which I did miracles. But assaying to make more of it, I never could effect it, having forgott the Composition; but now I am confident the Eagle was in it, for I ever remember the manner of the first fume that came out, and could never see the like againe, but when I worked on ye Eagle, though I never afterwards worked on her præpared as at that time. I know allso by experience, that Talc and Baysalt together will yeeld 6 times more spirit, than either of both will yield by it self. And that passage of Rhasis confirms mee, when hee mentions Aqua Salis trium generum: but above all that one word of Lullie, namely, Petra Salis, and especially that enumeration of materials, which hee makes in his *Ars Intellectiva*, Nitrum, Sal, Sulphur, vapor, then which nothing could have been sayd more expressly. And yet I doubt I shall bee much troubled, before I finde what I have lost, soe little difference there is between Forgetfulness and Ignorance.   T. R. V. 1658.

Quos Deus conjunxit quis separabit?

1658.

[This happened on a Sunday night, towards the Day-break, and indeed I think, it was morning light.]

On the 13th of June I dreamed that one appeared to mee, and purged herself from the scandalous contents of certaine letters, which were put into my hands by a certaine false friend. Then shee told mee, that her father had informed her, that shee should dye againe about a Quarter of a yeare from that time shee appeared to mee: which is just the 14th of September next, and on the 28th of the same month wee were married. It may bee, my mercifull God hath given mee this notice of the Time of my dissolution by one that is soe deare unto mee, whose person representing mine, signified my death, not hers, for shee can dye no more. Great is the love and goodness of my God, and most happy shall I bee in this Interpretation, if I may meete her againe so soone, and begin the Heavenly and Æternall life with her, in the very same month, wherein wee began the earthly: which I beseech my good God to grant us for his Deare Son, and our Saviour's sake, Christ Jesus. Amen!

[Written on the 14th of June, the day after I dreamed it. 1658.]

N.B.—N.B.—N.B. 1658.

On Friday the 18th of July, I myself sickened at Wapping, and that night I dream'd, I was pursued by a stone horse, as my dear wife dream'd before shee sickened, and I was grievously troubled all night with a suffocation at the heart, which continued all next day most violently, and still it remaines, but with some little remission. On the Saturday following being the 17th of July, I could not, for some secret instinct of spirit, stay any longer at Wapping, but came that very night to Sir John Underhill, and the Sunday following after that night, I understood that Mr Highgate was dead, as my heart gave mee at Wapping, a few dayes before. The will of my God bee done : Amen and Amen !

That night I came to Sir John, I dream'd, I had lent 20 pounds to my cousin J. Wakebross, and that his mother had stole the money, and I was like to loose it. But my cousin advised mee to give out I had received it, and hee would secure it for mee. I pray God, my dear wife's things do not miscarrie !

My most deare wife sickened on Friday in the Evening, being the 16th of April, and dyed the Saturday following in the Evening, being the 17. And was buried on ye 26th of the same month, being a Monday in the afternoone, at Mappersall in Bedfordshire. 1658. Wee were married in the yeare 1651, by a minister whose name I have forgott, on ye 28 of September.

God of his infinite, and sure mercies in Christ Jesus, bring us together againe in Heaven, whither shee is gone before mee, and with her my heart, and my faith not to bee broken, and this thou knowest, oh my God ! Amen !

Left at Mrs Highgate's.

1. One flatt Trunk of my deare wife's, with her mayden name upon it.

2. Another Cabinet Trunk of my deare wife's, in which is her small rock and Bible, and her mayden Bible I have by mee.

3. One grate wodden Box of my deare wife's, in which is all her best Apparell, and in that is her grate Bible, with her practice of pietie, and her other Bookes of Devotion.

4. Another wooden Box with pillowes in it, and a sweet Basket of my deare wife's.

5. One large Trunk of my deare wife's, with my name upon it, in which are the silver spoons. And in the Drawers are two small Boxes, one with a lock of my deare wife's hayre, made up with her own Hands ; and another with severall small Locks in it.

6. One pare of grate Irons with Brass-Knobs, and a single pare with Brass-Knobs, a fire-shovell, Tongs, and Bellowes: my deare wife's little chaire, a round Table, Joynt stoole, and Close stoole, with

a great glass full of eye-water, made at the Pinner of Wakefield, by my deare wife, and my sister Vaughan, who are both now with God.

To the end we might live well, and exercise our charitie, which was wanting in neither of us, to our power: I employed my self all her life time in the Acquisition of some naturall secrets, to which I had been disposed from my youth up: and what I now write, and know of them practically, I attained to in her Dayes, not before in very truth, nor after: but during the time wee lived together at the Pinner of Wakefield, and though I brought them not to perfection in those deare Dayes, yet were the Gates opened to mee then, and what I have done since, is but the effect of those principles. I found them not by my owne witt, or labour, but by God's blessing, and the Incouragement I received from a most loving, obedient wife, whom I beseech God to reward in Heaven, for all the Happiness and Content shee afforded mee. I shall lay them down here in their order, protesting earnestly, and with a good Conscience, that they are the very truth, and here I leave them for his use and Benefit, to whom God in his providence shall direct them.

On the 28th of August, being Saturday morning, after daylight, God Almightie was pleased to reveale unto mee, after a wonderful manner, the most blessed estate of my deare wife, partly by her self, and partly by his own Holy Spirit, in an express disclosure, which opened unto mee the meaning of those mysterious words of S. Paul: "For wee know, that if our Earthly house of this Tabernacle, &c."

Bless the Lord, O my soul! and all that is within mee, bless his holy name!   T. R. V.

Quos Deus conjunxit, quis separabit?

1658.

The Dreame I writt on the foregoing page, is not to bee neglected: for my deare wife a few nights before, appeared to mee in my Sleepe, and foretold mee the Death of my deare Father, and since it is really come to passe, for hee is dead, and gone to my mercifull God, as I have been informed by letters come to my hand from the countrey. It concerns mee therefore to præpare my self, and to make a right use of this warning, which I received from my mercifull and most loving God, who useth not to deale such mercies to all men: and who was pleased to impart it to mee by my deare wife, to assure mee shee was a Saint in his Holy Heavens, being thus imployed for an Angell, and a messenger of the God of my salvation. To him, bee all prayse and glorie ascribed in Jesus Christ for ever! Amen!
                                                          T. R. V.

1658.

The month and the day I have forgott: but having prayed earnestly for Remission of sinns, I went to bed: and dreamed, that I lay full of sores in my feet, and cloathed in certaine Rags, under the shelter of the great Oake, which growes before the Court-yard of my father's house, and it rain'd round about mee. My feet that were sore with Boyles, and corrupt matter, troubled mee extremely, soe that being not able to stand up, I was layd all along. I dreamed that my father and my brother W. who were both dead, came unto mee, and my father sucked the corruption out of my feete, soe that I was presently well, and stood up with great Joy, and looking on my feete, they appeared very white and cleane, and the sores were quite gone!

Blessed be my good God! Amen!

1659. *April 8th. Die ♀*

In the evening I was surprised with a suddaine Heaviness of spirit, but without any manifest cause whatsoever: but, I thank God, a great tenderness of Heart came along with it: soe that I prayed most earnestly with abundance of teares, and sorrow for Sinn. I fervently sollicited my gratious God for pardon to my self and my most deare wife: and besought Him to bring us together againe in his Heavenly Kingdom, and that hee would shew mee his mercie, and answer my prayers by such means, and in such a way as might quicken my spirit, that I might serve him cheerfully, and with Joy prayse his name.

I went that night to bed after earnest prayers, and teares, and towards the Day-Breake, or just upon it, I had this following dreame. I thought, that I was againe newly married to my deare wife, and brought her along with mee to shew her to some of my friends, which I did in these words. Heere is a wife, which I have not chosen of my self, *but my father did choose her for mee,** and asked mee if I would not marry her, for shee was a beautifull wife. Hee had no sooner shewed her to mee, but I was extremely in love with her, and I married her presently. When I had thus sayd, I thought, wee were both left alone, and calling her to me, I tooke her into my Armes, and shee presently embraced mee, and kissed mee: nor had I

* This was not true of our temporall marriage, nor of our naturall parents, and therefore it signifies some greater mercie.

in all this vision any sinnfull desyre, but such a Love to her, as I
had to her very soule in my prayers, to which this Dreame was an
Answer. Hereupon I awaked presently, with exceeding great inward Joy. Blessed be my God! Amen!

April the 9th. Die ♄. 1659.

I went to Bed after prayers and hearty teares, and had this Dreame
towards Day-Breake. I dreamed I was in some obscure, large House,
where there was a tumultuous, rageing people, amongst whom I knew
not any but my brother H. My deare wife was there with mee, but
having conceived some discomfort at their disorder, I quitted the
place, and went out leaving my deare wife behind mee. As I went
out, I consydered with my self, and called to mind some small, at
least seeming, unkindnesses I had used towards my deare wife in her
life-time, and the remembrance of them being odious to mee, I
wondred with my self, that I should leave her behind mee and
neglect her companie, having now the opportunitie to converse with
her after death. These were my Thoughts, whereupon I turned in,
and taking her along with mee, there followed us a certaine person,
with whom I had in former times revelled away many yeares in drinking. I had in my hand a very long cane, and at last wee came to
a churchyard, and it was the Brightest Day-light, that ever I
beheld: when wee were about the middle of the churchyard,
I struck upon the ground with my cane at the full length,
and it gave a most shrill reverberating eccho. I turned back to
look upon my wife, and shee appeared to mee in green silk downe
to the ground, and much taller, and slenderer then shee was in her
life-time, but in her face there was so much glorie, and beautie, that
noe Angell in Heaven can have more. Shee told mee the noyse of
the cane had frighted her a little, but saying soe, shee smiled upon
mee and looked most divinely. Upon this I looked up to Heaven,
and having quite forgot my first Apprehension, which was true,
namely that she appeared thus to me after her Death, I was much
troubled in mind lest I should dye before her, and this I feared
upon a spirituall Accompt, least after my death shee might bee
tempted to doe amiss, and to live otherwise than shee did at present.
While I was thus troubled, the cane that was in my hand suddainly
broke, and when it was broken, it appeared noe more like a cane,
but was a brittle, weake reede. This did put mee in mind of her
death againe, and soe did put mee out of my feare, and the Doubts
I conceived, if I dyed before her. When the Reede was broken,

shee came close to mee, and I gave her the longer half of the reed, and the furthest end, and the shortest I kept for my self: but looking on the broken end of it, and finding it ragged, and something rough, shee gave mee a knife to polish it which I did. Then wee passed both out of the churchyard, and turning to the gentleman that followed mee, I asked him, if hee would goe along with us, but hee utterly refused, and the truth is, hee still followes the world too much. Then I turned to my deare wife, to goe along with her, and having soe done, I awaked.

By this dreame, and the shortest part of the Reed left in my hand, I guess, I shall not live soe long after her, as I have lived with her. Praysed bee my God! Amen!

April the 16th, at night. 1659.

I dreamed that a flame of a whitish colour should breake out at the toes of my left foot, and this was told mee in my dreame by a strange person, and of a dark countenance. It is to bee noted, that this was the very night, on which my deare wife died, 1658: it being a Saturday night, and but one short of the number, or true Accompt. It may bee the disease that shall occasion my death, was shewed mee on the night wherein shee dyed, for true it is, that in my left foote there is now a dangerous humor fallen down, and lodgeth under my very heel, and upon the lifting of my leg upward, it paineth mee strangely. It fell first into my knee, and what it may come to, I know not, unless it will end in a gout: but it first of all troubled mee in the sinews, and caused a contracture of them, and then I had a dull paine, and still have in the uppermost joynt of the Thigh. T. R. V.

Many years ago, at Paddington, before my distemper in the Liver seized mee, there appeared to mee twice in the same night in two severall dreames, a young, strange person, not unlike to him, who appeared in a strange manner to mee at Edmond Hall in Oxford. His countenance was dark, and I believe it is the Evill Genius, but in this last dreame, I saw him not soe clearly, my life, I bless God for it, being much amended. The evill hee soe gladly signifies to mee, frights mee not, for I am ready for Death, and with all my heart shall I wellcome it, for I desyre to bee dissolved, and to bee with Christ, which is farr better for mee, than to live, and sinn in this sinnfull Body. T. R. V. 1659.

God is. T. R. V. Amen and Amen!

These private memoranda constitute a touching testimony to the tenderness and humanity of their writer, and, as a mystic, are conclusive proof of his sincerity. They establish the fact of his marriage with a lady whose genealogy is unknown; they bear evidence of his profound religious conviction and of the intensity of his devotional fervour; they, moreover, enable us to reconcile the manner of his death, as related by Ashmole and Wood, with the declamations contained in his books against the merely physical side of alchemy. We are no longer perplexed by inquiring how an adept in the spiritual side of the *Magnum Opus* came to meet his death through an experiment in common chemistry. He confesses in these memoranda that he had recourse to the inferior science with the hope of increasing his means in order to extend his charities, and he claims the success which appears to have been deserved by his motives from the standpoint of poetical justice. It is improbable that future researches will elicit further facts in the life of this interesting mystic, but I think I am right in affirming that the fragments which I have fortunately recovered bring us nearer to the man than any writings of the professed magician, and that our estimation of his character must increase in proportion to the proximity of our view.

I need only add that in this edition of some of his most celebrated treatises a number of long Latin extracts have been translated into English, and that in so doing I have followed his own method when he has given an English version of his recondite citations—that is to say, I have attempted, where necessary, an illustrative and interpretative translation, to elucidate as much as possible the ambiguous meaning of ultra-mystic writers.

INTRODUCTORY ESSAY

ON THE ESOTERIC LITERATURE OF THE MIDDLE AGES, AND ON THE
UNDERLYING PRINCIPLES OF THEURGIC ART AND
PRACTICE IN WESTERN CHRISTENDOM.

THE magical writings of Thomas Vaughan constitute an explanatory prolegomena not only to the general history of practical transcendentalism, and to the philosophy of transcendental art, from the standpoint of a Christian initiate, but they are specially directed to the interpretation of alchemical symbolism; they claim to provide the intelligent reader with a substantially fresh revelation of that mysterious First Matter of the *Magnum Opus* which endows those who know it, and can avail themselves of its manifold potencies, with a full and perfect power for the successful conduct of all classes of theurgic experiment. Adopting the terminology of Hermetic adepts, Thomas Vaughan enlarges the theoretical scope of alchemical processes, and delineates the spiritual evolution of humanity, completely and scornfully rejecting the merely mineral work, and claiming for the true hierophants of mystic science a personal interest and participation in the whole creative *opus*. In offering for the first time to the modern student of ancient mysteries a reprint of these curious and really important treatises, it seems needful to attempt a plain statement of the reasons which have led to their reproduction, and of the exact nature of the interest which now attaches to them. The vast literature of ancient occultism has till recently possessed little but an archæological interest, of a naturally relative kind, as the remains of discredited high thinking in past ages, and a certain bibliographical value, on account of the extreme rarity of all esoteric works. This interest and this value would be an insufficient warrant for their revival in an era of positive science

b

or in the absence of any message of vital import to this veridic age, and, therefore, on philosophical, as well as practical and, I may add, commercial grounds, they would have remained archæological monuments and book-lovers' treasures alone. But the sudden revival of psychic research amongst us, and certain discoveries made in the psychic world, of which many are now well known, and others remain *in abscondito*, have placed the position of old mystics in an utterly different light, and have created a presumptive probability that prior claimants have also a right to be heard, and that the conductors of early psychic experiments in ages of single purpose may have advanced beyond ourselves, and may be qualified for our teachers and guides. Here are the broad *à priori* grounds for the revived interest in the entire circle of esoteric literature. But when the whole faculty of an impartial and sympathetic mind, cognisant already of those ascertained facts to which I have just alluded, is brought to the adequate study of "the philosophers," as they were collectively termed, this general interest is speedily merged in a far more absorbing feeling, for we find ourselves in the presence of a titanic claim, advanced in a number of cases by intellectual giants and joined to a height of aspiration, a wealth of spiritual suggestiveness, a cosmic breadth of view, and a degree of apparent personal sanctity, which are sufficient to profoundly impress the most unemotional minds, while vistas of vast possibilities unveil to the prepared imagination at the magic word of the hierophants. Here are the more particular grounds for the new interest in ancient esoteric literature, and here once more the accepted facts of modern psychology are presumptive evidence for the truth of these claims, and evidence, moreover, which is, in my opinion, sufficiently strong not only to warrant their exhaustive and practical investigation on the lines of the mystics, but to make investigation imperative with those who, like myself, are unconditionally devoted to the progress of psychic science. To place within the reach of like-minded students the works of an acknowledged adept, which are otherwise almost *introuvable*, and thereby to set new sympathetic investigators on the track of the grand mysteries, is the *raison d'être* of this reprint. It is due to the work of the modern theosophists to state that they were substantially the first to draw attention to the connecting link between the psychic phenomena of to-day and the ancient thaumaturgy, and the second spring of magic and of magian thought in England is directly owing to their influence.

Having paid this just tribute, it becomes necessary to explain the nature of the psychic facts to which I have several times alluded, as much to prevent misconception as for the use of inquirers at the early stages of their progress.

. The ascertained facts which I consider, in common with numerous qualified persons, to be presumptive evidence for the truth of the magical claim, taken broadly in its totality, are quite independent of any mystical theory, are not confined to any special circle of esoteric students, and are wholly unconnected with the results which may or may not have been attained by such colleges of oriental adepts as theosophists proclaim to exist among the politically unapproachable fastnesses of the Thibetan highlands. I speak with all deference of an opinion which is held by several intellectual persons, and with due appreciation of such evidence as exists on the subject; I am personally quite uncommitted to any opinion in the matter, except on the *à priori* ground of magical possibility. The psychic facts in question may be verified by any intelligent person who is possessed of sufficient perseverance, and is capable of appreciating the issues which are at stake in such a manner as to conduct his researches with a view to those issues. They are concerned with the higher classes of hypnotic phenomena, with ecstatic and trance clairvoyance, with thought-transference, the transcorporeal action of mind upon matter, and with such phenomena of modern spiritualism as unbiassed inquirers agree to be well substantiated. These facts offer a rational basis for the belief in another form of subsistence than that of the physical life of man on earth, and naturally terminate the age of spiritual faith in the first auroral light of an age of spiritual knowledge, revealing for the first time, openly and to all mankind, that it is possible, even in earthly life, to enter into another form of perception and to establish communication with planes of intelligent existence which are normally beyond our range.

This communication at present is exceedingly hampered, and the progress, which has at best been slow, seems at the present moment to be almost completely arrested, partly owing to the insincerity of experiment, which is attempted on the lowest planes of physical subsistence, with coarse, degraded, and sometimes diseased instruments, yet is concerned with the spiritual altitudes, while the ignorance of a proper method of procedure—the "true process" of alchemical allegory—creates another and apparently insurmountable barrier. In this difficulty, the earnest student who turns for illumination to the sanctuaries of ancient mystic wisdom and for counsel to its grand hierophants, finds himself face to face with the departed but still eloquent representatives of a sacerdotal and royal science which claims to be exclusively acquainted with the One Way of Rectitude

and the Unerring Path of Light. He discovers that the prodigies of
the elder world are substantially identical with those modern phenomena with which he is already familiar, of whose actuality he is con-
vinced, and which have prompted him in his further quest. The
hypnotic trance, as we know it to-day, is clearly and frequently
alluded to in ancient writings; modern clairvoyance is paralleled by
the magical "vision at a distance;" for thought-transference, we
have mystical methods of communication with persons however
remote and in the absence of any material means; while an exact
fundamental correspondence may be easily established between many
marvels of American Spiritualism and the ghostly mysteries of necromantic and magical evocation. But whereas our modern phenomena have all the characteristics of a merely initial experience, the
thaumaturgic results obtained by the initiates of old are of another
and loftier order, the fruit of matured methods and of a long
sequence of experimental investigations. There is no doubt or
hesitation in the teachings or claims of the hierophants; they are ever
positive, unflinching, and practically unanimous, and they write under
the shadow of a vast and unlimited subject, embracing the depths and
the heights, and fortified by the sublime consciousness of eternity.

As at present conducted, our modern experiments are devoid of
practical results; the lines of investigation reach a certain point and
there leave us, but the old pioneers of mysticism would appear to
have discovered some hitherto inscrutable means of passing the
barriers which confront us, and in so doing they tell us that they
have come into the possession of a tremendous secret, which they
declare to be of a divine character, and which they dare not publicly
reveal, for incalculable penalties attach to the profanation of the
Grand Mysteries. In their books they protected their knowledge
from the vulgar by means of allegorical language and the use of
symbols, leaving their veritable meaning to be divined by the sincere
student with the help of an insight imparted from the spiritual world.
They also perpetuated their secrets by the initiation of tested
disciples of undoubted discretion, to whom they seem to have
liberally laid open the precious treasures of their knowledge, and in
this manner some of the secret colleges of magic, once apparently
numerous, came to be formed in the West.

Thus, the study of the mystics presents us with obvious difficulties which at the beginning appear insurmountable, but, speaking
from personal experience, I do not hesitate to say that there is no
ground for discouragement in a pure, patient, and active intelligence,
for the elementary phenomena are identical, and thus the modern

psychologist is already in possession of the outer doors of the sanctuary; but he must carefully bear in mind that a large proportion of Hermetic literature is concerned with a physical process for the conversion of "base metals" into gold, and that it is equally vicious and fruitless to force upon merely alchemical writings a psychic meaning which is completely at variance with the lives and undoubted aims of their authors. The literature of esoteric psychology in the past is large enough without the wholesale annexation which has been rashly, though not inexcusably, attempted by several critics.

The theurgic and mystical literature of Western Christendom, with which I am exclusively concerned in the present essay, is only a branch of universal occultism, but it admits of classification into several distinct divisions, all requiring consideration which will be much simplified by a brief preliminary reference to the history of Christian magic, or rather of magic as it was practised in the Christian countries of Europe.

The philosophical principles which underlie the theory and practice of theurgic art are mainly derived from the Platonic School of Alexandria—the school of Ammonius Saccas, Proclus, and Hypatia, the school of Synesius, the theosophical dream-interpreter, and of the angelical mysticism of pseudo-Dionysius. The neo-platonists were practically the inheritors of the Magian wisdom of Egypt, Greece, and Rome, and the mystical works of Hermes Trismegistus, which were the product of this period of Alexandrian illumination, were no mere inventions of a semi-Christianized sage, but probably embodied the traditional secrets and cosmic theories of a very considerable antiquity. The central doctrine of the high theurgic faith, professed by the grand masters of Alexandrian philosophy, was that by means of certain invocations, performed solemnly by chaste, sober, abstinent, and mentally illuminated men, it was possible to come into direct communication with those invisible powers which fill the measureless distance between man and God. A divine exaltation accompanied this communication with the superior intelligences of the universe, and man entered into a temporal participation of deific qualities, while the power and wisdom thus acquired submitted many hierarchies of spiritual beings to the will of the Magus.

The proscription of the old pagan cultus and the bitter and continual persecution of all professors of secret and magical arts, which took place in the reign of the infamous emperor Constantine, and was continued by Valentinian, Theodosius, and other shining lights of imperial Christianity, did not eradicate polytheism or destroy the adepts. The old religion and the old theurgic art took refuge in remote places; they were practised in stealth and in silence, and thus were presumably originated many of those mysterious secret societies which perpetuated the traditions of the Magi through the whole period of the Middle Ages, and in numerous magical rituals betray their connection with neo-platonism.

The proscription of magic and paganism was eventually followed by the proscription and persecution of the Jews, who, in like manner, were reduced to practise their religious rites in secret, and whose oriental vindictiveness was frequently roused to frenzy by their intolerable sufferings and humiliations. Professors of Kabbalistic arts, firm believers in the virtues of invocations and verbal formulæ, and addicted from time immemorial to every species of superstitious practice, they directed their mystic machinery to do injury to their enemies, and the infernal magic of the Middle Ages, with its profanation of Christian mysteries, its black masses and impious invocations, is, in part at least, their creation.

Thus, mediæval occultism was essentially of a composite character. It borrowed, on the one hand, from the rabbinical wisdom of Israel, and, on the other, from pagan sources. The crusades made it subject to Arabic influence, which was definitely increased by the spread of alchemical notions from east to west, while from the debris of every vanished cultus which in barbaric times had ever flourished among the Teutonic and Celtic nations was built up the mythology of nature-spirits, the elfin world, and the strange doctrines concerning elementary intelligences.

Over this many-coloured garment was invariably spread the sacerdotal cope of Christianity, which may have been adopted at first as a disguise, but which in the majority of cases came eventually to be beyond suspicion the official religious belief of most European adepts. The voice of esoteric literature is positively unanimous on this point. Whatever the secret teachings which entered into the traditional science of the Magi, they were not of a nature to interfere with the sincere profession of Christianity among their later initiates, or they were modified into harmony with orthodox Christian teaching. Admitting the claims of magic, it is indeed probable that the secret knowledge which was perpetuated was concerned more with esoteric power than with esoteric doctrine—a view which is wholly consistent with the universal history of magic, for in all ages and nations we find the same claims to the same preternatural powers advanced in the interests of the most various systems of religion.

The magical literature of Europe abounds in potent formulæ for the evocation and control of all classes of spiritual beings, and these to a large extent are directly taken from the hierarchic liturgies of Christendom, the miraculous powers inherent in the names of Jehovah, Jesus, Mary, and similar sacred names, are explained in the rituals, and the numerical mysticism of Pythagoras is interpreted in the interests of Trinitarian doctrine.

There is therefore no ground for supposing that western initiates had discovered a " religion behind all religions "; they were simply Christian mystics who never dreamed of looking further than Christianity for light, and what they pretend to have possessed was the key of miracles and not the key of religious symbolism. The professors of goetic magic and the infamous frequenters of the Sabbath may have denied and rejected Christ, but they did not deny his power, and if they served another master it was in search of an immediate recompense, and with a full consciousness of the penalties that they incurred.

The amount of misunderstanding which exists on this point among even sympathetic inquirers calls for a positive statement to check the general tendency to read into the writings of Christian adepts a significance that utterly eliminates all the positive elements of their faith, which generally was held in sincerity, and too often in the midst of persecution at the hands of their fellow-believers.

The sincere profession of Christianity by mediæval and later adepts is, on a cursory view, unfavourable to the gigantic claim of magian art and science, for, at least in its exoteric presentment, I recognize, in common with the general concensus of modern mystical thinking, that the Christian scheme does not provide us with an intelligible theory of the universe, and we might reasonably expect that illuminated persons, who "enjoy free perspicuity of thought in universal consciousness," would have entered into possession of a more adequate cosmogonical doctrine.

As one who is a partisan of no special opinion, and as one who deplores the extreme intellectual folly of making haste towards unstable and futile convictions on the most important problems by help of premature theories, I have no wish to minimise the importance of difficulties like this, but it is equally easy to overstate their value. Our modern discoveries in psychology have hitherto assisted us towards no definite theory of the universe, and it is impossible in their present condition that they should ever provide us with such. Their possibly indefinite development in the hands of the ancient mystics may have equally failed to enlighten them, for the power of working wonders within the domain of natural law and the exaltation of the intuitive faculties so as to enlarge the sphere of perception within the Cosmos may not place the observer in such a position as to make successful philosophic generalisations. On the other hand, if the Great Secret which is declared to be possessed by the Magi involves a veritably universal science, if it takes the observer without the domain of natural law, he is possibly wrapt beyond the domain of thêory, and the temporary enjoyment of a transcendent and deific form of subsistence eliminates for the time from the mind all consciousness of the common forms of thought and normal intellectual limitation.

There are three broad divisions of mediæval esoteric knowledge. The first is described as Natural Magic, the second as Spiritual or Transcendental Magic, and the third, under the comprehensive title of Alchemy, embraces a philosophy and a physical practice which are of the first and consummate importance to the modern student. The philosophy of the whole subject is embodied in two priceless collections, the so-called works of Hermes Trismegistus and the Jewish Kabbalah, which to all intents and purposes is contained in the Baron de Rosenroth's *Kabbala Denudata*, a part of which has been recently translated into English. The expositions of these philosophical text-books are numerous, and they vary considerably in value. There is much interesting and important matter to be found in Cornelius Agrippa's "Three Books of Occult Philosophy," albeit this author, so exalted by Thomas Vaughan, is not included among adepts of the loftiest order.[1] The Hermetic and Kabbalistic writings are both in great part devoted to the mystical history of creation, to which the evolution of humanity is considered rigorously parallel, in virtue of the magical doctrine of correspondence, and thus an esoteric significance is attributed to those portions which deal with the development of the material cosmos out of the chaotic storm of elementary forces.

The Kabbalistic books, in addition to this, treat largely of pneumatology, of the hierarchy and classification of spirits, the circular progression of the soul, its nature, origin, and destiny, the divine progress of

---

[1] "Cornelius Agrippa, who was a seeker all his life, and who attained neither knowledge nor peace, belongs to another category. His books abound in erudition and audacity; his personal character was fantastic and independent, which obtained him the reputation of an abominable sorcerer and the persecution of priests and princes; he subsequently wrote in condemnation of studies from which he had derived no happiness, and he perished in desolation and misery."— Eliphas Lévi, *Histoire de la Magie*, pp. 346, 347.

the Royal Intellectual Essence from star to star and from sun to sun through the endless chain of existence, and of the highest problems of transcendental psychology. Their philosophical interest at the present stage of exoteric spiritual investigation is scarcely diminished by the uncertainty of their origin, and the occasionally fraudulent manner in which individual treatises have been given to the world, for they undoubtedly embody an antique tradition, and are wholly in harmony with the sombre sublimity of Jewish genius.

An important division of the Kabbalah is devoted to practical magic, and may be described as at once the source and synthesis of all the existing rituals from the days of the Enchyridion, not excepting those of the Black Art, which are simply infernal perversions of normal and lawful magic.

The nature, processes, and results of Natural Magic have been variously described by its professors, and its scope is frequently extended till it includes a large proportion of the spiritual or transcendental branch, as, for instance, the prediction of future events which are beyond the calculus of probabilities, and therefore can only be ascertained by the ecstatic transference of the intellectual faculties into another form of subsistence. It is properly the manifestation of the arcana of physical nature by means of art. In more common and definite terms, it is the production of apparently thaumaturgic effects by means of physical laws which are not generally known, and it has therefore no connection with psychology. Experimental chemistry produces at the present day innumerable phenomena which to the vulgar mind are distinctly thaumaturgic. "That most secret and arcane department of physical science, by which the mystical properties of natural substances are developed, we denominate Natural Magic," says Robert Fludd in his "Compendious Apology for the Fraternity of the Rosy Cross;" he cites the three Magi, who were led by the Star in the East to the cradle of the Grand Christian Initiator, and the mythical King Solomon, among the most illustrious adepts of this elementary branch of esoteric wisdom, which culminates in the celestial science of astrology, for astrology is the calculation of future contingencies, based on the traditional and observed facts of stellar influence on the life of humanity at large. It is impressive in its antiquity, and important by the respect which it has commanded from great minds in the past, but neither this nor any species of Natural Magic are of service to the psychic student.

Spiritual or Transcendental Magic comprises in itself several distinct subdivisions of esoteric art and science. Considered in its totality, it is the synthesis of those methods and processes by which the ancient mystics claim to have developed their psychic potencies so as to establish communication with such forms of intelligent finite subsistence as are without the physical horizon, and therefore normally invisible, to form a correspondence with the underlying principles of nature, and thus develop the possibilities which are secreted like seeds in the heart of all material substances, and so perform on the physical plane what is beyond the scope of common physical science, and, lastly, as the crowning aim and *magnum opus* of experimental mysticism, to enable the "highest fact in man" to hold "immediate intercourse with the highest fact in the universe."

The wonders of Spiritual Magic are said to be accomplished by means of a certain method of life and a certain sequence of ceremonies, all of symbolical significance, but unanimously considered by the highest adepts to be devoid of inherent virtue, and simply adopted to direct and develop the psychic faculties of will and imagination which are the grand agents in every magical process. Éliphas Lévi recommends the postulant in the pronaos of the Spiritual Temple to "rise daily at the same hour, and at an early hour, bathe summer and winter before daybreak in spring water, never wear soiled clothes, to wash them himself if necessary, to exercise himself by voluntary privations that he may be better able to bear involuntary ones; finally, to impose silence on all desires save that of achieving the *magnum opus*." But this is simply the preliminary discipline; the preparation of the mystic "sulphur of the wise" is of another and higher kind; the student of Thomas Vaughan will find it described in various parts of his writings, and especially in the *Anima Magica Abscondita;* it is a process of psychic chemistry of a triadic and absolutely supernatural character, for the diatribes of modern mystics against the use of the term supernatural are founded on a fundamental misapprehension of occultism, and are due to the influence of materialistic philosophy. It is a doctrine of magical science that there is an inherent imperfection in Nature, and that there is an absolute perfection which transcends Nature; now, the testimony of the visible universe and the unceasing aspiration of man's higher consciousness are in harmony with this doctrine.

The triadic process of which I have spoken is the transmutation of the physical body by the soul within it, the exaltation and transfiguration of the soul by the overshadowing spirit, and the illumination and deification of the spirit by contact with the Universal Consciousness. This process accomplishes that regeneration of the whole man, which is the true object of transcendental philosophy and the only safe basis of practical magic. All operations attempted by the vulgar and the uninitiated, in other words, by unregenerate persons, are either dangerous or unsuccessful, or, as in the case of Black Magic, of a dark and abominable nature.

Contemplation and quietism are the keys of this mysterious process, which seems to have been carried to its highest point among Oriental nations. It is described by Roger Bacon as the modification of the body by alchemy, which puts much of Hermetic allegory in a new and more intelligible light.

When this modification, or New Birth, has been accomplished, the Magus is placed in communication with the creative forces of the universe, and the avenues of spiritual perception, which are narrow, difficult, and full of barriers to the psychologist of to-day, are freely thrown open for unlimited exploration—such, at least, is the claim of the magical text-books—and the initiated epopt may proceed to the invocation of the celestial intelligences, the souls of the great departed, and to the assertion of intellectual dominion over the hierarchies of elementary being. The depths and heights of his own immortal nature are also revealed to him, and from the pinnacles of his spiritual life he may soar into ecstatic yet conscious communion with God Himself. On the physical plane he may perform, by the adaptation of natural laws, many prodigies which seem to the uninitiated observer in defiance of all law; he may endue inert substance with the potency of his individual will, and this is the philosophical principle of talismanic magic; he can search all hearts and read all destinies; perceive events happening at a remote distance; and can impart to suitable subjects a portion of his own prerogatives, inducing trance, clairvoyance, prophetic foresight, &c.

Such is the great claim of Spiritual Magic, and it involves at least an aspiration of the highest conceivable kind. Its antithesis exists in the counter claim of the Black or Infernal Art, with all its grotesque horrors and barbarous, perverse processes, by which the initiates of forbidden knowledge employed their developed physical faculties in operations of darkness and destruction.

The third division of mediæval esoteric science is, in some respects, the most important of all, for alchemy is not only the foundation of that experimental method which has transformed the face of the earth; it is not only the historical radix of modern physics, including chemistry, it is not only an arcane process for the manufacture of material gold, but it has originated a theory which is of the utmost importance to all present students of psychology.

I have traced the connection between ancient thaumaturgic mysticism and modern mystic action, I have shown that the hierophants of old were familiar with the spiritual phenomena of to-day, and they claim to have made such advances in the paths wherein we are slowly and painfully travelling, that they had entered into the permanent possession of a power and knowledge which it was dangerous or impossible for them to reveal, which they consequently spoke of in veiled language, but which they nevertheless endeavoured to extend to others, in order that it might be perpetuated, and to this end they invented their symbols and allegories in the hope that a divine light would illuminate deserving seekers and enable them to penetrate to their inner significance. Now, the grand initiates of ancient magic were the princes of alchemy in a large number of cases, and these two branches of esoteric wisdom are intimately and curiously connected both in principle and practice. The doctrines of mystical and magical regeneration were expounded by alchemical philosophers, and the psychic manufacture of gold was taught in return by the magicians. Astrology lent to both the assistance of her traditional observations and the resources of her archaic symbolism. Alchemists and magicians lay claim to the possession of the same tremendous secret, the same indicible power; they worked with the same weapons after rigorously identical methods but in various fields of achievement — the material world was the province of the followers of Geber; to the disciples of the Magi were delivered the realms of mind. The highest inspirations of both schools appear to have been derived from the Hermetic books, and though the practical alchemy of the Christian age originated with the Arabian Geber, its sources must thus be sought in the theosophy of the later Platonists.

Now, whether from hints contained in the Hermetic books or whether from some adaptation of Kabbalism, or from what source soever the seeds came which germinated in the minds of the alchemists, a theory of universal development, capable of application in almost any direction, was enunciated in this division of esoteric literature, and constitutes the general and explainable principle of the Secret Doctrine of Mysticism. I have described this theory at considerable length, and, I believe, with a certain precision, in an account of the true principles of the *magnum opus*, prefixed to the "Lives of Alchemistical Philosophers," recently published in London. This biographical work endeavours, by a consideration of the careers of adept philosophers, to determine the true nature and object of practical alchemy, and, so far as this plan is fulfilled, it constitutes a suitable and necessary introduction to the study of historical Hermetics. I do not propose to make in the present essay any substantial repetition of what I have already stated there. The alchemical theory of universal development includes a philosophical forestatement of the modern evolutionary hypothesis which, considering the scientific ignorance and darkness of the Middle Ages, is simply bewildering, and justifies the indignant demand of one theosophical writer for the restitution of its rightful property to "a spoliated past." But the alchemical theory was originated by thinkers who believed in the paramount reality of spiritual things, and their doctrine of evolution was extended to the soul and spirit of man, though its practical application was scarcely attempted by alchemists outside the metallic kingdom.

I would direct the particular attention of earnest psychological inquirers to this grand and important doctrine, the highest outcome of Hermetic speculation which has been openly transmitted from antiquity. It is founded on a general assumption that the philosophers claim to have demonstrated as experimentally true in at least one kingdom of Nature, namely, that all existing substances whatsoever—the substance of spirit and soul, of animal and vegetable life, of metals and of stones—contain elements or seeds of a higher perfection in any given direction than they can normally manifest, that there is no practical limit to their progress towards perfection, and that man is the agent and dispenser of Divine power for the development of his own and the latent energies of all earthly things. The union of individual consciousness in the universal consciousness of God was the culminating point of this theory in its extension to man, and the extraction of a tincture which would transform a million times its own weight into gold was its last assigned development in its relation to metals.

The unity and solidarity of Nature in the midst of infinite formal differentiation was the first logical outcome of this assumption, the universal potentiality of improvement constituting the bond of union. From this dual doctrine of fundamental solidarity and latent power a practical conclusion was drawn—that the processes for the development of inherent energies in the various kingdoms of Nature should be rigorously parallel, but with due regard to formal difference. *Quod superius sicut quod inferius, et quod inferius sicut quod superius ad perpetranda miracula rei unius.*

The alchemical doctrine of evolution is the philosophical basis of the sublime claim of transcendental or spiritual magic which I have already considered at such length, and the full consequent psychic importance of the literature of alchemy may be shown in a few words. Though it conceals the first matter of the *magnum opus*, it describes the processes which, given the first matter, will ultimately eliminate the imperfections of metals. These processes are parallel by the theory in every department of Nature, and thus the magical evolution, transfiguration, or reconstruction of man is to be accomplished in a manner which is rigorously similar to the reconstruction in the mineral world. As man is the subject of spiritual chemistry, the first matter does not need seeking in this division of the art, and as man, in the same manner, is that mystic *vas philosophorum* which has been always a *crux* for seekers from the days of Geber downwards, it is a plain case that the development of his latent spiritual energies may be accomplished along the lines of the avowed Hermetic processes as they are described in alchemical works, provided the assumptions contained in the general Hermetic theory have a basis, as claimed, in fact. Now the processes in question are delineated with a tolerable amount of perspicuity, and I submit to those numerous students of psychology who are turning for light to the writings and to the alleged achievements of the old mystics, that here is an adequate warrant for their earnest and exhaustive study, and some ground for believing that we may strike upon an unwrought mine of spiritual possibilities in the hidden but not unattainable mysteries of alchemy.

The practical outcome of my own studies in this direction must be reserved for the present, as it would be unwise in the limited space of the present essay to forestall what I subsequently hope to treat in a comprehensive and complete manner. My present object is to draw the attention of other investigators to the only lines of research which are likely to produce a definite and desired result, and if possible to elicit their collaboration in the first serious attempt at the mystical reconstruction of humanity. From the practical magic of the Middle Ages we may learn the identity of new and old psychological phenomena, from theurgic philosophers we may ascertain the true nature of the psychic achievements which transcendental magic claims to have accomplished, for the actual processes by which it attained its grand results we must study the *turba philosophorum*—the long line of alchemists—and that in a consecutive and exhaustive manner. But we must carefully bear in mind that we are in search of the psycho-chemical process, which is connected, but not identical, with the metallic process of the *turba*, that the transmutation of material substances into material gold was the object of alchemy itself, and that it can only provide us with a parallel. But the exactitude of this parallel is guaranteed by the theory, "From the greater to the lesser, from the lesser to the greater, the consequences are identically connected, and the proportions progressively rigorous."

The student will also do well to avoid discouragement at the antiquated forms of reasoning and the exploded physical notions of all the Hermetic philosophers. Their conceptions are crude enough, and sometimes seem scarcely consonant with sanity, but their psychic knowledge is not to be measured by their progress in physics, and even a true process for metallic transmutation is not incompatible with a disconcerting ignorance of numerous natural laws.

All persons connected with the present revival of mysticism should endeavour by its logical and consistent study, on an unbiassed historical method, to recover some positive knowledge from its secluded sanctuaries. That is an inconsequent interest which is manifested only in spasmodic investigation; rash and illiberal theories are its normal results. The secrets of esoteric literature will only surrender to the searching analysis of sympathetic minds which have been duly equipped for the task by an acquaintance with psychic progress in the present, and are endowed with a height of aspiration which is parallel to the aspiration of the hierophants.

ANTHROPOSOPHIA THEOMAGICA:

OR

A DISCOURSE OF THE NATURE OF MAN AND HIS STATE AFTER DEATH;

GROUNDED ON HIS CREATOR'S PROTO-CHIMISTRY, AND VERIFI'D BY A PRACTICALL EXAMINATION OF PRINCIPLES IN THE GREAT WORLD.

BY

EUGENIUS PHILALETHES:

DAN: Many shall run to and fro, and knowledge shall be increased.
Zoroaster in OracuL.—AUDI IGNIS VOCEM.

TO THE MOST ILLUSTRIOUS AND TRULY REGENERATED BRETHREN R.C.,

TO THE PEACE-LOVING APOSTLES OF THE CHURCH IN THIS CONTENTIOUS AGE,

SALUTATION FROM THE CENTRE OF PEACE.

IN so much as this votive offering doth entreat the high priest alone at the high altar, not without sacrilege may it seem to be thrust upon you. Even devotion hath its limits; who so approaches unbidden is guilty of audacity, not of service. That aforetime gigantomachia of the poets was concerned with those who did indeavour to carry Heaven by storm, nor are fatuous and vicious sparklings wanting in our own day, who dream themselves stars and believe that they are equal to the sun. Be far from Eugenius this arrogance and climax of ambition! This were "to pile Pelion upon Ossa."

I, most noble Brethren, am in the vestibule of the Sacrarium, nor do I set my offering upon the altar, but, more modestly, upon the threshold. If admitted into the ranks such things would I offer unto you

> Quæ secula posterique possint
> Arpinis quoque comparare chartis.

But there is no reason why I should despair. There shall come those in the last times who will præfer this my torchlet to the sun of Tuscany. And indeed I am a colleague by that shewing of Marcus Tullius, *quod in eandem immortalem tendit noster consulatus.* I have wandered, like the bees (not those of Quintillian in poisoned gardens), touching lightly the Cœlestiall Flowres, which derive their scents from the Aromatic Mountains. If here there be aught of honey, I offer unto you this honey-comb and bee-hive. Roses, however, are wont to be soiled upon the breasts of most persons; peradventure also this handfull is sullied, for it is of my gathering. What is error is of Eugenius, what remains is of Truth. Yet to what purpose is this testimony of Truth, to you emancipated ones, who enjoy the unveiled manifestation of the triplex *Martyrium* of Spirit, of Water, and of Blood? This is no voice of help, however small, but a thing superfluous. Wise is he who is silent in the presence of Heaven! Receive therefore, most illustrious Brethren, this my mite not as such that I ought to offer unto you, but as all that I am able. My good will is in my willing service. This also doth my poverty premise: weigh not the gift itself but the obedience of

Your suppliant,

E. S.

THE AUTHOR TO THE READER.

LOOK on this life as the Progresse of an Essence Royall: the Soul but quits her court to see the countrey. Heaven hath in it a Scene of Earth; and had she been contented with Ideas, she had not travelled beyond the map. But excellent patterns commend their mimes: Nature that was so fair in the type, could not be a slut in the Anaglyph. This makes her ramble hither to examine the medall by the flask, but whiles she scannes their Symmetrie, she formes it. Thus her descent speaks her Original. God in love with his own beauty frames a Glasse to view it by reflection; but the frailety of the Matter excluding Eternity, the composure was subject to dissolution. Ignorance gave this release the name of Death, but properly it is the Soule's Birth, and a charter that makes for her liberty; she hath severall wayes to break up house, but her best is without a disease. This is her mysticall walk, an exit only to return.* When she takes air at this door, it is without prejudice to her tenement. The Magicians tell me, *Anima unius entis egreditur, et aliud ingreditur.* Some have examined this, and state it an expence of influences, as if the Soul exercised her royalty at the Eye, or had some blinde jurisdiction at the pores. But this is to measure magicall positions by the slight, superficial strictures of the common philosophy. It is an age of intellectuall slaveries; if they meet anything extra-ordinary, they prune it commonly with distinctions, or dawb it with false glosses, till it looks like the traditions of Aristotle. His followers are so confident of his principles they seek not to understand what others speak, but to make others speak what they understand. It is in Nature as it is in Religion; we are still hammering of old elements, but seek not the America that lyes beyond them. The apostle tells us of leaving the first principles of the Doctrine Hebrews of Christ, and going on to perfection: not laying again the founda-

* Note I.

tion of repentance from dead works; and of faith towards God, of
the doctrine of Baptism, and laying on of hands, of resurrection, and
the eternal judgement. Then he speaks of illumination, of tasting
of the Heavenly gift, of being partakers of the Holy Ghost, of
tasting of the good word of God, and the powers of the world to
come. Now, if I should question any sect (for there is no communion in Christendom) whither these later intimations drive, they
can but return me to the first rudiments, or produce some emptie
pretence of spirit. Our naturall philosophers are much of a cast
with those that step into the prerogative of prophets, and antedate
events in configurations and motions. This is a consequence of
as much reason as if I saw the Suede exercising, and would finde
his designes in his postures. Friar Bacon walked in Oxford between two steeples, but he that would have discovered his thoughts
by his steps had been more his fool then his fellow. The Peripateticks when they define the Soul, or some inferior principle,
describe it onely by outward circumstances, which every childe
can do, but they state nothing essentially. Thus they dwell,
altogether in the face, their indeavours are mere titillations,
and their acquaintance with Nature is not at the heart. Notwithstanding, I acknowledge the schoolmen ingenious: they
conceive their principles irregular, and prescribe rules for
method, though they want matter. Their philosophie is like
a church that is all discipline and no doctrine; for bate me their
prolegomena, their form of arguing, their reciting of different
opinions, with severall other digressions, and the substance of these
Tostati will scarce amount to a Mercury. Besides, their Aristotle
is a poet in text, his principles are but fancies, and they stand
more on our concessions than his bottom. Hence it is that his
followers, notwithstanding the assistance of so many ages, can fetch
nothing out of him but Notions; and these indeed they use, as he
sayeth Lycophron did his Epithets, not as spices, but as food.
Their compositions are a meer tympanie of termes. It is better
then a fight in Quixot to observe what duels and digladiations they
have about him. One will make him speak sense, another non-
sense, and a third both. Aquinas palps him gently, Scotus makes
him winch, and he is taught like an ape to shew severall tricks. If
we look on his Adversaries, the least among them hath foyld him,
but Telesius knocked him in the head, and Campanella hath quite
discomposed him. But as that bald haunter of the circus had his
skull so steeled with use it shivered all the tiles were thrown at
it, so this Aristotle thrives by scuffles, and the world cryes him up

L. Verulam
in his N. H.

when Truth cryes him down. The Peripatetickes look on God, as they do on carpenters who build with stone and timber, without any infusion of life. But the world, which is God's building, is full of spirit, quick and living. This spirit is the cause of multiplication, of severall perpetuall productions of minerals, vegetables, and creatures ingendred by putrefaction, all which are manifest, infallible arguments of life. Besides, the texture of the universe clearly discovers its animation. The earth, which is the visible natural basis of it, represents the gross, carnal parts. The element of water answers to the bloud, for in it the pulse of the Great World beates ; this most men call the flux and reflux, but they know not the true cause of it. The air is the outward refreshing spirit, where this vast creature breathes, though invisibly, yet not altogether insensibly. The interstellar skies are his vital, æthereall waters, and the stars his animal, sensuall fire. Thou wilt tell me perhaps, this is new philosophy, and that of Aristotle is old. It is indeed, but in the same sense as religion is at Rome. It is not the primitive truth of the creation, not the ancient, reall Theosophie of the Hebrews and Egyptians, but a certain preternaturall upstart, a vomit of Aristotle, which his followers with so much diligence lick up and swallow. I present thee not here with any clamourous opposition of their patrone, but a positive expresse of principles as I finde them in Nature. I may say of them as Moses said of the FIAT: "These are the generations of the heavens, and of the earth, in the day that the Lord God made the heavens and the earth." They are things "beyond reasoning," sensible practicall truths, not meer vagaries and rambles of the braine. I would not have thee look on my indeavours as a designe of captivity: I intend not the conquest but the exercise of thy reason, not that thou shouldest swear allegiance to my dictates, but compare my conclusions with Nature, and examine their correspondency. Be pleased to consider that obstinacy inslaves the Soule, and clips the wings which God gave her for flight and discovery. If thou wilt not quit thy Aristotle, let not any prejudice hinder thy further search. Great is their number who perhaps had attained to perfection, had they not already thought themselves perfect. This is my advice, but how wellcome to thee I know not. If thou wilt kick and fling, I shall say with the Cardinall, "My ass also doth kick up his heels," for I value no man's censure. It is an age wherein truth is neer a miscarriage, and it is enough for me that I have appeared thus far for it in a day of necessity.

E. S.

ANTHROPOSOPHIA THEOMAGICA.

WHEN I found out this truth, that man in his originall was a branch planted in God and that there was a continuall influxe from the Stock to the Scion, I was much troubled at his corruptions, and wondered his fruits were not correspondent to his roote. But when I was told he had tasted of an other Tree, my admiration was quickly off, it being my chiefe care to reduce him to his first simplicitie, and separate his mixtures of good and evill. But his Fall had so bruised him in his best part that his Soule had no knowledge left to study him a cure, his punishment presently followed his trespasse : "All things became hidden and oblivion, the mother of ignorance, did enter in." This Lethe remained not in his body, but passing together with his nature made his posterity her channel. Imperfection's an easy inheritance, but vertue seldome finds any heires. Man had at the first, and so have all Souls before their intrance into the body, an explicit methodicall knowledge, but they are no sooner vesselied than that liberty is lost, and nothing remaines but a vast confused notion of the creature. Thus had I only left a capacity without power, and a will to doe that which was far enough above me. In this perplexity I studied severall arts, and rambled over all those inventions which the folly of man called sciences ; but these endeavours sorting not to my purpose, I quitted this booke-businesse, and thought it a better course to study Nature then Opinion. Hereupon I considered with my selfe that man was not the primitive immediate worke of God, but the world, out of which he was made. And to regulate my studies in point of methode, I judged it convenient to examine his principles first, and not him. But the world in generall being too large for inquisition, I resolved to take part for the whole, and to give a guesse at the frame by proportion. To perfect this my essay, I tooke to task the fruits of one Spring. Here I observed a great many vegetables fresh and beauteous in their time, but when I looked

C. Agrip.
De Vanit.
Scient.

back on their original, they were no such things as vegetables.   This
observation I applyed to the world, and gained by it this inference:
that the world in the beginning was no such thing as it is,* but some
other seed or matter out of which that fabric which I now behold
did arise.   But, resting not here, I drove my conclusion further; I
conceived those seeds whereof vegetables did spring must be something else at first then seeds, as having some præ-existent matter
whereof they were made, but what that matter should be I could
not guesse.   Here was I forced to leave off speculation, and come
up to experience.   Whiles I sought the world, I went beyond it,
and I was now in quest of a substance which without Art I could
not see.   Nature wrapps this most strangely in her very bosome,
neither does she expose it to any thing but her own Vitall Cœlestiall
Breath.   But in respect that God Almighty is the onely proper
immediate Agent which actuates this Matter, as well in the work
of generation as formerly in his creation, it will not be amisse to
speak something of him, that we may know the Cause by his
creatures, and the creatures by their Cause.

My God, my Life, whose Essence man
Is no way fit to know or scan,
But should approach thy Court a guest
In thoughts more low then his request;
When I consider how I stray,
Methinks 'tis pride in mee to pray.
How dare I speake to Heaven, nor feare
In all my sinns to court Thy eare?
But as I looke on moles that lurke
In blind intrenchments, and there worke
Their owne darke prisons to repaire,
Heaving the earth to take in aire:
So view my fetter'd Soule, that must
Struggle with this her load of dust,
Meet her addresse, and add one ray
To this mew'd parcell of thy day.
She would, though here imprison'd, see
Through all her dirt thy Throne and Thee.
Lord guide her out of this sad night,
And say once more, Let there be Light.

It is God's own positive truth: In the beginning, that is, in that
dead silence, in that horrible and empty darknesse when as yet
nothing was fashioned, then (saith the Lord) did I consider those
things, and they all were made through me alone, and through none
other, by me also they shall be ended and by none other.   That

Esdras.

* Note 2.

meditation forerunns every solemne worke, is a thing so well knowne to man that he needs no further demonstration of it then his owne practice. That there is also in God something analogicall to it from whence man derived this customary notion of his, as it is most agreeable to reason, so withall is it very suitable to Providence. "The Gods (saith Jamblichus) did conceive within themselves the whole design before they generated it." And the Spirit here to Esdras, Then did I consider these things; He considered them first and made them afterwards. God in his Æternall Idea foresaw that whereof as yet there was no materiall copy. The goodnesse and beauty of the one moved him to create the other, and truly the image of this prototype being imbosomed in the second made Him so much in love with his creature, that when sin had defaced it, he restored it by the suffering of that patterne by which at first it was made. Dyonisius the Areopagite, who lived in the primitive times,* and received the mysteries of Divinity immediately from the apostles, stiles God the Father sometimes "the Arcanum of Divinity," sometimes "that hidden supersubstantial Being," and elsewhere he compares him to a roote whose flowers are the Second and Third Persons. This is true; for God the Father is the basis or supernaturall foundation of his creatures: God the Son is the Patterne in whose expresse image they were made: And God the Holy Ghost is the "Spirit-Fabricator," or the Agent, who framed the creature in a just symmetrie to his Type. This consideration or type God hath since used in the performance of inferiour workes. Thus in the institution of his Temple, he commands Moses to the Mount, where the Divine Spirit shews him the idea of the future fabrick : And let them make me a sanctuary that I may dwell amongst them, according to all that I shew thee, after the patterne of the Tabernacle, and the patterne of all the instruments thereof, even so shall you make it. Thus the Divine Mind doth instruct us "by setting forth ideas by a certain self-extension beyond himself," and sometimes more particularly in dreames. To Nebuchadnezzar he presents a tree strong and high, reaching to the heavens, and the sight thereof to the ends of the earth. To Pharaoh he shews seven ears of corn. To Joseph he appears in sheafes, and then resembles the Sun, Moon, and Stars. To conclude he may expresse himself by what he will, for in him are innumerable, eternall prototypes, and he is the true Fountaine and Treasure of Formes. But that we may come at last to the scope proposed: God the Father is the Metaphysicall, Supercelestiall Sun,

Exodus.

---

* The mystical writings attributed to Dionysius the Areopagite are now almost universally rejected as forgeries of the fifth century.

the Second Person is the Light, and the Third is "Fiery Love," or a Divine Heate proceeding from both. Now, without the presence of this Heate there is no reception of the Light, and by consequence no influx from the Father of Lights. For this "Love" is the medium which unites the Lover to that which is beloved, and probably 'tis the Platonicks "Chief Daimon, who doth unite us to the Rulers of Spirits." I could speak much more of the offices of this Loving Spirit, but these are "Grand Mysteries of God and of Nature," and require not our discusse so much as our reverence. Here also I might speak of that supernaturall generation, whereof Trismegistus: "The one begetteth one, and doth reflect upon itself its own brightness;" but I leave this to the Almighty God as his own essentiall, centrall mystery. It is my onely intention in this place to handle exterior actions, or the process of the Trinity from the Center to the Circumference. And that I may the better do it, you are to understand that God before his work of creation was wrapped up and contracted in himself. In this state the Egyptians stile him "Solitary Monad," and the Cabalists "Dark Aleph;" but when the decreed instant of creation came, then appeared "Bright Aleph," and the First Emanation was that of the Holy Ghost into the bosom

Genesis.

of the matter. Thus we read that Darknesse was upon the face of the deep, and the Spirit of God moved upon the face of the waters. Here you are to observe that notwithstanding this processe of the Third Person, yet was there no Light, but darknesse on the face of the deep, illumination properly being the office of the second. Wherefore God also when the Matter was prepared by Love for Light, gives out his *Fiat Lux*, which was no creation as most think, but an Emanation of the Word, in whom was life, and that life is the light of men. This is that life whereof Saint John speaks, that it shines in the darknesse and the darknesse comprehended it not. But lest I seem to be singular in this point, I will give you more evidence. Pimandras, informing Trismegistus in the work of the creation, tells him the self-same thing. "I am that Light, the Pure Intelligence, thy God, more ancient than the aqueous nature which shone forth out of the shadow." And Georgius Venetus in his book *De Harmonia Mundi*: "Whatsoever liveth doth subsist by virtue of its inward heat; thence that substance of heat, indiscriminately distributed through the world, is held to contain within itself a vital strength; yea, Zoroaster testifieth that all things were made out of fire, when he sayeth: all things were produced by a single fire, that fire, to wit, which God, the inhabitant of essential flame (as Plato hath it), did bid appear in the substance of Heaven, and Earth, at that time created rude and formless that it might assume life and symmetrie. Hereupon, the Fabricator did straightway bring out the *Sit Lux* — let there be Light — into these creations, for which term a mendacious rendering doth substitute FIAT LUX, let Light be made; but the Light is no way made, but communicated and admitted to things formerly obscure, that they may be clarified and made splendid in its beauties." But to proceed: no sooner had the Divine Light pierced the bosom of the Matter, but the Idea or Pattern of the whole material world appeared in those primitive waters like an image in a glasse. By this pattern it was that the Holy Ghost framed and modelled the universal structure. This mystery or appearance of the Idea is excellently manifested in the magicall analysis of bodies; for he that knows how to imitate the proto-chymistrie of the Spirit by the separation of the principles wherein the life is imprisoned may see the impresse of it experimentally in the outward naturall vestiments. But lest you should think this my invention, and no practicall truth, I will give you another man's testimony. "I inquire (saith one) what such great philosophers would say, if they beheld the plant born as in a moment in the glass vial, with its colours as in life, and then again die, and reborn, and that daily, and whenever they choose? But the power to deceive human senses I believe they include in the art magic of the demons."* They are the words of Doctor Marci in his *Defensio Idearum Operatricium*. But you are to be admonished, there is a twofold Idea—Divine and Naturall. The naturall is a fiery, invisible, created spirit, and properly a meer inclosure, or vestiment of the true one. Hence the Platonicks called it " the Nimbus of the descending Divinity." Zoroaster, and some other philosophers, think it is " the Soul of the World," but, by their leave, they are mistaken; there is a wide difference betwixt *Anima* and *Spiritus*. But the Idea I speak of here is the true, primitive, exemplar one, and a pure influence of the Almighty. This Idea before the coagulation of the seminall principles to a grosse, outward fabrick, which is the end of generation, impresseth in the vitall ethereall principles a modell or pattern after which the body is to be framed, and this is the first inward production, or draught of the creature. This is it which the Divine Spirit intimates to us in that Scripture where he saith, that God created every plant of the field before it was in the ground, Genesis. and every herb of the field before it grew. But notwithstanding this presence of the Idea in the matter, yet the creation was not performed " by the projection of anything outside of the essential

* Note 3.

archetype," for it is God that comprehends his creature, and not the creature God.

Thus farre have I handled this primitive supernaturall part of the creation. I must confesse it is but short in respect of that which may be spoken, but I am confident it is more then formerly hath been discovered: some authors having not searched so deeply into the centre of Nature, and others not willing to publish such spiritual mysteries. I am now come to the gross work or mechanicks of the Spirit, namely, the separation of severall substances from the same masse: but in the first place I shall examine that Lymbus or huddle of matter wherein all things were so strangely contained. It is the opinion of some men, and those learned, that this sluggish empty rudiment of the creature was noe created thing. I must confesse the point is obscure as the thing it selfe, and to state it with sobriety, except a man were illuminated with the same Light that this Chaos was at first, is altogether impossible. For how can wee judge of a nature different from our owne, whose species also was so remote from anything now existent that it is impossible for fancy to apprehend, much more for reason to define it. If it be created, I conceive it the effect of the Divine Imagination, acting beyond it selfe in con-templation of that which was to come, and producing this passive darknesse for a subject to worke upon in the circumference. Trismegistus, having first exprest his Vision of Light, describes the matter in its primitive state thus:—"And in a short time after (he saith), the Darkness was thrust downwards, partly confused and dejected, and tortuously circumscribed, so that I appeared to behold it transformed into a certain humid substance, and afterwards, one might say, excited and vomiting forth smoke as from fire, and giving forth a lugubrious and inexpressible sound." Certainly these *Tenebræ* he speakes of, or fuliginous spawne of Nature, were the first created matter, for that Water we read of in Genesis was a product or secondary substance. Here also he seemes to agree further with the Mosaicall tradition; for this "Smoke" which ascended after the transmutation can be nothing else but that Darknesse which was upon the face of the Deepe; but to expresse the particular mode or way of the Creation, you are to understand that in the Matter there was a horrible confused qualme, or stupifying spirit of moysture, cold, and darknesse. In the opposite principle of Light there was heate and the effect of it, siccitie; for these two are noe elemental qualities, as the Galenists and my Peripateticks suppose. But they (if I may say so) the hands of the Divine Spirit by which He did worke upon the Matter, applying every agent to his proper patient. These two are active and masculine, those of moysture and cold are passive and feminine. Now as soone as the Holy Ghost and the Word (for it was not the one nor the other, but both—"the formative intelligence conjoined with the Word," as Trismegistus hath it—I omit that speech, *Let us make man*, which effectually proves their union in the worke) had applyed themselves to the Matter, there was extracted from the bosome of it a third Spirituall Cœlestiall Substance, which receiving a tincture of heat and light proceeding from the Divine Treasures, became a pure, sincere, innoxious Fire. Of this the bodyes of angells consist, as also the Empyræall Heaven, where Intellectual Essences have their residence. This was "the primeval marriage of God and Nature," the first and best of compositions. This extract being thus settled above, and separated from the Masse, retained in it a vast portion of Light, and made the first day without a sun. But the Splendour of the Word expelling the Darknesse downwards, it became more settled and compact towards the centre, and made a horrible thick night. Thus God (as the Hebrew hath it) was betweene the Light and the Darknesse, for the Spirit remained still on the face of the inferior portion to extract more from it. In the second separation was educed "the nimble atmosphere," as Trismegistus calls it—a spirit not so refined as the former, but vitall, and in the next degree to it. This was extracted in such abundance that it filled all the space from the masse to the Empyræall Heaven, under which it was condensed to a water, but of a different constitution from the Elementall, and this is the Body of the Interstellar Skie. But my Peripateticks, following the principles of Aristotle and Ptolomie, have imagined so many wheeles there with their final diminutive epicycles that they have turned that regular fabrick to a rumbling confused labyrinth. The inferior portion of this second extract from the Moon to the Earth remained Air still, partly to divide the inferior and superior waters, but chiefly for the respiration and nourishment of the creatures. This is that which is properly called the Firmament, as it is plain out of Esdras :—"On the second day thou didst create the spirit of the Firmament"; for it is "the bond of all Nature," and in the outward geometricall composure it answers to "the Middle Nature," for it is spread through all things, hinders vacuity, and keeps all the parts of Nature in a firm, invincible union.

This is "the sieve of Nature," as one wittily calls it, a thing Author appointed for most secret and mysterious offices, but we shall *Philos.* speake further of it when we come to handle the Elements particu- *Restitut.* larly. Nothing now remained but the two inferior principles, as we

commonly call them—Earth and Water. The Earth was an
impure, sulphureous subsidence, or *caput mortuum* of the creation.
The water was also phlegmatick, crude, and raw, not so vitall as
the former extractions. But the Divine Spirit, to make his work
perfect, moving also upon these, imparted to them life and heate,
and made them fit for future productions. The Earth was so
overcast and mantled with the Water that no part thereof was to be
seen; but that it might be the more immediately exposed to the
Cœlestiall Influences which are the cause of vegetation, the Spirit

Job. orders a retreat of the Waters, "breaks up for them his decreed
place, and sets them bars and doors." The Light as yet was not
confined, but retaining his vast flux and primitive liberty, equally
possest the whole creature. On the fourth day it was collected to a
sun, and taught to know his fountain. The Darknesse, whence
proceed the corruptions and, consequently, the death of the creature,
was imprisoned in the centre, but breaks out still when the day
gives it leave, and like a baffled gyant thrusts his head out of doors
in the absence of his adversary. Thus Nature is a lady whose face
is beauteous but not without a black bag. Howsoever when it shall
please God more perfectly to refine his creatures, this tincture shall
be expelled quite beyond them, and thus it will be an outward
darknesse from which Good Lord deliver us!

Thus I have given you a cursory and short expresse of the
creation in generall. I shall now descend to a more particular
examination of Nature and especially her inferior, elementall parts,
through which man passeth daily, and from which he cannot be
separated. I was about to desist in this place to prevent all future
acclamations, for when a Peripatetick findes here but three, nay, but
two genuine elements—Earth and Water—for the Air is something
more—will he not cry out I have committed sacrilege against
Nature and stole the fire from her altar? This is noise indeed, but
till they take coach in a cloud and discover that idol they prefer
next to the moon, I am resolved to continue my heresie. I am not
onely of opinion, but I am sure there is no such principle in Nature.
The Fire which she useth is "the physicall and incorporeall
horizon, the interbinding of both worlds, and the Seal of the Holy
Ghost." It is no chymæral, commentitious quirck like that of the
school-men. I shall therefore request my friends the Peripateticks
to return their fourth element to Aristotle, that he may present it to
Alexander the Great as the first part of a new world, for there is no
such thing in the old.

To proceed then: the Earth (as you were told before) being the subsidence or remaines of that primitive masse which God formed out of Darknesse, must needs be a fæculent, impure body, for the extractions which the Divine Spirit made were pure, oleous, æthereall substances, not the crude, phlegmatick, indigested humors settled like lees towards the centre. The Earth is spongy, porous, and magneticall, of composition loose, the better to take in the severall influences of heate, rains, and dewes for the nurture and conservation of her products. In her is the principle residence of that Matrix which attracts and receives the sperme from the Masculine part of the World. She is Nature's Ætna; here Vulcan doth exercise himself—not that limping, poeticall one which halted after his fall, but a pure, cœlestiall, plastick Fire. We have Astronomy here under our feet, the stars are resident with us, and abundance of jewels and pantauras; she is the nurse and receptacle of all things, for the Superior Natures ingulph themselves into her: what she receives this age, she discovers to the next, and, like a faithfull treasurer, conceales no part of her accounts. Her proper, congeneall quality is cold.

I am now to speak of the Water. This is the first element we read of in Scripture, the most ancient of principles and the Mother of all things among visibles. Without the mediation of this, the Earth can receive no blessing at all, for moysture is the proper cause of mixture and fusion. The Water hath severall complexions according to the severall parts of the creature. Here below, and in the circumference of all things, it is volatile, crude, and raw. For this very cause Nature makes it no part of her provision, but she rectifies it first, exhaling it up with her heat, and thus condensing it into rains and dews, in which state she makes use of it for nourishment. Some where it is interior, vitall, and cœlestiall, exposed to the breath of the First Agent, and stirred with spirituall æternall windes. In this condition it is Nature's wanton—*Fœmina Satacissima*, as one calls it. This is that Psyche of Apuleius, and the Fire of Nature is her Cupid. He that hath seen them both in the same bed will confesse that love rules all. But to speak something of our common, elementall Water. It is not altogether contemptible; there are hidden treasures in it, but so inchanted we can not see them, for all that the chest is transparent. "The congelated spirit of the Invisible Water is better than the whole earth," saith the noble and learned Sendivogius. I doe not advise the reader to take this phlegm to task, as if he would extract a Venus from the sea, but I wish him to study Water that he may know the Fire.

I have now handled the two Elements, and more I cannot finde:

B

I know the Peripateticks pretend to four, and, with the help of their master's quintessence, to a fifth principle. I shall at leysure diminish their stock, but the thing to be now spoken of is Air. This is no element, but a certain miraculous Hermaphrodite, the cæment of two worlds, and a medley of extremes. It is Nature's common place, her index, where you may finde all that ever she did, or intends to do. This is the World's panegyrick, the excursions of both globes meet here, and I may call it the rendezvous. In this are innumerable magicall forms of men and beasts, fish and fowls, trees, herbs, and all creeping things. This is "the sea of things invisible," for all the conceptions "in the bosom of the superiour Nature" wrap themselves in this tiffany before they imbark in the shell. It retaines the species of all things whatsoever, and is the immediate receptacle of spirits after dissolution, whence they passe to a Superior Limbus. I should amaze the reader if I did relate the severall offices of this body, but it is the Magician's back door, and none but friends come in at it. I shall speak nothing more—onely

Corn.
Agrippa.

this I would have you know: the Air is "the envelope of the life of our sensitive spirit," our animal oyl, the fuell of the vital, sensual fire, without which we cannot subsist a minute.

I am now come to the fourth and last substance, the highest in "the Scale of Nature." There is no fifth principle, no quintessence, as Aristotle dreamed, but God Almighty. This Fourth Essence is a moyst, silent Fire. This Fire passeth thorough all things in the world, and it is Nature's chariot; in this she rides; when she moves, this moves; and when she stands, this stands, like the wheels in Ezekiel whose motion depended on that of the Spirit. This is the mask and skreen of the Almighty;* wheresoever He is, this train of Fire attends Him. Thus, he appears to Moses in the bush, but it was in Fire; the prophet sees him break out at the north, but like a Fire catching it self. At Horeb he is attended by a mighty strong winde rending the rocks to pieces, but after this comes the Fire, and with it a still small voice. Esdras also defines Him a God whose service is conversant in Winde and Fire. This Fire is the vestiment of the Divine Majesty—his back parts which he shewed to Moses, but his naked, royall essence none can see and live— the glory of his presence would swallow up the naturall man and make him altogether spirituall. Thus Moses his face, after conference with Him, shines, and from this small tincture we may guesse at our future state in the Regeneration. But I have touched the veyle and must return to the outer court of the Sanctuary.

* Note 4.

I have now in some measure performed that which at first I promised, an exposition of the World and the parts thereof; but in respect of my affection to Truth and the dominion I wish her, I shall be somewhat more particular in the examination of Nature, and proceed to a further discovery of her riches. I advise the reader to be diligent and curious in this subsequent part of the discourse, that having once attained to the fundamentalls of science, he may the better understand her superstructures.

Know then that every Element is threefold, this triplicity being the expresse image of their author, and a seall He hath laid upon his Creature. There is nothing on earth, though never so simple, so vile and abject, in the sight of man, but it bears witnesse of God even to that abstruse mystery, his Unity and Trinity. Every compound whatsoever is three in one and one in three. The basest reptile even in his outward symmetrie testifies of his Author, his severall proportions answering to their æternall superior Prototype. Now man hath the use of all these creatures, God having furnished him with a Living Library wherein to imploy himself. But he, neglecting the works of his Creator, prosecutes the inventions of the creature, laps up the vomit of Aristotle and other illiterate ethnicks —men as concerning the faith, reprobate, and in the Law of Nature altogether unskilfull, scribbling blasphemous atheists "whose souls hearken to be distracted and torn asunder, and who behold hell" (as Agrippa hath it). He is much troubled at those mysteries of the Trinity and the Incarnation ; one denies, another grants them ; but if they did once see the Light of Nature, they might find those mysteries by reason which are now above their faith. When I speak of a naturall triplicity, I speake not of kitchen-stuffe—those three pet-principles, Water, Oyle, and Earth—but I speake of cœlestiall hidden natures, knowne onely to absolute magicians, whose eyes are in the centre, not in the circumference, and in this sense every element is threefold. For example, there is a threefold earth ; first there is "the elementary earth," then there is "the cœlestiall earth," and, lastly, "the spirituall earth." The influences of the spirituall earth by mediation of the cœlestiall are united to the terrestriall, and are the true cause of life and vegetation. These three are the fundamentalls of Art and Nature. The first is a visible, tangible substance— pure, fixed and incorruptible—of quality cold, but, by application of a superior agent, drie, and by consequence a fit receptacle of moysture. This is "Created Aleph," the true "Adamic Earth," the basis of every building in Heaven and Earth. It answers to God the Father, being the naturall foundation of the creature, as He is

the supernaturall.   Without this nothing can be perfected in Magick.
The second principle is the infallible Magnet, the Mystery of Union.
By this all things may be attracted, whether physicall or metaphysicall,
be the distance never so great.   This is Jacob's ladder; without this
there is no ascent or descent, either infiuentiall or personall.   The
absence of this.I conceive to be that Gulph between Abraham and
Dives.   This answers to God the Son, for it is that which mediates
between extremes, and makes inferiors and superiors communicate.
But there is not one in ten thousand knows either the substance or
the use of this nature.   The third principle is properly no principle.
It is not "from whom," but "by which all things are."   This can do all
in all, and the faculties thereof are not to be exprest.   It answers to
the Holy Ghost, for amongst naturalls it is the onely agent and
artificer.   Now he. that knows these three perfectly with their
severall graduations, or annexed links, which differ not in substance,
but complexion—he that can reduce their impurities to one sincere
consistence, and their multiplicities to a spirituall, essentiall simplicity, he is an absolute compleat magician, and in full possibility to
all strange miraculous performances.   In the second place you are
to learn that every Element is twofold.   This duplicity or confusion
is that *Binarius*, whereof Agrippa, *in scalis numerorum*, as also both
himself and Trithemius in their epistles.   Other authors who dealt
in this science were pragmaticall scribblers, and understood not this
"Secret of the Shades."   This is it in which the creature prevaricates
and falls from his first Harmonicall Unity.   You must therefore
subtract the Duad, and then the magicians' Triad may be reduced
"by the Tetrad into the extreme simplicity of Unity," and, by consequence, "into a metaphysicall union with the Supreme Monad."

The sun and moon are two magicall principles, the one active, the
other passive, this masculine, that fœminine.   As they move, so
move the wheeles of corruption and generation.   They naturally
dissolve and compound, but properly the moon is " the instrument of
the transmutation of the inferiour Nature."   These two luminaries are
multiplied and fructifie in every one particular generation.   There is
not a compound in all nature but hath in it a little sun and a little
moon.   The little sun is "the Son of the Sun cœlestiall," the little
moon is "the Daughter of the Moon cœlestiall."   What offices soever
the two great luminaries perform for the conservation of the great
world in generall, these two little luminaries perform the like for the
conservation of their small cask, or Microcosm, in particular.   They
are " Miniatures of the greater Animall"—Heaven and Earth in a
lesser character.   God, like a wise Architect, sits in the centre of all,

repaires the ruins of his building, composeth all disorders, and continues his creature in his first, primitive harmony. The moon is "that well-watered and many-founted moist principle," at whose top sit Jove and Juno in a throne of gold. Juno is an incombustible, eternall oyl, and therefore a fit receptacle of Fire. This Fire is her Jove, the little sun we spoke of formerly; these are the philosophers *Sol* and *Luna*, not gold and silver, as some mountebanks and carbonadoes would have it. But in respect I have proceeded thus far, I will give you a true receipt of the Medecine—"Ten parts of cœlestiall slime, separate the male from the female, and each afterwards from its earth, physically, mark you, and with no violence. Conjoin after separation in due, harmonic, vitall proportion; and, straightway, the Soul descending from the pyroplastic sphære, shall restore, by a mirific embrace, its dead and deserted body. The conjoined substances shall be warmed by a natural fire in a perfect marriage of spirit and body. Proceed according to the Vulcanico-Magical theory, till they are exalted into the Fifth Metaphysical Rota. This is that world-renowned medecine, whereof so many have scribbled and which so few have known."*

It is a strange thing to consider that there are in Nature incorruptible, immortall principles. Our ordinary kitchin fire, which in some measure is an enemy to all compositions, notwithstanding doth not so much destroy as purifie some parts. This is clear out of the ashes of vegetables, for although their weaker exterior elements expire by the violence of Fire, yet their Earth cannot be destroyed, but vitrified. The fusion and transparency of this substance is occasioned by the radicall moysture or seminall water of the compound. This water resists the fury of the fire, and cannot possibly be vanquished. "The rose lieth hidden through the winter in this water" (sayth the learned Severine). These two principles are never separated, for Nature proceeds not so far in her dissolutions. When death hath done her worst, there is an union between these two, and out of them shall God raise us at the last day, and restore us to a spirituall condition. Besides, there remaines in them that primitive universall tincture of the Fire; this is still busie after death, brings Nature again into play, produceth wormes, and other inferiour generations. I do not conceive there shall be a Resurrection of every species, but rather their terrestrial parts together with the element of water (for "there shall be no more sea") shall be united _{Revelations.} in one mixture with the Earth, and fixed to a pure, diaphanous substance. This is St John's Chrystall Gold, a fundamental of the

* Note 5.

New Jerusalem, so called not in respect of colour, but constitution.
Their spirits, I suppose, shall be reduced to their first Limbus, a
sphære of pure, ethereall Fire, like rich eternall tapestry spread
under the throne of God. Thus, Reader, have I made a plenary
but short inquisition into the Mysteries of Nature. It is more then
hitherto hath been discovered, and therefore I expect the more
opposition. I know my reward is calumnie, but he that hath already
condemned the vanity of opinion is not like to respect that of
censure. I shall now put the creatures to their just use, and from
this shallow contemplation ascend to mine and their Author.

Lord God ! this was a stone
As hard as any one
Thy Laws in Nature fram'd :
'Tis now a springing Well,
And many drops can tell,
Since it by Art was tam'd.

My God ! my Heart is so,
'Tis all of flint, and no
Extract of teares will yield :
Dissolve it with thy fire,
That something may aspire,
And grow up in my field.

Bare teares I'll not intreat,
But let thy Spirit's seat
Upon these waters bee,
Then I, new form'd with Light,
Shall move without all Night,
Or excentricity.

It is requisite now, if we follow that method which God Himself
is Author of, to examine the nature and composition of Man, having
already described those Elements, or principles whereof he was made
and consists. Man, if we look on his materiall parts, was taken out
of the great world as woman was taken out of man. I shall therefore to avoyd repetitions, refer the reader to the former part of this
discourse, where if things be rightly understood, he cannot be
ignorant in his materiall frame or composure. We read in Genesis
that God made him out of the Earth : this is a Great Mystery. For
it was not the common pot-clay, but another, and that of a far better
nature. He that knowes this, knowes the subject of the philosophical medecine, and, by consequence, what destroyes or preserves
the temperament of Man. In this are principles homogeneall with
his life, such as can restore his decayes and reduce his disorders to
a harmony. They that are ignorant in this point are not competent

judges of life and death, but quacks and piss-pot doctors. The learned Arias Montanus calls this matter "the unique particle of the multiplex earth." If these words be well examined, you may possibly find it out, and so much for his body. His Soule is an essence not to be found in the texture of the great world, and therefore meerely divine and supernaturall. Montanus calls it "the Wind of the Divine Spirit and the Breath of the Life Divine." He seemes also to make the creation of man a little Incarnation, as if God in this worke had multiplyed Himself. Adam (saith he) received his Soule "by a wonderfull and unparalleled inspiration and fructification of God (if it be lawfull so to speake)." St Luke also tells us the same thing, for he makes Adam the son of God, not in respect of the exterior act of creation, but by way of descent, and this St Paul confirms in the words of Aratus. "For we also are his generation." The soul of man consists chiefly of two portions —Ruach and Nephes—inferior and superior. The superior is masculine and eternall, the inferior fœminine and mortall. In these two consists our spirituall generation. "As, however, in the rest of the animal world, and also in man himself, the conjunction of male and female tends towards a fruit and propagation worthy of the nature of each; so in man that interior and secret association of male and female, to wit, the copulation of the rational soul and the animal life, is appointed for the production of fitting fruit of Divine Life. And unto this does that arcane benediction and endowed fecundity, that revealed faculty, and warning, refer—Increase, and multiply, and replenish the earth, and subdue it, and have dominion." Out of this, and some former passages, the understanding reader may learne, that marriage is a comment on life, a meere hieroglyphick, or outward representation of our inward vitall composition. For life is nothing else but an union of male and fœmale principles, and he that perfectly knowes this secret, knowes the Mysteries of Marriage, both spiritual and naturall, and how he ought to use a wife. Matrimony is no ordinary triviall business, but in a moderate sense sacramentall. It is a visible signe of an invisible union to Christ, which S. Paul calls a Great Mystery, and if the thing signified be so reverend, the signature is no *ex tempore* contemptible agent. But of this elsewhere. When God had thus finished his last and most excellent creature, he appointed his residence in Eden, made him his viceroy, and gave him a full jurisdiction over all his workes, that as the whole man consisted of body and spirit, so the inferiour earthly creatures might be subject to the one, and the superiour Intellectual Essences might minister to the other. But this royalty continued not long, for pre-

Acts.

Arias Montanus.

sently upon his preferment there was a faction in the Heavenly
Court, and the Angels scorning to attend this piece of clay, contrived
how to supplant him.   The first in this plot was Lucifer—Montanus tells me his name was Hilel.   He casts about to nullifie that
which God had inacted, that so at once he might overreach Him
and his Creature.   This pollicy he imparts to some others of the
Hierarchy, and strengthens himself with conspirators.   But there is
no counsel against God : the mischief is no sooner hatched but he
and his confederates are expelled from Light to Darknesse, and thus
rebellion is as the sin of witchcraft—a witch is a rebel in physicks,
and a rebell is a witch in politicks : the one acts against nature, the
other against order, the rule of it ; but both are in league vith the
devil, as the first father of discord and sorcerie.   Satan being thus
ejected, as the condition of reprobates is, became more hardened in
his resolutions, and to bring his malice about arrives by permission
at Eden.   Here he makes Woman his instrument to tempt Man, and
overthrowes him by the same means that God made for an help to
him.   Adam having thus transgrest the commandment was exposed
to the lash, and in him his posterity.   But here lyes the knot ; how
can we possibly learne his disease, if we know not the immediate
efficient of it ?   If I question our divines what the Forbidden Fruit
was, I may be long enough without an answer.   Search all the school-
men from Ramus to Peter Hispan, and they have no logick in the
point.   What shall we doe in this case ?   To speake anything contrary to the sting of Aristotle (though perhaps we hit the mark) is to
expose ourselves to the common hue ; but in respect I prefer a
private truth to a publick errour, I will proceed.   And now reader,
" prick up thine ears," come on without prejudice, and I will tell thee
that which never hitherto hath been discovered.

That which I now write must needs appeare very strange, and
incredible to the common man, whose knowledge sticks in the barke
of allegories and mysticall speeches, never apprehending that which
is signified by them unto us.   This I say must needs sound strange,
with such as understand the Scriptures in the litterall plaine sence,
considering not the scope and intention of the Divine Spirit, by
whom they were first penned and delivered.   Howsoever, Origen
being " one chosen out of many," and, in the judgement of many
wise men, the most learned of the Fathers, durst never trust himselfe
in this point, but alwaies in those Scriptures where his reason could
not satisfie, concluded a mystery.

Certainly, if it be once granted (as some stick not to affirm) that
the Tree of Knowledge was a vegetable and Eden a Garden, it may

be very well affirmed, that the tree of life being described in the same category, as the schoolemen expresse it, was a vegetable also. But how derogatory this is to the power of God, to the merits and passion of Jesus Christ, whose gift eternall life is, let any indifferent Christian judge. Here then we have a certain entrance into Paradise, where we may search out this Tree of Knowledge, and (haply) learn what it is. For seeing it must be granted that by the Tree of Life is figured the Divine Spirit (for it is the Spirit that quickeneth, and shall one day translate us from corruption to incorruption), it will be no indiscreet inference on the contrary, that by the Tree of Knowledge is signified some sensuall nature, repugnant to the spirituall, wherein our worldly sinfull affections, as lust, anger, and the rest, have their seat, and predominate.

I will now digresse a while; but not much from the purpose, whereby it may appear unto the reader that the letter is no sufficient expositor of Scripture, and that there is a great deal of difference between the sound and the sense of the text. Dionysius the Areopagite in his Epistle to Titus gives him this *caveat.* " And to know this is, notwithstanding, the worth of the business—that the tradition of theologists is twofold—the one mystical and secret, the other manifest and more known." And in his Book of the Ecclesiastical Hierarchie, written to Timotheus, he affirms that in the primitive, Apostolical times, the mysteries of Divinity were delivered " partly in written and partly in unwritten canons." Some things, he confesseth, were written in the theological books, and such are the common doctrinals of the Church now; in which, notwithstanding (as St Peter saith), " there are many things hard to be understood." Some things again " which wholly transcended carnal understanding were transmitted without writing from mind to mind, being concealed between the lines of the visible word." And certainly this orall tradition was the cause that in the subsequent ages of the Church, all the mysteries of Divinity were lost. Nay, this very day there is not one among all our school-doctors, or late ex-temporaries, that knows what is represented unto us by the outward element of Water in Baptism. True indeed, they tell us it betokens the washing away of sin, which we grant them, but this is not the full signification for which it was ordained. It hath been the common errour of all times to mistake *signum* for *signatum*, the shell for the kernel, yet to prevent this it was that Dionysius wrote his book of the Cœlestiall Hierarchie, and especially his *Theologia Significativa*, of which there is such frequent mention made in his works. Verily, our Saviour Himself, who is blessed for evermore, did sometimes speak in parables, and commanded further that pearles should not be cast forth unto swine, for " it is not given to all men to know the mysteries of the Kingdome of God." Supposing then (as is most true) that, amongst other mystical speeches contained in Scripture, this of the Garden of Eden and the trees in it is one. I shall proceed to the exposition of it in some measure, concealing the particulars notwithstanding.

Man in the beginning (I mean the substantiall inward Man), both in and after his creation, for some short time, was a pure Intellectual Essence, free from all fleshly, sensuall affections. In this state the *Anima*, or Sensitive Nature, did not prevail over the spirituall as it doth now in us. For the superior mentall part of man was united to God " by an essentiall contact," and the Divine Light being received in, and conveyed to, the inferiour portions of the Soul, did mortifie all carnal desires, insomuch that in Adam the sensitive faculties were scarce at all imployed, the spirituall prevailing over them in him, as they do over the spirituall now in us. Hence we read in Scripture, that during the state of innocence he did not know that he was naked, but no sooner eats he of the Tree of Knowledge but he saw his nakednesse, and was ashamed of it, wherefore also he hides himself amongst the trees of the Garden, and when God calls

Genesis.   to him, he replies : " I heard thy voice in the Garden, and I was afraid because I was naked, and I hid myself." But God, knowing his former state, answeres him with a question : " Who told thee that thou wast naked? Hast thou eaten of the tree, whereof I commanded thee thou shouldest not eat ? " Here we see a twofold state of man—his first and best in the spirituall substantiall union of his intellectual parts to God, and the mortification of his æthereall sensitive nature, wherein the fleshly, sinfull affections had their residence—his second, or his fall, in the eating of the Forbidden Fruit, which did cast asleep his intellectual faculties, but did stir up

Genesis.   and exalt the sensuall. For (sayeth the Serpent) "God doth know that in the day you eat thereof, then your eyes shall be opened, and you shall be as gods, knowing good and evill. And when the woman saw that the Tree was good for food, and that it was pleasant to the eyes and a tree to be desired to make one wise ; shee took of the Fruit thereof, and did eat, and gave also unto her husband, with her, and he did eat ; and the eyes of them both were opened, and they knew that they were naked." Thus we see the sensuall faculties revived in our first parents and brought " from potentiality into activity," as the schoolmen speak, by vertue of this Forbidden Fruit. Neither did this eating suppresse the intellectuall powers in Adam onely, but in all his generations after him, for the influence of this fruit past together with his nature into his posterity. We are all born like Moses with a veil over the face; this is it which hinders the prospect of that intellectual shining light which God hath placed in us. And to tell a truth that concerns all mankind, the greatest mystery both in divinity and philosophy is how to remove it.

It will not be amiss to speak something in this place of the nature and constitution of man, to make that more plain which hath already been spoken.

As the Great World consists of three parts—the Elemental, the Cœlestial, and the Spiritual, above all which God himself is seated in that infinite, inaccessible Light which streames from his own nature, even so man hath in him his earthly, elemental parts, together with the cœlestial and angelical natures, in the center of all which moves and shines the Divine Spirit. The sensuall, cœlestial, æthereal part of man is that whereby we do move, see, feel, taste, and smell, and have a commerce with all material objects whatsoever. It is the same in us as in beasts, and it is derived from Heaven, where it is predominant, to all the inferiour earthly creatures. In plain terms it is part of the Soul of the World, commonly called the Medial Soul, because the influences of the Divine Nature are conveyed through it to the more material parts of the creature, with which of themselves they have no proportion. By meanes of this Medial Soul, or Æthereal Nature, man is made subject to the influence of stars, and is partly disposed of by the Cœlestial Harmony. For this middle part (middle I mean between both extreames, and not that which actually unites the whole together), as well that which is in the outward heaven as that which is in man, is of a fruitfull, insinuating nature, and carried with a strong desire to multiply itself, so that the Cœlestiall Form stirs up and excites the Elementall. For this spirit is in man, in beasts, in vegetables, in minerals, and in everything it is the mediate cause of composition and multiplication. Neither should any wonder that I affirm this spirit to be in minerals because the operations of it are not discerned there. For shall we conclude therefore that there is no inward agent that actuates and specifies those passive, indefinite principles whereof they are compounded? Tell me not now of blind Peripateticall formes and qualities! A forme is that which Aristotle could not define substantially, nor any of his followers after him, and therefore they are not competent judges of it. But, I beseech you, are not the faculties of this spirit supprest in man also when the organs are corrupted, as it appeareth in those that are blind? But, notwithstanding the eye onely is destroyed and not the visible power, for that remaines, as it is plain in their dreames. Now this vision is performed by a reflexion of the visuall radii in their inward, proper cell. For Nature imployes her gifts onely where she findes a conveniencie and fit disposition of organs, which being not in minerals, we may not expect so clear an expression {of the naturall powers in them. Notwithstanding in the flowers of severall vegetables (which in some sort represent the eyes), there is a more subtile, acute perception of heat and cold, and other cœlestiall influences then in any other part. This is manifest in those herbs which open at the rising and shut towards the sunset, which motion is caused by the spirit being sensible of the approach and departure of the sun. For indeed the flowers are (as it were) the spring of the spirit, where it breakes forth and streames, as it appeares by the odours that are more cœlestiall and comfortable there. Again, this is more evident in the plant-animalls, as the Vegetable Lamb, the *Arbor Casta*, and severall others. But this will not sink with any but such as have seen this spirit separated from his elements, where I leave it for this time.

Next to this sensuall nature of man is the angelicall or rationall spirit. This spirit adheres sometimes to the *mens*, or superior portion of the Soul, and then it is filled with the Divine Light, but most commonly it descends into the æthereal inferior portion, which St Paul calls the natural man, where it is altered by the cœlestiall influences, and diversely distracted with the irregular affections and passions of the sensuall nature.

Lastly, above the Rational Spirit is the *Mens*, or Concealed Intelligence, commonly called *Intellectus Illustratus*, and of Moses the Breath of Life. This is that spirit which God himselfe breathed into man, and by which man is united again to God. Now, as the Divine Light, flowing into the *Mens*, did assimilate and convert the inferior portions of the Soul to God, so, on the contrary, the Tree of Knowledge did obscure and darken the superior portions, but awaked and stirred up the animal, sinfull nature. The sum of all is this—Man, as long as he continued in his union to God, knew the good only, that is, the things that were of God; but, as soon as he stretched forth his hand, and did eate of the Forbidden Fruit, that is, the Medial Spirit, or Spirit of the Greater World, presently upon his disobedience and transgression of the commandement, his union to the Divine Nature was dissolved, and his spirit being united to the spirit of the world, he knew the evill only, that is, the things that were of the world. True it is, he knew the good and the evill, but the evill in a far greater measure then the good.

Some sparks of grace were left, and though the perfection of innocence was lost upon his fall from the Divine Light, yet conscience remained still with him, partly to direct, partly to punish. Thus you see that this *Anima Media,* or Middle Spirit, is figured by the Tree of Knowledge, but he that knows why the Tree of Life is said to be in the middest of the Garden, and to grow out of the ground, will more fully understand that which we have spoken.* We see, moreover, that the faculties which we have ascribed to the Tree of Knowledge are to be found only in the Middle Nature. First, it is said to be a tree to be " desired to make one wise," but it was fleshly, sensuall wisdom, the wisdom of this world and not of God. Secondly, it is said to be " good for food and pleasant to the eyes ;" so is the Middle Nature also, for it is the onely medecine to repaire the decayes of the naturall man, and to continue our bodies in their primitive strength and integrity.

Lastly, that I may speake something for my selfe : this is no new unheard of fansie, as the understanding reader may gather out of Trismegistus. Nay, I am verily of opinion that the Egyptians received this knowledge from the Hebrews, who lived a long time amongst them, as it appears out of Scripture, and that they delivered it over to the Grecians. This is plain out of Jamblichus in his book *De Mysteriis,* where he hath these words. " The intellectual man, considering within himself, was formerly joined to the contemplation of the gods : afterwards, however, there did enter in another soul, coeval with the human kind of shape, and on that account he was bound by the same bond of fate and of necessity." And what else, I beseech you, is signified unto us in that poeticall fable of Prometheus ?—that he should steale a certaine fire from Heaven, for which trespasse afterwards, God punished the world with a great many diseases and mortality.

But some body may reply :—Seeing that God made all things good, as it appeares in his review of the creatures on the sixth day, how could it be a sin in Adam to eat that which in it self was good? Verily, the sin was not grounded in the nature of that which he did eate, but it was the inference of the commandment, in as much as he was forbidden to eate it. And this is that which St Paul tells us, that he had not known sin had it not been for the law; and again, in another place, " the strength of sin is the law." But presently upon the disobedience of the first man, and his transgression of the commandement, the creature was made subject to vanity, for the curse followed, and the impure seeds were joyned with the pure, and

* Note 6.

they reigne to this houre in our bodies, and not in us alone, but in every other naturall thing.   Hence it is we read in Scripture, that "the Heavens themselves are not clean in his sight," and to this alludes the apostle in that speech of his to the Colossians, that "it pleased the Father to reconcile all things to himselfe by Christ, whether they be things in earth or things in Heaven."   And here you are to observe that Cornelius Agrippa mistook the act of genera- tion for originall sin, which indeed was the effect of it, and this is the only point wherein he hath miscarried.

I have now done—only a word more concerning the situation of Paradise, and the rather because of the diversitie of opinions con- cerning that place, and the absurdity of them.   St Paul in his second Epistle to the Colossians discovers it in these words : " I knew a man in Christ above fourteen yeares ago (whether in the body or out of the body, I cannot tell, God knoweth) such a one caught up to the third Heaven.   And I knew such a man (whether in the body or out of the body, I cannot tell, God knoweth) how that he was caught up into Paradise."   Here you see that Paradise and the Third Heaven are convertible tearms, so that the one discovers the other. Much more I could have said concerning the Tree of Knowledge, being in it selfe a large and very mysticall subject, but, for my part, I rest contented with my owne particular apprehension and desire not to enlarge it any further.   Neither had I committed this much to paper but out of my love to the Truth, and that I would not have these thoughts altogether perish.

You see now, if you be not men of a most uncouth head, how man fell, and, by consequence, you may guesse by what meanes he is to rise.   He must be united to the Divine Light, from whence by disobedience he was separated.   A flash or tincture of this must come, or he can no more discerne things spiritually then he can dis- tinguish colours naturally without the light of the sun.   This Light descends, and is united to him, by the same meanes as his Soule was at first.   I speake not here of the symbolicall, exteriour descent from the prototypicall-planets to the created spheres and thence "into the night of the body," but I speake of that most secret and silent lapse of the Spirit "through the sequence of naturall formes," and this is a mystery not easily apprehended.   It is a Cabalisticall maxime— *Nulla res spiritualis descendens inferius operatur sine indumento*— " No spirituall entity descending into our inferiour plane can mani- fest therein without an envelope."   Consider well of it with your selves, and take heed you wander not in the circumference.   The Soul of man, whiles she is in the body, is like a candle shut up in a dark lanthorn, or a fire that is almost stifled for want of aire. Spirits (say the Platonicks) when they are " in their own country," are like *Proclus— De Anima* the inhabitants of green fields, who live perpetually amongst flowers in a spicy, odorous aire, but here below, " in the circle of generation," they mourn because of darkness and solitude, like people lockt up in a pest-house. " Here do they fear, desire and grieve." This is it makes the Soule subject to so many passions, to such a Proteus of humours. Now she flourishes, now she withers, now a smile, now a tear, and when she hath played out her stock, then comes a repetition of the same fancies, till at last she cries out with Seneca, " How long shall these things continue ? " This is occasioned by her vast and infinite capacity, which is satisfied with nothing but God, from whom at first she descended. It is miraculous to consider how she struggles with her chaynes when man is in extremity, how she falsifies with fortune, what pomp, what pleasure, what a paradise doth she propose to her selfe ! She spans kingdomes in a thought, and enjoyes all that inwardly which she misseth outwardly. In her are patterns and notions of all things in the world. If she but fancies her selfe in the midst of the sea, presently she is there, and heares the rushing of the billowes. She makes an invisible voyage from one place to an other, and presents to her selfe things absent as if they were present. The dead live to her ; there is no grave can hide them from her thoughts. Now shee is here in dirt and mire, and in a trice above the moone :

> Above the region of the storms she soars,
> Beneath her feet she hears devolving clouds,
> And under foot she thrusts the thunders blind.

But this is nothing. If she were once out of the body, she could act all that which she imagined. " In a moment (saith Agrippa) whatsoever she desires shall follow." In this state she can " act on the fluids of the Macrocosm," make generall commotions in the two spheres of air and water, and alter the complexions of times. Neither is this a fable, but the unanimous tenet of the Arabians, with the two Princes Avicebron and Avicenna. She hath then an absolute power in miraculous and more than naturall transmutations. She can in an instant transfer her own vessell from one place to an other. She can (by an union with universall force) infuse and communicate her thoughts to the absent, be the distance never so great. Neither is there any thing under the sun but she may know it, and remaining onely in one place, she can acquaint her selfe with the actions of all places whatsoever. I omit to speak of her Magnet, wherewith she can attract all things, as well spirituall as naturall.   Finally, "there is

no achievement in the whole series of nature, however arduous, however excellent, however even miraculous, that the human Soul, when connected with the source of its divinity, which the Magi term the Soul Standing, and not Falling, shall not be able to effect by its own powers and devoid of any external support whatsoever." But who is he " amid so many myriads of philosophers," that knows her nature substantially, and the genuine, speciall use thereof?   This is

Abraham's "Grand Secret, wonderful exceedingly and very occult, sealed with seven seals, and out of these flow fire, water, and air, which are divided into males and females."   We should therefore pray continually, that God would open our eyes, whereby we might see to imploy that talent which he hath bestowed upon us, but lies buried now in the ground, and doth not fructifie at all.   He it is to whom we must be united by "an essentiall contact," and then we shall know all things, "manifested face to face by a clear seeing into the Divine Light."   This influx from Him is the true, proper efficient of our regeneration, that *sperma* of St John, the seed of God which remaines in us.   If this be once obtained, we need not serve under Aristotle or Galen, nor trouble ourselves with foolish Utrums and Ergos, for his unction will instruct us as in all things.   But indeed the doctrine of the Schoolmen, which in a manner makes God and nature contraries, hath so weakened our confidence towards Heaven that we look upon all receptions from thence as impossibilities.   But if things were well weighed, and this cloud of tradition removed, we should quickly finde that God is more ready to give then we are to receive, for He made man (as it were) for his playfellow, that he might survey and examine his workes.   The inferiour creatures he made not for themselves but his own glory, which glory he could not receive from any thing so perfectly as from man, who, having in him the spirit of discretion, might judge of the beauty of the creature and consequently praise the Creatour.   Wherefore also God gave him the use of all his works, and in Paradise how familiar

is he, or rather how doth he play with Adam?   " Out of the ground (saith the Scripture) the Lord God formed every beast of the field, and every fowl of the air, and brought them unto Adam to see what he would call them ; and whatsoever Adam called every living creature, that was the name thereof."   These were the books which God ordained for Adam, and for us his posterity, not the quintessence of Aristotle, nor the temperament of Galen the Antichrist. But this is "tormenting the hornets."   Now will the Peripateticks brand me with their *contra principia*, and the schoole-divines with a *tradatur Satanæ.* I know I shall be hated of most for my paines, and perhaps scoffed at like Pythagoras in Lucian. "Who buyeth Eugenius? Who wisheth to be above the best of men? or to know the Harmony of the World and to live anew?" But because, according to their own master, ορχὸς τὸ τιμ-εαταρον ἐστι, and that an affirmative of this nature cannot fall to the ground with a Christian, I will come to my oath. I do there-fore protest before my glorious God, I have not written this out of malice, but out of zeal and affection to the truth of my Creatour. Let them take heed then, least whiles they contemn Mysteries, they violate the Majesty of God in his creatures, and trample the Blood of the Covenant under foot. But shall I not be counted a conjurer, seeing I follow the principles of Cornelius Agrippa, that grand Archimagus, as the antichristian Jesuits call him? He indeed is my author, and next to God I owe all that I have unto him. Why should I be ashamed to confesse it? He was, reader, by extraction noble, by religion a Protestant, as it appeares out of his owne writings, besides the late but malitious testimony of Promondus, a *Promondus —In Crisi* learned Papist. For his course of life, a man famous in his person *sua ad Cau-* both for actions of war and peace, a favorite to the greatest princes *sam despera-tam Gisberti* of his time, and the just wonder of all learned men. Lastly, he was *Voe.* one that carried him selfe above the miseries he was borne to, and made fortune know man might be her master. This is answer enough to a few sophisters, and, in defiance to all calumnies thus I salute his memory.*

Great glorious penman! whom I should not name,
Lest I might seem to measure thee by fame,
Nature's apostle and her choice high-priest,
Her mysticall and bright Evangelist,
How am I rapt when I contemplate thee,
And winde my self above all that I see?
The spirits of thy lines infuse a fire
Like the World's Soul, which makes me thus aspire.
I am unbodied by thy books and thee,
And in thy papers finde my extasie;
Or if I please but to descend a strain,
Thy elements do skreen my Soul again.
I can undresse myself by thy bright glasse,
And then resume th' inclosure as I was.
Now I am earth, and now a star, and then
A spirit; now a star and earth agen.
Or if I will but ransack all that be,
In the least moment I ingrosse all three.

* Note 7.

C

I span the Heaven and earth, and things above,
And which is more joyn natures with their love.
He crowns my soul with fire, and there doth shine
But like the rainbow in a cloud of mine.
Yet there's a law by which I discompose
The ashes and the fire it self disclose,
But in his em'rald still he doth appear,
They are but grave-clothes which he scatters here.
Who sees this fire without his mask, his eye
Must needs be swallowed by the Light, and die.
    These are the mysteries for which I wept,
Glorious Agrippa, when thy language slept,
Where thy dark texture made me wander far,
Whiles through that pathless night I traced the star;
But I have found those mysteries for which
Thy book was more then thrice-piled o'er with pitch.
Now a new East beyond the stars I see
Where breaks the day of thy Divinitie:
Heav'n states a commerce here with Man, had he
But grateful hands to take and eyes to see.
    Hence you fond school-men, that high truth deride,
And with no arguments but noise and pride—
You that damn all but what yourselves invent,
And yet finde nothing by experiment;
Your fate is written by an unseen hand,
But his Three Books with the Three Worlds shall stand.

Thus far, reader, I have handled the composure and royalty of man; I shall now speak something of his dissolution, and close up my discourse, as he doth his life, with death. Death is "the recession of life into the Unknown," not the annihilation of any one particle, but a retreat of hidden natures to the same state they were in before they were manifested. This is occasioned by the disproportion and inequality of the matter, for when the harmony is broken by the excesse of any one principle, the vitall twist (without a timely reduction of the unity) disbands and unravells. In this recesse the several ingredients of man return to those severall elements from whence they came at first in their accesse to a compound, for to think that God creates anything from nothing in the work of generation is a pure metaphysicall whymsey. Thus the Earthly parts, as we see by experience, return to the Earth, the cœlestial to a superiour, heavenly Limbus, and the Spirit to God that gave it. Neither should any wonder that I affirm the Spirit of the living God to be in man, when God himself doth acknowledge it for his own. "My
Genesis. spirit (saith he) shall not alwaies be sheathed (for so the Hebrew signifies) in man, for that he also is flesh, yet his dayes shall be an hundred and twenty years." Besides, the breathing of it into Adam

proves it proceeded from God, and therefore the Spirit of God. Thus Christ breathed on his Apostles, and they received the Holy Ghost. In Ezeckiel, the Spirit comes from the four winds and breathes upon the slain, that they might live. Now this Spirit was the Spirit of Life, the same with that Breath of Life which was breathed into the first man, and he became a living Soul. But, without doubt, the Breath or Spirit of Life is the Spirit of God. Neither is this Spirit in man alone but in all the Great World, though after another manner. For God breathes continually, and passeth through all things like an air that refresheth—wherefore also he is called of Pythagoras "the animating principle of all." Hence it is that God in Scripture hath severall names according to those severall offices he performes in the preservation of the creature. "Nay also (sayeth the Areopagite) they declare him to be present in our minds, and in our souls, and in our bodies, and to be in Heaven equally with earth, and in himself at the same time; the same also they declare to be in the world, around the world, above the world, above the Heaven, the superior Essence, sun, star, fire, water, spirit, dew, cloud, the very stone, and rock, to be in all things which are, and himself to be nothing which they are." And most certain it is because of his secret passage and penetration through all, that other simile in Dionysius was given him. " He joyns himself to the nature of Adam (saith hee), and to that which is most mean and irrational, to the worm itself—so has it come down to us from those who in former times were versed in things Divine."

Now this figurative kind of speech, with its variety of appellations, is not only proper to Holy Writ, but the Ægyptians also (as Plutarch tells me) called Iris, or the most secret part of Nature, myrionymos, and certainly that the same thing should have a thousand names is no news to such as have studied the Philosophers' Stone. But to return thither whence we have digressed. I told you the severall principles of man in his dissolution part, as sometimes friends do, severall wayes—earth to earth, as our liturgie hath it, and Heaven to Heaven, according to that of Lucretius.

> And that which first did issue from the earth
> Doth now disintegrate to earth again ;
> And what was mission'd from æthereall shores,
> That Heaven's resplendent temples welcome back.

But more expressly the Divine Virgil, speaking of his Bees—

> And by these signs, by this example set,
> Within the bees a part of Mind Divine
> And the ethereall sources they discern.

For through the length and breadth of every land,
Dim ocean's depths and Heaven's effulgent heights ;
Extends that active God, from whom the kine,
The beasts of burthen, and the race of man,
With all the raging dwellers of the wild,
Their life derive ; who summons to himself
Brief lives but just begun.   To him 'tis plain
Must every life dissolved, be late or soon
Surrendered back, nor is there room for death,
But living still the Spirit is enrolled
Among the starry hosts, and refuge finds
In highest Heaven.

This vanish or ascent of the inward ethereall principles doth not presently follow their separation, for that part of man which Paracelsus calls the Sydereall Man, and more appositely "the Brute part of man," but Agrippa "the spectre" and Virgil

"Th' æthereall sense, and heat of simple breath,"

this part, I say, which is the Astral Man,* hovers sometimes about the dormitories of the dead, and that because of the magnetism, or sympathie, which is between him and the radical, vital moysture.   In this "Spectre" is the seat of the Imagination, and it retaines after death an impresse of those passions and affections to which it was subject in the body.   This makes him haunt those places where the whole man had been most conversant, and imitate the actions and gestures of life.   This magnetism is excellently confirmed by that memorable accident at Paris which Dr Fludd proves to be true by the testimonies of great and learned men.   Agrippa also, speaking of the apparitions of the dead, hath these words :—"But what I myself have seen with my own eyes and touched with my own hands, I will not refer to in this place, lest it be my lot to be accused by the ignorant of falsehood on account of the stupendous strangeness of the occurrences."   But this scæne exceeds not the circuit of one year, for when the body begins fully to corrupt, the Spirit returnes to his originall element.   These apparitions have made a great noise in the world, not without some benefit to the pope.   But I shall reserve all for my great work, where I shall more fully handle these mysteries.

I am now to speak of man as he is subject to a supernaturall judgement.   And, to be short, my sentiment is this.   I conceive there are, besides the Empyræall Heaven, two inferiour Mansions, or Receptacles of Spirits.   The one is that which our Saviour calls "the outer darkness," and this it is whence there is no redemption

* Note 8.

—whence the souls may never come forth, as the divine Plato hath it. The other, I suppose, is somewhat answerable to the Elysian Fields, some delicate, pleasant region, the Suburbs of Heaven, as it were. Those Seven Mighty Mountaines, whereupon there grow Roses and Lilies, or the outgoings of Paradise in Esdras. Such was that place where the oracle told Amelius the soul of Plotinus was—

> Where friendship is, where Cupid fair to see,
> Replete with purest joy, enriched from God
> With sempiternall streames ambrosiall,
> Whence are the bonds of love, the gentle breath,
> The tranquil air of great Jove's golden race.

Stellatus supposeth there is a successive, gradual ascent of the Soul, according to the process of expiation, and he makes her inter-residence in the Moon. But, let it be where it will, my opinion is, that this middlemost mansion is appointed for such souls whose whole man hath not perfectly repented in this world, but, notwithstanding, they are "of the number of the saved," and reserved in this place to a further repentance in the spirit for those offences they committed in the flesh. I do not here maintain that Will o' the Wisp of Purgatory, or any such painted, imaginary Tophet; but that which I speak (if I am not mistaken) I have a strong Scripture for. It is that of St Peter, where he speaks of Christ being "put to death in the flesh, but quickened by the Spirit; by which also he went, and preached unto the spirits that were in prison, which sometimes were disobedient when once the long-suffering of God waited in the dayes of Noah, while the ark was a preparing, wherein few, that is, eight, souls were saved by water." These spirits were the souls of those who perished in the Floud, and were reserved in this place till Christ should have come, and preached repentance unto them. I know Scaliger thinks to evade this construction with his *Qui tunc*, that they were then alive, namely, before the Floud, when they were preached unto. But I shall overthrow this single nonsense with three solid reasons, drawn out of the body of the text. First, it is not said that the Spirit it self precisely preached unto them, but He who went thither by the Spirit, namely, Christ in the hypostaticall union of his Soul and Godhead, which union was not before the Floud, when these dead did live. Secondly, it is written that he preached unto spirits, not to men, to those which were in prison, not to those which were "in life," which is quite contrary to Scaliger. And this exposition the apostle confirms in another place— "to them that are dead," the dead were preached to not the living. ¹ Pet. iv. 6. Thirdly, the apostle says: these spirits were but sometimes disobedient, and withall tells us when, namely, in the dayes of Noah, whence I gather they were not disobedient at this time of preaching, and this is plain out of the subsequent chapter.

"For this cause (sayeth the apostle) was the gospel preached also to them that are dead, that they might be judged according to men in the flesh, but live according to God in the Spirit." Now this judgement in the flesh was grounded on their disobedience in the dayes of Noah, for which also they were drowned, but salvation according to God in the Spirit proceeded from their repentance at the preaching of Christ, which was after death. I do not impose this on the reader as if I sate in the infallible chaire, but I am confident the text of it self will speak no other sense. As for the doctrine, it is no way hurtfull, but, in my opinion, as it detracts not from the mercy of God, so it addes much to the comfort of man.

I shall now speak a word more concerning my self, and another concerning the common philosophy, and then I have done. It will be questioned perhaps what I am, and especially what my religion is. Take this short answer; I am neither Papist nor sectary, but a true resolute Protestant in the best sense of the Church of England. For philosophy, as it now stands, it is altogether imperfect, and withall false—a meer apothecary's drug, a mixture of inconsistent, contrary principles which no way agree with the harmony and method of Nature. In a word, the whole Encyclopædia (as they call it) bateing the demonstrative, mathematicall part, is built on meer imagination without the least light of experience. I wish, therefore, all the true sons of my famous Oxford mother to look beyond Aristotle, and not confine their intellects to the narrow and cloudy horizon of his text, for he is as short of Nature as the grammarians are of steganography. I expect not any thanks for this my advice or discovery, though perhaps I deserve well for both; but, verily, the time will come when this truth shall be more perfectly manifested, and especially that great and glorious mystery, whereof there is little spoken in this book. "The alone King Messias, the Word made flesh of the Father, doth reveal this Arcanum, hereafter to be more openly manifested in a certain fulness of time"— Cornelius Agrippa's own prediction, and I am confident it shall finde patrons enough when nothing remaines here of me but memory.

John.

> My sweetest Jesus! 'twas thy voice: "If I
> Be lifted up, I'll draw all to the skie."
> Yet I am here; I'm stifled in this clay,
> Shut up from Thee, and the fresh East of Day.

I know thy hand's not short; but I'm unfit—
A foul, unclean thing !—to take hold of it.
I am all dirt, nor can I hope to please,
Unless in mercy thou lov'st a disease.
Diseases may be cur'd, but who'd reprieve
Him that is dead? Tell me, my God, I live.
'Tis true I live, but I so sleep withall,
I cannot move, scarce hear, when Thou dost call.
Sin's lullabies charm me when I would come,
But draw me after thee, and I will run.
Thou know'st I'm sick; let me not feasted be,
But keep a diet, and prescribed by thee.
Should I carve for my self, I would exceed
To surfeits soon, and by self murder bleed.
I ask for stones and scorpions, but still crost,
And all for love—should'st Thou grant, I were lost;
Dear Lord, deny me still, and never signe
My will but when that will agrees with thine;
And when this conflict's past, and I appear
To answer what a patient I was here—
How I did weep when Thou didst woo, repine
At thy best sweets, and in a childish whyne
Refuse thy proffer'd love, yet cry and call
For rattles of my own to play withall—
Look on thy Cross and let Thy Blood come in
When mine shall blush as guilty of my sin;
Then shall I live, being rescu'd in my fall—
A text of mercy to thy creatures all,
Who, having seen the worst of sins in me,
Must needs confesse the best of loves in Thee.

I have now done, reader, but how much to my own prejudice I cannot tell. I am confident this shall not passe without noise, but I may do well enough if thou grantest me but one request. I would not have thee look here for the paint and trim of rhetorick, and the rather because English is a language the author was not born to. Besides this piece was composed in haste, and in my dayes of mourning on the sad occurrence of a brother's death. "And who knoweth how to write amidst a strife of teares and inke?"

To conclude—if I have erred in anything (and yet I followed the rules of creation) I expose it not to the mercy of man, but of God, who as he is most able, so also is he most willing to forgive us in the day of our accounts.

AN ADVERTISEMENT TO THE READER.

If the old itch of scribbling, a disease very proper to Galenists, surprise any of their tribe, I shall expect from them these following performances. First, a plain, positive exposition of all the passages in this book, without any injury to the sense of their author, for if they interpret them otherwise then they ought, they but create errours of their own, and then overthrow them.

Secondly, to prove their familiarity and knowledge in this art, let them give the reader a punctuall discovery of all the secrets thereof. If this be more then they can do, it is argument enough they know not what they oppose, and if they do not know, how can they judge? or if they judge, where is their evidence to condemn.

Thirdly, let them not mangle and discompose my book with a scatter of observations, but proceed methodically to the censure of each part, expounding what is obscure, and discovering the very practise, that the reader may finde my positions to be false, not onely in their theorie, but, if he will assay it, by his own particular experience.

I have two admonitions more to the ingenuous and well-disposed reader. First, that he would not slight my endeavours because of my years, which are but few. It is the custom of most men to measure knowledge by the beard, but look thou rather on the Soul,

Proclus.

an essence of that nature "which requireth not the courses of time for its perfection." Secondly, that he would not conclude anything rashly concerning the subject of this art, for it is a principle not easily apprehended. It is neither earth nor water, air nor fire. It is not Gold, Silver, Saturn, Antimonie, or Vitriol, nor any kind of minerall whatsoever. It is not bloud, nor the seed of any individuall, as some unnaturall, obscene authors have imagined. In a word, it is no minerall, no vegetable, no animall, but a system, as it were, of all three. In plain terms, it is *Sperma Majoris Animalis*, the seed of Heaven and earth, our most secret, miraculous Hermaphrodite. If you know this, and, with it, the Hydro-pyro-magical art, you may with some security attempt the work—if not, practice is the way to poverty. Assay nothing without science, but confine yourself to those bounds which Nature hath prescribed you.

THE END.

ANIMA MAGICA ABSCONDITA:

OR

A ·DISCOURSE OF THE UNIVERSALL SPIRIT OF NATURE,

WITH HIS STRANGE, ABSTRUSE, MIRACULOUS ASCENT, AND DESCENT.

BY

EUGENIUS PHILALETHES.

Stapul: in Dion:

Est autem universum speculum unum, ad quod astans Amor, suum efformat idolum.

Dû a Digon: Hêb Dhû, Hêb Dhim.

TO THE READER.

OW God defend! what will become of me? I have neither consulted with the stars, nor their urinals, the almanacks. A fine fellow, to neglect the prophets who are read in England every day! They shall pardon me for this oversight. There is a mystery in their profession they have not so much as heard of—"the Christian starry Heaven" —a new Heaven fansied on the whole earth. Here the twelve Apostles have surprised the zodiak, and all the saints are ranged on their North and South sides. It were a pretty vanity to preach when St Paul is ascendent, and would not a papist smile to have his pope elected under St Peter? Reader, if I studied these things, I should not think myself worse imployed then the Roman Chaucer was in Troilus. I come out as if there were no houres in the day, nor planets in the houres, neither do I care for anything but that interlude of Perrendenga in Michael Cervantes: "Let the old man, my master live, and Christ be with us all." Thou wilt wonder now where this drives, for I have neither a Conde de lemos, nor a cardinal to pray for. I pray for the dead, that is, I wish him a fair remembrance whose labours have deserved it. It happened in exposing my former discourse to censure (a custom hath strangled many truths in the cradle), that a learned man suggested to me some bad opinion he had of my author, Henricus Cornelius Agrippa. I have ever understood it was not one but many in whose sentiment that miracle suffered. It is the fortune of deep writers to miscarry because of obscurity; thus the spots in the moon with some men are earth, but it is more probable they are water. There is no day so clear, but there are lees towards the horizon; so, inferior wits, when they reflect on higher intellects, leave a mist in their beames. Had he lived in ignorance, as most do, he might have past hence like the last yeare's cloudes, without any more remembrance. But as I believe the truth a maine branch of that end to which I was born, so I hold it my duty to vindicate him from

whom I have received it.   The world then being not able to confute
this man's principles by reason, went about to do it by scandal, and
the first argument they fastened on was that of the Jews against his
Saviour: "Thou art a Samaritan, and hast a devil."   The chief in
this persecution is Cicognes, and after him Delrio in his fabulous
"Disquisitions."   But Paulus Jovius stirred in the vomit, who
amongst other men's "lives" hath put my author to death.   It is
done indeed emphatically betwixt him and his poet, whom he hired
(it seems) to stitch verse to his prose, and so patched up the legend.
"Who would believe (saith he) a monstrous disposition to have been
concealed by the sedate countenance of Henry Cornelius Agrippa!"
In his subsequent discourse he states his question, and returns my
author's best parts as a libell on his memorie.   But that which
troubles him most of all is that Agrippa should prove his doctrine
out of the Scriptures.   Then he inculcates the solemn crambo of
his dog-devil, whose collar, emblematically wrought with nailes, made
the *russe* to his familiar.   For a close to the story, he kills him at
Lyons, where, being near his departure, he unravelled his magick in
this desperate dismission: "Begone, abandoned beast, who hast lost
me everything!"   This is the most grosse lie, and the least probable
in every circumstance that ever was related.   Devils are use not to
quit their conjurors in the day of death, neither will they at such
times be exterminated.   This is the hour wherein they attend their
prey, and from seeming servants become cruell masters.   Besides, is
it not most gross, that any should dog this devil from Agrippa's
lodging to Araria, where (sayth this prelate) he plunged himself?
Certainly spirits passe away invisibly, and with that dispatch no
mortall man can trace them.   Believe this, and believe all the fables
of Purgatory.   Now, reader, thou hast heard the worst, lend a just eare
and thou shalt hear the best.   Johannes Wierus, a profest adversarie to ceremonial magick, and sometimes secretary to Cornelius
Agrippa, in his *Dæmonomania* speaks thus.   He wonders that some
learned Germans and Italians were not ashamed to traduce his
master in their publick writings.   That he had a dog whose call
was *Monsieur* he confesseth, and this spaniell during his service he
used to leade, when Agrippa walked abroad, by a hair chain.   "And
certainly the dog was a natural male animal" (saith he), to which
also Agrippa coupled a bitch of the same colour called *Made-
moyselle*.   It is confest that he was fond of this dog as some men
are, and having divorced his first wife would suffer him for a
sarcasm to sleep with him under the sheets.   In his study too, this
dog would couch at the table by his master, whence this great

philosopher, "absolutely surrounded by his extraordinary manuscript treasures," would not sometimes stir out for a whole week
together. So studious was he for the good of posterity, who have
but coldly rewarded him for his pains. I have observed also in his
"Epistles," that when he was resident at Malines, his domesticks
used to give him an account in their letters how his dogs fared, so
fond was he of those creatures. But to come to the rest of the
legend; Paulus Jovius tells you he died at Lyons "in a squalid and
gloomy inn." But Wierus, who had more reason to be inquisitive
after his master's death, tells me he died at Granople, and that "in
the Lord," not desperately as his enemies would have it. Here
now was a noble stride from Gratianopolis to Lugdunum; sure this
Paul was a scant geographer. But, reader, it is not my intention to
conceal anything in this matter; know therefore that Agrippa had
another dog, his Filioli, and this last died in more respect then
most of his master's adversaries. For my author, by some secret
meanes having strangely qualified him, divers learned men writ
epitaphs upon him, whereof some have been published and are yet
extant. Out of this fable of the Cerberus, Baptista Possevinus
pumpt these verses.

> All ye who, living, gaze upon this tomb,
> And deem what lies therein deserving rest,
> Know, here entombed, abysmal Styx's king,
> On earth protected by a guard from hell,
> But in perdition as his warder's prey
> Surrendered now. Oh! had he check'd his mind,
> He might have risen to the heights as far
> As in perdition he is deeply plunged.

Thus have they all-to-be-devilled him; but why may not truth run
in verse as well as scandal?

> Thus great Agrippa did the two fold world
> Illuminate, and in a weakly frame
> His manifold abilities revealed.
> By earth he conquered earth, by Heaven he gain'd,
> And master'd heavenly things; alive, he wrote
> Amidst the acclamations of the wise,
> By naturall things attracting Nature's self,
> And so for things supernal. Life Divine
> Did recognize this spirit for its own.
> He taught in life, and teaches still in death,
> And while up starry heights his course ascends
> Some magic potence still his hands dispense.

Now, reader, if thou wouldest be further satisfied in his distaste
of black magick, I wish thee to read his most christian invective

against the German conjurer entertained in the French court. Nay, so zealous and nice of conscience was he, that being solicited by some divines for a comment on Trismegistus, he returned them a very tart answer, referring all true knowledge to the Scripture. In a word, he did not onely hate impious but vaine arts, for he lost the favour of the Queen-Mother, because he would not be imployed by her in Astrologie. A science in whose true naturall part, which concernes generation and corruption, he was skilled to a miracle, but he knew it was bootless to look for fatal events in the planets, for such are not written in Nature, but in the superior Tables of Prædestination. Having thus then sufficiently proved his integrity, I will in a few words discover the grounds of his persecution. He was a man reformed in his religion, and had I the leisure to cite his workes I could quickly prove he was not of the Roman Church. For in his book on the "Vanity of all the Sciences," he allows not of monks and friars, but calls them sects "of which the Church at its best was devoid." And certainly that notable jest of his on the cowle nettles the papists to this day. He disclaimes also their images, their invocation of saints, their purgatory and pardons, and would have the laity communicate "in both kindes." He corrects the pope himself sufficiently, and is utterly against the Inquisition Office. What also his opinion was of Luther is not hard to guesse out of his Epistles, for in a letter to Melancthon he hath these words, "Salute through me that invincible heretic, Martin Luther, who (as Paul sayeth in the Acts) serveth God according to that sect which they call heretical." Lastly, he was altogether for the written word, preferring it to humane constitutions, which is contrarie to the papist, who will not allow it to be the judge of controversies. This is the man, and thus qualified at home, howsoever the world hath rendred him abroad. Now for his more mysterious principles, thou hast their name in this discourse, which if thou can'st apprehend, I know thou wilt style him in particular, as Trismegistus doth man in generall "the expounder of God," or as Panætius did his Plato, "the most divine, most holy, most wise man, and the Homer of philosophers." But this sluttish shuffle fits not his memorie, and things fall from me now as strictures, not compositions. I shall say nothing more, but leave thee to thy studies, whiles I translate this epitaph of Platina to his Tom. 6.

Who e'er thou art, if piously inclined,
  Seek not the dead Agrippa to molest,
Nor what with him lies narrowly enshrined,
  And only asks to be alone in rest.

ANIMA MAGICA ABSCONDITA.

O build castles in the air is a common proverb with all men, but a common practice with the Peripateticks onely. I have sometimes admired, that the very end and result of their philosophy did not clearly discover its falsity. It is a mere help to discourse. Moode and figure are their two pillars, their limit; their heptarchy ends in a syllogism, and the best professor amongst them is but a scold well disciplined. Their seven years' studie are seven years of famine; they leave the Soul "not satisfied," and are more a dream Genesis. than that of Pharaoh. For verily if the stage and reign of dreams be no where beyond fansie, then the fansies of these men being no where beyond their authors may rest on the same pillow. This sect then may be styled "an assembly of dreamers;" their conceptions are not grounded on any reason existent in Nature, but they would ground Nature on reasons framed and principled by their own conceptions. Their philosóphie is built on generall empty maxims, things of that stretch and latitude they may be applied to any thing, but conduce to the discovery of nothing. These are the first lineaments of their—monster, and in reference to them they have many subordinate errors, which prætend a symmetrie with their fundamentalls, but in truth have none at all. These latter quillets are so minced with divisions and distinctions that their very patrons are dubious how to state them. I could compare their physiologie to a chase in Arras, where there is much of similitude but nothing of truth. 'Tis the childe of fancie, a romance in syllogisms, a texture of their own brain, like that cob-web campagnia which Lucian's spiders planted betwixt the Moon and Venus. "Nature in generall (say they) is the principle of motion and rest." A form is "the outward expression of an inward essence," a definition they know not what to make of, and the Soul is ἐντελέχεια or, the actuating principle of a mechanical body. These two last descriptions (for they are no

substantial definitions) are such riddles, that I verily believe Aristotle
made use of those words "form" and "actuality," because he
would not discover his ignorance in these points. For why should
a form be called *Logos*, or in what other author do we find this
"actuality"? But because Nature in generall, that is, in her active
and passive portions, namely, matter and form, together with the
Soul of man, are the main fundamentals whereon to build a philosophie, and that this Aristotle is so sainted by his clients, that the
divines of Colleni tell us he was "præcursor of Christ in things
naturall" as John Baptist was in things of grace, I shall further
examine these his definitions, and acknowledge the benefit when I
finde it.

In the first place, then, it may be thought I am beholden to this
man for telling me that Nature is a principle. So, I may tell the
reader the Magician's Passive Spirit is a principle, but if I tell him
not what kind of substance it is, I will allow him ten years of studie,
and if the Sun went back every day ten degrees in his diall, he shall
not, without a supernaturall assistance, know what or where it is.
But you will reply: He tells me further; it is a principle causeth
bodies to move and rest. I thank him for his nothing. I desire
not to know what this principle doth, for that is obvious to every eye;
but I would know what it is, and therefore he may pocket his definition. Again you will object. He tells me not onely that Nature is
a principle, but that "Nature is form," and, by consequence, "form
is Nature." This is *idem per idem ;* he retains me in a circle of
notions but resolves nothing at all essentially. Besides "form," in
the genuine scope of the language signifies the outward symmetrie
or shape of a compound. But the Peripateticks who impose no
tongues, as they do on Nature, render it otherwise in their books,
and mistake the effect for the cause. I shall therefore take it in
their sense, and be content for once to subscribe to their comments.
Form then in their conception is the same with *vis formatrix* or
"Formative Power," which Aristotle defines "the outward expression of the inward essence." I must confesse I do not understand
him, and therefore I shall take him upon trust as his disciples
expound him. "It is the Logos (saith Magirus) in so much as it
completes, doth improve and inform natural substance, so that one
thing may thereby be distinguished from another." This is an
expresse of the office and effect of formes, but nothing at all to their
substance or essence.

Now let us see what he sayth to the Soul of man. The Soul
(sayth he) is in plain terms the consummation, or barbarously

but truly *Finitatio*, though his own followers falsely render it " the actuating principle of an organised body." But this definition is common to beasts and plants, and therefore he hath stumbled on another; "the Soul is that principle in which we live, feel, move, and comprehend." Now, both these descriptions concerne only the operations and faculties which the Soul exerciseth on the body, but discover not her nature or originall at all. It was ingenuously done of Galen, who confessed his ignorance concerning the substance of the Soul, but this fellow, who had not so much honestie, is voiced " prince of philosophers," and the positions of more glorious authors are examined by his dictates, as it were by a touchstone. Nay, the Scripture itself is oftentimes wrested and forced by his disciples to vote a *placet* to his conclusions. It is a miserable task to dwell on this ethnick, to gather his straw and stubble most of our dayes, and after all to be no better acquainted with our selves, but that the Soul is the cause of life, sense, motion, and understanding. I pitie our customarie follies, that we binde our selves over to a prentiship of expence and study, onely to compasse a few superficiall truths which every plow-man knows without book. Verily, Nature is so much a tutor that none can be ignorant in these things, for who is so stupid as not to know the difference between life and death, the absence and presence of his Soul? Yet these very definitions, though looked upon as rare, profound, philosophicall determinations, instruct us in nothing more. Away then with this Peripatetickall philosophy, this "vain babbling" as St Paul justly styles it, for, sure enough, he had some experience of it at Athens in his dispute about the resurrection. Let us no more look on this Olla Podrida, but on that spirit which resides in the elements, for this produceth real effects by the subsequent relations of corruption and generation, but the spirit of errour, which is Aristotle's, produceth nought but a multiplicity of notions. Observe, then, that this Stagirite and Nature are at a great distance, the one ends in works, the other in words; his followers refine the old notions, but not the old creatures. And, verily, the mystery of their profession consists onely in their terms; if their speculations were exposed to the world in a plaine dress, their sense is so empty and shallow, there is not any would acknowledge them for philosophers. In some discourses I confesse they have Nature before them, but they go not the right way to apprehend her. They are still in chase but never overtake their game, for who is he amongst them whose knowledge is so entire and regular that he can justifie his positions by practice? Againe, in some things they are quite

D

besides the cushion; they scold and squabble about whymzies and problems of their own which are no more in Nature then Lucian's Lachanopters or Hyppogypians. Now the reason of their errours is this, because they are experienced in nothing but outward accidents or qualities, and all the performance they can do in philosophie is to pronounce a body hot or cold, moyst or dry; but if they minde the essentiall temperament, they are grossly mistaken in stating these qualifications, for it is not the touch or sight that can discern intrinsecal, true complexions. A body that is outwardly cold to the sense may be hotter in the inmost part where the genuine tempera-ment lies, then the Sun himself is outwardly. But they know not the providence of Nature, how she interposeth a different resisting quality in the circumference of everything, lest the qualities of ambient bodies should conspire in too great a measure with the center, and so procure a dissolution of the compound. Thus she interposeth a passive, refreshing spirit between the Centrall Fire and the Sulphur; again she placeth the Sulphur between the Liquor of the Cœlestiall Luna and her outward Mercurie—a rare and admirable texture, infallibly proving that none but God onely wise, who fore-saw the conveniencies and disconveniencies of his creatures, could range them in that daring order and connexion. But to go further with these Peripateticks: their philosophy is a kinde of physiog-nomy; they will judge of invisible, inward principles (formes, as they call them), which are shut up in the closet of the matter, and all this in perusing the outside or crust of nature. 'Twere a foolish presumption if a lapidary should undertake to state the value or lustre of a jewell that is lockt up, before he opens the cabinet. I advise them therefore to use their hands, not their fansies, and to change their abstractions into extractions, for, verily, as long as they lick the shell in this fashion, and pierce not experimentally into the center of things, they can do no otherwise then they have done; they cannot know things substantially, but onely describe them by their outward effects and motions, which are subject, and obvious to every common eye. Let them consider, therefore, that there is in Nature a certain spirit which applies himself to the matter and actuates in every generation; that there is also a passive, intrinsecal principle where he is more immediately resident than the rest, and by mediation of which he communicates with the more gross, materiall parts. For there is in Nature a certain chain, or sub-ordinate propinquity of complexions between visibles and invisibles, and this is it by which the superiour, spirituall essences descend, and converse here below with the matter. But have a care lest you misconceive me. I speake not in this place of the Divine Spirit, but I speake of a certaine art by which a particular Spirit may be united to the universall, and nature by consequence may be strangely exalted and multiplied.* Now then, you that have your eyes in your hearts, and not your hearts in your eyes, attend to that which is spoken, and, that I may exhort you to Magick in the Magician's phrase—"Hear with the understanding of the heart."

It is obvious to all those whom Nature hath enriched with sense, and convenient organs to exercise it, that every body in the world is subject to a certain species of motion. Animals have their progressive outward, and their vitall inward motions. The Heavens are carried with that species which the Peripateticks call Lation, where, by the way, I must tell you, it proceeds from an intrinsecall principle, for intelligences are fabulous. The aire moves variously, the sea hath his flux and reflux. Vegetables have their growth and augmentation, which necessarily infer a concoction; and, finally, the earth with her mineralls and all other treasures, are subject to alteration, that is, to generation and corruption. Now, the matter of it selfe being merely passive, and furnished with no motive faculty at all, we must of necessity conclude that there is some other inward principle which acts and regulates it in every severall species of motion. But, verily, it is not enough to call this inward principle a Form, and so bury up the riches of Nature in this narrow and most absurd formality. We should rather abstaine from scribbling, or study to publish that which may make something for the author's credit, but much more for the benefit of the readers. To be plaine then, this principle is the Soule of the World, or the Universall Spirit of Nature. This Soule is retained in the matter by certain other proportionate natures, and missing a vent doth organize the shapeless mass. She labours what she can to resume her former liberty, frames for her selfe a habitation here in the center, puts her prison into some good order, and brancheth into the severall members, that she may have more roome to act and employ her faculties. But you are to observe that in every frame there are three leading principles. The first is this Soule whereof we have spoken something already. The second is that which is called the Spirit of the World, and this Spirit is the medium whereby the Soul is infused and doth move its body. The third is a certain oleous æthereall water; this is the Menstruum and Matrix of the World, for in it all things are framed and preserved. The Soule is a compound of "an ether of excessive tenuity and of the most

* Note 9.

uncompounded form of light." Hence that admirable Platonicall poet styled it "the fire of purest ether." Virgil.

Neither should you wonder that I say it is a compound, for there is no perfect specificall Nature that is simple and void of composition but only that of God Almighty. Trust not then to Aristotle, who tells you that the elements are simple bodies, for the contrary hath been manifested by absolute infallible experience. The passive spirit is a thin æriall substance, the only immediate vestiment wherein the Soule wraps her selfe when she descends and applies to generation. The radicall vitall liquor is a pure cœlestiall nature, answering in proportion and complexion to the superiour interstellar waters. Now, as soone as the passive spirit attracts the Soule, which is done when the first link in the chain moves (of which we shall speake in its due place), then the æthereall water in a moment attracts the passive spirit, for this is the first visible receptacle wherein the superiour natures are concentrated. The Soule being thus confined and imprisoned by lawfull magick in this liquid chrystall, the light which is in her streams thorough the water, and then it is "the Light made openly visible to the eye," in which state it is first made subject to the artist. Here now lies the mystery of the magician's denarius, his most secret and miraculous pyramid, whose first unity or cone is alwaies in the "horizon of eternity," but his basis or quadrate is here below in the "horizon of the temporal." The Soule consists of three portions of light and one of the matter. The passive spirit hath two parts of the matter and two of the light, wherefore it is called the "natural medium" and the "sphere of equilibrium." The cœlestiall water hath but one portion of light to three of the matter. Now the chaine of descent which concernes the spirituall is grounded on a similitude, or symboll of natures, according to that principle of Osthanes ἡ φύσις τῇ φύσει τέρπεται—"One Nature delights in another." For there being three portions of light in the Soule and two in the passive spirit, the inferiour attracts the superiour. Then there being but one portion in the cœlestiall nature, and two in the middle spirit, this solitary shining Unity attracts the other Binarius to fortifie and augment it selfe, as light joynes with light or flame with flame, and thus they hang in a vitall, magneticall series. Again, the chayne of ascent which concerns the matter is performed thus. The cœlestiall nature differs not in substance from the æriall spirit but only in degree and complexion, and the æriall spirit differs from the aura, or materiall part of the Soule, in constitution only, and not in nature, so that these three being but one substantially may admit of a perfect hypostaticall union, and be carried by a certaine intellectuall light "into the plane of the super-cœlestiall world, and so swallowed up of immortality.* But one thinks Nature complaines of a prostitution, that I goe about to diminish her majesty, having almost broken her seall, and exposed her naked to the world. I must confesse I have gone very far, and now I must recall my selfe, for there is a necessity of reserving as well as publishing some things, and yet I will speake of greater matters. The Soule, though in some sense active, yet is she not so essentially, but a mere instrumentall agent, for she is guided in her operations by a Spirituall Metaphysicall Graine, a Seed or Glance of Light, simple and without any mixture, descending from the first Father of Lights. For though his full-eyed love shines on nothing but man, yet every thing in the world is in some measure directed for his preservation by a spice or touch of the first Intellect. This is partly confirmed by the Habitation and Residence of God, for He is seated above all his creatures, to hatch, as it were, and cherish them with living eternall influences which daily and hourely proceed from him. Hence he is called of the cabalists Kether, and it answers to Parmenides his " Burning Crown," which he placed above all the visible sphæres. This flux of immateriall powers, Christ himself, in whom the fullnesse of the Godhead resided, confirmed and acknowledged in the flesh, for when the diseased touched his garment, though the press was great, he questioned who it was, adding this reason—" I perceive (said he) that vertue is gone out of me." But, laying aside such proofs, though the Scripture abounds in them, let us consider the exercise and practice of Nature here below, and we shall finde her game such she can not play it without this tutor. In the first place then, I would faine know who taught the spider his mathematicks? How comes he to lodge in the center of his web, that he may sally upon all occasions to any part of the circumference? How comes he to premeditate and forecast? For if he did not first know and imagine that there were flies, whereupon he must feede, he would not watch for them, nor spin out his netts in that exquisite form and texture. Verily, we must needs confesse that He who ordained flyes for his sustenance gave him also some small light to know and execute His ordinance. Tell me, if you can, who taught the hare to countermarch, when she doubles her trace in the pursuit to confound the scent and puzzle her persecutors? Who counsels her to stride from the double to her form, that her steps may be at a greater distance, and, by consequence, the more difficult to finde out? Certainly, this is a well-ordered policy, enough to prove that God is not absent from his creatures, but that " Wisdom reacheth mightily Wisdom.

* Note 10.

from one end to another," and that "his Incorruptible Spirit filleth all things." But to speak something more immediately apposite to our purpose, let us consider the severall products that are in Nature, with their admirable features and symmetrie. We know very well there is but one matter out of which there are found so many different shapes and constitutions.* Now, if the agent which determinates and figures the matter were not a discerning spirit, it were impossible for him to produce anything at all. For let me suppose Hyliard with his pencill and table ready to pourtray a rose; if he doth not inwardly apprehend the very shape and proportion of that which he intends to limne, he may as well do it without his eyes as without his intellectualls. Let us now apply this to the Spirit that worketh in Nature. This moves in the center of all things, hath the matter before him, as the potter hath his clay, or the limner his colours, and first of all he exerciseth his chymistry in severall transformations, producing sinews, veines, blood, flesh, and bones, which work also includes his arithmetic, for he makes the joynts and all integrall parts, nay, as Christ tells us, the very hairs of our heads in a certain determinate number, which may conduce to the beauty and motion of the frame. Again, in the outward lineaments or symmetrie of the compound, he proves himself a most regular mathematician, proportioning parts to parts, all which operations can proceed from nothing but a Divine, Intellectuall Spirit. For if he had not severall ideas or conceptions correspondent to his severall intentions, he could not distinguish the one from the other; and if he were not sensible, if he did not foresee the work he doth intend, then the end could be no impulsive cause, as the Peripateticks have it.

The consideration of these severall offices which this spirit performs in generation made Aristotle himself grant, that in the seeds of all things there were "potencies similar to designes." We should therefore examine who weaves the flowers of vegetables? who colours them without a pencill? who bolts the branches upwards, and threads (as it were) their roots downwards? For all these actions include a certain artifice which cannot be done without judgement and discretion. Now our Saviour tells us: "My Father worketh hitherto;" and in another place, it is "God cloathes the lilie of the field;" and again, "not one sparrow falls without your Father." Verily, this is the truth, and the testimony of truth, notwithstanding Aristotle and his problems. Neither should you think the Divine Spirit disparaged in being president to every generation because some products seem poor and contemptible, for, verily, as

* Note II.

long as they conduce to the glory of their Author, they are noble enough, and if you reflect upon Egypt, you will finde the basest of his creatures to extort a Catholick Confession from the wizards—*Digitus Dei est hic,* " the Finger of God is here." That I may come then to the point, these invisible, centrall Artists are Lights seeded by the First Light, in that primitive emanation, or *Sit Lux*— " let there be light"—which some falsely render *Fiat Lux*—" let light be made." For Nature is " the Voice of God," not a meer sound or command, but a substantiall, active breath, proceeding from the Creatour, and penetrating all things. God himself is " a spermatick Forme ; " and this is the only sense in which a form may be defined as " the outward expression of an inward essence." I know this will seem harsh to some men, whose ignorant zeal hath made them adversaries to God, for they rob him of his glory, and give it to his creature, nay sometimes to fancies and inventions of their own. I wish such philosophers to consider whether in the beginning there was any life or wisdom beyond the Creatour, and, if so, to tell us where. Verily (to use their own term) they can never find this *Ubi.* For they are gratious concessions or talents which God of his free will hath lent us, and if he should resume them, we should presently return to our first nothing. Let them take heed therefore whiles they attribute generation to qualities, lest the true Author of it should come against them with that charge which he brought sometimes against the Assyrians. " Shall the ax boast it self against him that heweth therewith ? or shall the saw magnifie it self against him that shaketh it ? as if the rod should shake it self against them that lift it up, or as if the staffe should lift up it self as if it were no wood ? " Let them rather cashier their Aristotle, and the errors wherewith he hath infatuated so many generations. Let them approach with confidence to the Almighty God, who made the world, for none can give a better account of the work than the Architect. Let them not despair to attain his familiarity, for he is a God that desires to be known, and will reveale himself both for the manifestation of his own glory and the benefit of his Creature. There is no reason then why we should decline this great and glorious School-Master, whose very invitation speaks more then our ordinary encouragement. " Thus sayth the Lord, the Holy One of Israel, and our Maker : Ask me of things to come concerning my sons, and concerning the work of my hands command you me. I have made the Earth, and created man upon it ; I, even my hand, have stretched out the Heavens, and all their hosts have I commanded." But it will be questioned perhaps,

Exodus.

Isaiah.

Is. xlv.

how shall we approach to the Lord, and by what means may we finde him out? Surely, not with words, but with workes, not in studying, ignorant, heathenish authours, but in perusing and trying his creatures. For in them lies his secret path, which though it be shut up with thornes and briars, with outward, worldly corruptions, yet if we would take the pains to remove this luggage, we might enter the Terrestriall Paradise, that *Hortus conclusus*, that Encompassed Garden, of Solomon, where God descends to walk, and drink of the Sealed Fountain. But, verily, there is such a generall prejudice, such a customary opposition of all principles which crosse Aristotle, that truth can no sooner step abroad but some sophister or other flings dirt in her face. It is strange that none of these schoolmen consider how the severall distinctions and divisions translated from logick to divinity have set all Christendom on fire, how they have violated the peace of many flourishing kingdoms, and occasioned more sects in religion then there are opinions in philosophie. Most seasonable then and Christian is that petition

In Gen. of St Augustine, "Deliver us from logick, O Lord!" And here I must desire the reader not to mistake me. I do not condemn the use but the abuse of reason, the many subtleties and fetches of it, which man hath so applied that truth and errour are equally disputable. I am one that stands up for a true naturall knowledge, grounded, as Nature is, on Jesus Christ, who is the true foundation of all things visible and invisible. I shall therefore in this discourse touch meerly upon those mysteries which some few have delivered over to posterity in difficult, obscure termes, that if possible the majesty of truth and the benefit they shall receive from it may settle men in a new way, and bring them at last from vain, empty fansies to a reall, sensible fruition of Nature.

You may remember how in my former discourse of the nature of man I mentioned a certain triplicity of elements according to their severall complexions in the severall regions of the world. I shall now speak of another triplicity much more obscure and mysticall, without which you can never attain to the former, for these three principles are the KEY of all magick, without whose perfect knowledge you can never truely understand the best idioms in Nature. The first principle is One in One, and One from One. It is a pure white Virgin, and next to that which is most pure and simple. This is the first created unity. By this all things were made, not actually, but mediately, and without this nothing can be made, either artificiall or naturall. This is "the Bride of God and of the Stars."*

* Note 12.

By mediation of this, there is a descent from One into Four, and an ascent from three by four to the invisible, supernaturall Monas. Who knows not this can never attain to the Art, for he knows not what he is to look for. The second principle differs not from the first in substance and dignity but in complexion and order. This second was the first, and is so still essentially, but by adhæsion to the matter it contracted an impurity, and so fell from its first unity, wherefore the magicians stile it Binarius. Separate therefore the circumference from the centre through the line of the diameter, and there will appear unto thee the philosopher's Ternarius, which is the third principle. This third is properly no principle, but a product of art. It is a various nature, compounded in one sence and decompounded in another, consisting of inferior and superior powers. This is the Magician's Fire. This is the Mercury of the philosophers, that most celebrated Microcosmos, and Adam. This is the Labyrinth and Wild of magick, where a world of students have lost themselves, a thing so confusedly and obscurely handled by such as knew it that it is altogether impossible to find it in their records. There is no late writer understands the full latitude and universality of this principle, nor the genuine metaphysicall use thereof. It moves here below in shades and tiffanies, above in white, æthereall vestures, neither is there anything in nature exposed to such a publick prostitution as this is, for it passeth thorough all hands, and there is not any creature but hath the use thereof. This Ternarius, being reduced by the Quaternary, ascends to the magicall Decad which is " the exceeding single Monad," in which state " it can perform whatsoever things it pleases," for it is united thus, " face to face," to the First, Eternall, Spirituall Unity. But of these Three, hear the oracle of magick, the great and solemn Agrippa. " There are then, as we have said, four Elements, without the perfect knowledge of which we can effect nothing in Magick. Now, each of them is threefold, that so the number of four may make up the number of twelve ; and by passing the number of seven into the number of ten, there may be a progress to the supreame Unity, upon which all vertue and wonderfull operation depends. Of the first order are the pure Elements, which are neither compounded nor changed, nor admit of mixtion, but are incorruptible, and not of which but through which the vertues of all naturall things are brought forth into act. No man is able to declare their vertues, because they can do all things upon all things. He which is ignorant of these shall never be able to bring to compass any wonderfull matter Of the second order are elements that are compounded, changeable, and impure, yet such as may by art be reduced to their pure simplicity, whose vertue, when they are thus reduced to their simplicity, doth above all things perfect all occult and common operations of Nature, and these are the foundations of the whole naturall Magick. Of the third order are those elements which originally, and of themselves, are not elements, but are twice compounded, various, and changeable one into the other. They are the infallible medium, and therefore are called the middle nature, or Soul of the middle nature. Very few there are that understand the deep mysteries thereof. In them is, by means of certain numbers, degrees, and orders, the perfection of every effect in what thing soever, whether naturall, cœlestiall, or super-cœlestiall; they are full of wonders and mysteries, and are operative as in Magick Naturall, so Divine; for from these, through them, proceed the bindings, loosings, and transmutations of all things, the knowing and foretelling of things to come, also the driving forth of Evill, and the gaining of good, spirits. Let no man, therefore, without these three sorts of elements, and the knowledge thereof, be confident that he is able to work anything in the occult sciences of Magick and Nature. But whosoever shall know how to reduce those of one order into those of another, impure into pure, compounded into simple, and shall know how to understand distinctly the nature, vertue, and power of them in number, degrees, and order, without dividing the substance, he shall easily attain to the knowledge and perfect operation of all naturall things, and cœlestiall secrets.' This is he with the " black spaniell," or rather, this is he " who, even from his earliest age did ever appear as an inquiring and intrepid investigator into the abounding operations of things mysterious and of miraculous effects." Now, for your further instruction, hear also the dark disciple of the more dark Libanius Gallius. " The first principle doth consist in that one substance through which, rather than from whom, is every potentiality of naturall marvels developed into the actual. We have said ' through which,' because the Absolute which proceedeth out of unity is not compounded, neither hath it any vicissitude. Thereunto from the Triad, and from the Tetrad is an arcane progression to the Monad, for the completion of the Decad, because thereby is the regression of number into unity, and, in like manner, the descent unto the Tetrad and the ascent unto the Monad. By this only can the Duad be completed. With joy and triumph is the Monad converted into the Triad. None who are ignorant of this principle which is after the principle of the Monad can attain unto the Triad, nor approach the most sacred Tetrad. Had they mastered all the books of the wise, were they perfectly conversant with the courses of the stars, with their virtues, powers, operations, and properties, did they keenly and clearly understand their types, signets, sigils, and their most secret things whatsoever, no performance of marvels could possibly follow these operations without the knowledge of this principle which cometh out of a principle, and returneth into a principle; whence all, without exception, whom I have found experimenting in natural magic have either attained nothing or, after long and unproductive operations, have been driven into vain, trifling, and superstitious pursuits. Now, the second principle, which is separated from the first in order and not in dignity, which alone existing doth create the Triad, is that which works wonders by the Duad. For in the one is the one and there is not the one; it is simple, yet in the Tetrad it is compounded, which being purified by fire cometh forth pure water, and reduced to its simplicity shall reveal unto the performer of arcane mysteries the completion of his labours. Here lieth the centre of all naturall magick, whose circumference united unto itself doth display a circle, a vast line in the infinite. Its virtue is above all things purified, and it is less simple than all things, composed on the scale of the Tetrad. But the Pythagoric Tetrad supported by the Triad, the pure and purified in one, can, if order and grade be observed, most assuredly perform marvels and secrets of nature in respect of the Duad within the Triad. This is the Tetrad within the capacity whereof the Triad joined to the Duad, maketh all things one, and which worketh wonderfully. The triad reduced to unity contains all things, *per aspectum*, in itself, and it doeth whatsoever it will. The third principle is by itself no principle, but between this and the Duad is the end of all science and mystic art, and the infallible centre of the mediating principle. It is no easier to blunder in the one than in the other for few flourish on earth who fundamentally comprehend its mysteries, both progressing by an eight-fold multiplication through the septenary into the triad, and remaining fixed. Therein is the consummation of the scale and series of Number. By this hath every philosopher, and every true Scrutator of naturall secrets, attained unto admirable results; by this, reduced in the Triad unto a simple element, they suddenly performed miraculous cures of diseases, and of all kinds of sickness in a purely naturall manner, and the operations of naturall and supernaturall Magick attained results through the direction of the Tetrad. By this the prediction of future events was truthfully performed, and no otherwise was the narrow entrance unto things kept secret wrested from Nature. By this only Medium was the secret of Nature laid bare unto Alchemists; without it no comprehension of the art can be acquired, nor the end of experiment discovered. Believe me, they do err, they do all err, who devoid of these three principles dream it possible for them to accomplish anything in the secret services of Nature." Thus far Trithemius, where for thy better understanding of him, I must inform thee there is a two-fold Binarius, one of light and confusion; but peruse Agrippa seriously "Of the Scales of numbers," and thou mayst apprehend all, for our abbot borrowed this language from him, the perusall of whose books he had before he published anything in this nature of his own. Now, for thy further instruction, go along with me, not to Athens or Stagyra but to that secretary and penman of God Almighty who stood on a cleft of the rock when he made all his goodnesse to passe before him. I am certain the world will wonder I should make use of Scripture to establish Physiologie, but I would have them know that all secrets, physicall and spirituall, all the close connexions, and that mysterious Kisse of God and Nature are clearly and punctually discovered there. Consider that mercifull mystery of the Incarnation, wherein the fullnesse of the Godhead was incorporated, and the Divine Light united to the Matter in a far greater measure then at the first creation. Consider it, I say, and thou shall finde that no philosophie hath perfectly united God to his creature but the Christian, wherefore also it is the onely true philosophie, and the onely true religion, for without this union there can neither be a naturall temporall, nor a spirituall æternall life. Moses tells us that in the beginning God created the Heaven and the Earth, that is the Virgin Mercury and the Virgin Sulphur. Now, let me advise you not to trouble yourselves with this Mercurie unlesse you have a true friend to instruct you, or an expresse illumination from the first Author of it, for it is a thing attained "by a marvellous Art." Observe then what I shall now tell you. There is in every star, and in this elementall world, a certain principle which is "the Bride of the Sun." These two in their coition do emit semen, which seed is carried in the womb of Nature, but the ejection of it is performed invisibly, and in a sacred silence, for this is the conjugall mystery of Heaven and Earth, their act of generation, a thing done in private between males and females, but how much more, think you, between the two universall natures? Know therefore that it is impossible for you to extract or receive any seed from the sun without this fœminine principle which is the Wife of the Sun. Now then my small sophisters of the Stone, you that consume your time and substance in making waters and oyles with a dirty *Caput Mortuum*, you that deal in gold and quick-silver, being infatuated with the legends of some late and former mountebanks, consider the last end of such men. Did they obtain any thing by it but diseases and poverty? Did they not in their old age, "the greybeards of an evil time," fall to clipping and counterfeiting of coyne? and for a period to their memory did they not die in despair, which is the childe of ignorance? Know then for certain that the magician's Sun and Moon are two universall peeres, male and female, or king and queen regents, alwayes young, and never old. These two are adæquate to the whole world, and coextend thorough the universe. The one is not without the other, God having united them in his work of creation in a solemn sacramentall union. It will then be a hard and difficult enterprise to rob the husband of his wife, to put those asunder whom God himself hath put together, for they sleep both in the same bed, and he that discovers the one must needes see the other. The love betwixt these two is so great, that if you use this Virgin kindly, shee will fetch back her Cupid, after he hath ascended from her in wings of fire. Observe, moreover, that materiall principles can be multiplied but materially, that is, by addition of parts, as you see in the augmentation of bodies, which is performed by a continual assumption of nutriment into the stomach, but it is not the body that transmutes the nutriment into flesh and bloud, but that spirit which is the light and life of the body. Materiall principles are passive, and can neither alter nor purifie, but well may they be altered and purified; neither can they communicate themselves to another substance beyond their own extension which is finite and determinate. Question not these impostors then who tell you of a *Sulphur Tingens*, and I know not what fables; who pin also that narrow name of *Chemia* on a science both ancient and infinite. It is the Light onely that can be truely multiplied, for this ascends to, and descends from, the first fountain of multiplication and generation. This Light, applied to any body whatsoever, exalts and perfects it after its own species. If to animals, it exalts animals; if to vegetables, vegetables; if to minerals, it refines minerals, and translates them from the worst to the best condition. Where note, by the way, that every body hath passive principles in it self for this Light to work upon, and therefore needs not borrow any from gold or silver. Consider then what it is you search for, you that hunt after the Philosophers' Stone, for "it is his to transmute who creates; you seek for that which is most high, but you look on that which is most low." Two things there are which every good Christian may and ought to look after—the true and the necessary. Truth is the Arcanum, the mystery and essence of all things, for every secret is truth, and every substantiall truth is a secret. I speak not here of outward historicall truths, which are but relatives to actions, but I speak of an inward essentiall truth which is Light, for Light is the truth, and it discovers falshood, which is darknesse. By this truth all that which is necessary may be compassed, but never without it. "I preferred wisdom (said the wise king) before scepters and thrones, and esteemed riches nothing in comparison of her. Neither compared I unto her any precious stone, because all gold in respect of her is as a little sand, and silver shall be counted as clay before her. I loved her above health and beauty, and chose to have her instead of light, for the light that cometh from her never goeth out. All good things came to me together with her, and innumerable riches in her hands. And I rejoyced in them all, because wisdom goeth before them, and I knew not that she was the mother of them. If riches be a possession to be desired in this life, what is richer then wisdom that worketh all things? for she is privy to the mysteries of the knowledge of God, and a lover of his works. God hath granted me to speak as I would, and to conceive as is meet for the things that are given me, because it is he that leadeth unto wisdom and directeth the wise, for in his hand are both we and our words, all wisdom also, and knowledge of workmanship. For he hath given me certain knowledge of the things that are, namely, to know how the world was made, and the operation of the Elements. The beginning, ending, and middest of the times, the alterations of the turning of the sun, and the change of seasons, the circuit of yeares and the position of stars, the natures of living creatures and the furies of wild beasts, the violence of windes and the reasoning of men, the diversities of plants and the vertues of rootes, and all such things as are either secret or manifest, them I know. For wisdom, which is the worker of all things, taught me. For in her is an understanding spirit, holy, onely begotten, manifold, subtil, lively, clear, undefiled, plain, not subject to hurt, loving the thing that is good, quick, which cannot be letted, ready to do good, kind to man, stedfast, free from care, having all power, overseeing all things, and going thorough all understanding, pure, and most subtill spirits. For wisdom is more moving then any motion, she passeth and goeth thorough all things by reason of her purenesse. For she is the brightnesse of the everlasting light, the unspotted mirror of the power of God, and the image of his goodnesse. And being but one she can do all things,

and remayning in her self she maketh all things new, and in all ages
entring into holy souls, she maketh them friends of God and
prophets. For God loveth none but him that dwelleth with wisdom.
For she is more beautifull then the sun, and above all the order of
stars, being compared with the light, she is far before it, for after
this cometh night, but vice shall not prevail against wisdom." Thus
Solomon, and again a greater then Solomon: "First seek you the
Kingdom of God, and all these things shall be given you." For, of
a truth, temporall blessings are but ushers to the spirituall, or to
speak more plainly, when once we begin to love the Spirit, then he
sends us these things as tokens and pledges of his love, for pro-
motion comes neither from the East nor from the West, but from
God that giveth it. "He truly is (saith one) from whom nothing is
absent, whom nothing supports, and whom nothing, much less, can
harm—that all necessary thing, having which it is impossible to be
destitute. Truth, therefore is the highest excellence and an impregnable fortress, having few friends abiding therein and assailed
by innumerable enemies, invisible in these days to well nigh all the
world, but an invincible security to those who possess it. In this
Citadel is contained the true and undoubted Philosophers' Stone
and the Treasure, which uneaten by moths and unstolen by thieves
remaineth to eternity, though all things else dissolve, set up for
the ruin of many and the salvation of some. This is the matter
which to the crowd is vile, exceedingly contemptible and odious,
yet not odious but love-worthy and precious to Philosophers above
gems and gold, itself the lover of all, to all well nigh an enemy,
to be found everywhere, yet by few, scarcely by any, discovered;
crying along the streets unto all, Come to me all ye who seek, and
I will lead you into the true path. This is that one thing proclaimed by the veritable Philosophers, which overcometh all, and is
itself overcome by nothing, searching heart and body, penetrating
everything stony and solid, and strengthening all things tender,
and establishing its own power on the opposition of that which is
most hard. It doth set itself before us all, crying and proclaiming
with uplifted voice: I am the way of truth, walk by me, for there is
no other path unto life; and yet we will not hearken to her. She
giveth forth the odour of sweetness, but we do not perceive it.
Daily doth she liberally in sweetness offer herself to us in the
holy festivals, and we will not taste her. Softly she draws us
to salvation, and resisting her pressure, we refuse to endure it.
For we are become as stones, having eyes and seeing not, having
ears and hearing not, having nostrils and smelling not, furnished

with mouth and tongue yet not tasting nor speaking, with hands and feet yet neither working nor walking. O most miserable race of men, which is not superior to stones, yea, so much the more inferior because to this and not to those is given knowledge of their acts. Be ye transmuted (she cries), be ye transmuted from dead stones into living philosophical stones. I am the true Medicine, rectifying and transmuting that which is no more into that which it was before corruption, and into something better by far, and that which is not into that which it ought to be. Lo, I am at the door of your conscience, knocking night and day, and ye will not open unto me, yet I stand mildly waiting; I do not, depart in anger; I suffer your insults patiently, hoping by that patience to lead you to that which I exhort you to. Come again and again, often come, ye who seek wisdom, and purchase gratis, not with gold nor with silver, still less with your own labours, what is voluntarily offered to you. O sonorous voice, O voice sweet and gracious to the ears of the sages, O fount of inexhaustible riches to those thirsting after truth and justice! O solace to the need of those who are desolate! Why seek ye further, anxious mortals? Why torment your minds with innumerable anxieties, ye miserable? Prithee, what madness blinds you? When in you, and not without you, is all that you seek outside you instead of within you. This characteristic is commonly the vice of the vulgar, that despising their own they desire ever what is foreign to them, and not altogether unreasonably, for of our own selves we possess nothing that is good; for if it be possible for us to have within us any goodness, we receive it from Him who alone is æternall Goodness, while, on the contrary, our disobedience hath appropriated the Evil of our nature out of an evil principle without us. Man, then, hath no possession of his own beyond the evil which he individualises within him. Whatsoever is good within him he receives from the Lord of goodness, not from himself; nevertheless, he hath the faculty of incorporating what he receives from the good principle. That Life which is the light of men shineth (albeit dimly) within us, that Life which is not of us, but from Him who possesses it from Everlasting. He hath implanted it in us, that in his Light, who dwelleth in light inaccessible, we may behold the Light; by this doe we surpass the rest of his perishable creatures; thus are we fashioned in his own likeness, because he hath given us one ray of his own inherent illumination. Truth must not, therefore, be sought in our lower selves, but in the likeness of God which is within us." This is he to whom the Brothers of R. C. gave the title of *Sapiens*, and from whose writings they borrowed

most of their instructions addressed to a certaine German postulant.
But that you may the better understand how to come by this Stone,
hear what he speaks in another place. "True knowledge begins
when after the comparison of the imperishable and the perishable,
of life and annihilation, the Soule forcibly attracted by the delights
of the supersensual doth elect to be made one with its divine
spirit. The intellectuall principle doth issue from this knowledge, and chooses the voluntary separation of the body, beholding
with the Soule, on the one hand, the foulness and corruption of the
body, and, on the other, the everlasting splendour and felicity of
the Spirit; with this (the Divine Pneuma so ordering) doth it yearn
to be connected, completely discarding the body, that it may seek
only what it knows is encompassed by God himself with salvation
and glory, but he is constrained nevertheless to permit the body
it self to participate in the union of Soule and Spirit; and this is
that marvellous philosophicall transmutation of body into spirit, and
of spirit into body about which this aphorism has come down to us
from the wise of old. 'Fix that which is volatile, and volatilise that
which is fixed, and thou shalt attain to our Grand Magisterium.'
That is to say, 'make the unyielding body pliant, which, by the
supreme vertue of the Spirit acting in concert with the Soule, will
endow the physicall organism itself with an invariable constancy,
and enable it to resist every test.' For gold is proven with fire, by
which process all that is not gold is cast aside. O præ-eminent
Gold of the philosophers with which the Sons of the Wise are
enriched, not with that which is coined. Come hither all ye who
seek with such multitudinous exertions for the Philosophicall Treasure, behold that Stone which you have rejected, and learn first what
it is before you set out in search of it. It is more astonishing than
any miracle that a man should seek he knows not what. It is un-
deniably foolish that an object should be sought by men, about the
truth of which the investigators know nothing, for such a search is
hopeless. Let those whosoever, who seek with so great toil first ascertain the existence and nature of the object they are in search of,
and thus they will not be frustrated in their attempts. The wise man
seeks what he loves and cannot love what he does not know, otherwise he would be a fool. Out of knowledge, therefore, springeth Love,
the truth which is in all things, and which alone flourishes in all true
philosophers." Thus he, and again : " Ye but labour in vain, all ye
exposers of the hidden secrets of Nature, when having entered upon
the wrong path ye endeavour to discover by material meanes the
informing vertues of things material. Learn therefore to know

E

Heaven by Heaven, not by earth, but the potentialities of the material learn to discern by the heavenly. No one can ascend into the Heaven which is thy ambition unless he who descended from a Heaven which thou seekest not, shall first vouchsafe him light. Ye seek an incorruptible medecine which shall not only transmute the body from corruption into a perfect organism but shall preserve that perfected body for an indefinite period, but except in Heaven it self never anywhere will you discover such a medecine. The cœlestiall virtue penetrates all the elements along invisible lines which, starting from all points, meet at the earth's centre; it generates and fosters the elementated worlds. No one can be brought forth therein save in the likeness thereof which also is drawn therefrom. In like manner the combined fœtus of either parent retains within itself its special nature, that both parents may be potentially and actually discoverable therein. What shall cleave more closely save the Stone in philosophicall generation? Learn from within thyself to know whatsoever is in Heaven and on Earth, that thou mayst be made wise in all things. Thou seest not that Heaven and the elements were once but one substance, and were separated one from another by divine skill to accomplish the generation of thy self and all that is. Didst thou know this the rest could not escape thee, else art thou devoid of all capacity. Again, in every generation such a separation is necessary as I have already told thee must thou make before setting sail in the study of the true philosophy. Never wilt thou extract the one thing which thou desirest out of the many which are round thee till from thy self be extracted that one thing which I have proclaimed to thee. For such is the will of God, that the devout should perform the devout work which they desire, and the perfect accomplish another on which they have been bent. To men of bad will shall there be no harvest other than they have sown; furthermore, on account of their malice, their good seed shall very often be changed into cockle. Perform then the work which thou seekest in such a manner that, so far as may be in thy power thou mayst escape a like misfortune." This is now the true, essentiall mystery of regeneration, or the spirituall death. This is, and ever was, the onely scope and upshot of Magick. But, for your further instruction, ruminate this his other mysticall speech. "Rouse up now, therefore, my Soule, and bodye alsoe; rise now, follow the flight of your Spirit. Let us goe up into that high mountain over against us, from whose pinnacle I will show you that two-fold road which Pythagoras spoke of in cloud and darkness. Our eyes are opened, now shineth forth the Sun of holiness and justice, guided by which we cannot possibly turn aside from the waye of truth. Turn first thine eyes to the right path, lest they behold vanity before they distinguish wisdome. See you not that splendid and impregnable tower? Therein is the Philosophical love from whose fount floweth living water, and he who once drinkes of it shall never more thirst after vanity. From that how pleasant and delightfull place is a plain path to that more delightfull yet, wherein the Divine Sophia tarries, from whose fount leap waters far more blessed than the first, and which they who give to an enemy, he is forthwith forced to grant them peace. Most of those who go there direct their course still higher, but not all can accomplish their desire. There is another place which mortals may scarcely attaine, unlesse they are received by the Divine Numen into the plane of immortality, and before they are introduced, they are constrained to put off the world, being weighted by the garments of perishable life. In those who attaine it there is no longer any fear of death, much rather do they from day to day welcome it with more favour because they judge that whatsoever is in nature is worthy of their embrace. Whosoever doth progresse beyond these three places vanishes from the eyes of men. If so be that it be granted us to behold the second and the third places, let us ascend higher. So, beyond the first chrystalline arch, ye behold a second of silver, beyond which there is a third of adamant, but the fourth falls not within sense till the third be passed under. This is the golden region of undying felicity, voide of care and filled wholly with perpetuall joy."

This is the pitch and place, to which if any man ascends he enters into chariots of fire with horses of fire, and is translated from the earth, soul and body. Such was Enoch, such was Elijah, such was Esdras, to whom this medecine was ministred by Uriel the angel. Such was St Paul, who was carried up to the third Heaven; such was Zoroaster, who was transfigured, and such was that Anonymous mentioned by Agrippa. "The same wise man (sayth he) did also appear in such wise that burning rays came from him with a great sound."

This, I suppose, was R. C., the founder of a most Christian and famous society, whose body also by vertue of that medecine he took in his life time is preserved entire to this day, with the epitomes of two worlds about it. Such Elijahs also are members of this Fraternitie, who, as their own writings testifie, walk in the supernatural light. "To join our assembly it is needful that thou shouldst perceive this Light, for without it, it is impossible to behold us, save when we ourselves may will it." I know some illiterate school divines will no sooner read this but they will cry

out with the Jewes: "Away with such a fellow through the Earth."
Truly they are the men to whom I also do advise that they read not
our writings, neither master, nor remember them; for they are
harmful and venomous to such, and for them the mouth of hell is in
this book. It utters not words but stones; let them beware lest it
cast them on their heads. Let them not mind it, buy it not, touch
it not—

"Hence, hence Profane ones!"

Go on still, and proceed in your own corrupt fancies, that the
occasion of justice may be upheld. Follow your old beggarly
elements, the rudiments of this world, which hitherto have done
despight to the Spirit of Grace, which have grieved that holy and
loving Spirit of God, whereby you are sealed to the day of redemption.
But consider whiles you are yet in the flesh, whiles it is to day with
you, and timely to consider, that God will use those men whom you
revile for his truth as witnesses against you in a day when you shall
have nothing to speak for your ignorance, unless you plead your
obstinacie. Of a truth, God himself discovered this thing to the
first man, to confirm his hopes of those three supernaturall mysteries,
the Incarnation, Regeneration, and Resurrection, for Jamblichus,
citing the Ægyptian records with "It is to be believed on the
authority of secret wisdom," hath these very words, "that a certain
substance has been handed down from the gods by means of sacred
shows, and that consequently it was known to those same men
who transmitted it." And our former Christian author in a certain
place speakes thus: "It is indisputable that Deity revealed to the
patriarchs, by the Holy Ghost, a certain medecine whereby they
healed the corruption of the flesh, and when he spake to them, did
enter into a most binding compact with them." Let me tell you
then that the period and perfection of magick is no way physicall
for this art

"Touches the seat of Jove, and things Divine essays."

In a word, it ascends "through the light of Nature to the light of
grace," and the last end of it is truely theologicall. Remember,
therefore, that Elijah deposed his mantle, and past thorow the
waters of Jordan before he met with the chariots of Israel. But as
Agrippa sayth: "The storehouse of truth is closed." The Scripture
is obscure and mysticall even in historicall passages. Who would
believe that in the history of Agar and Sarah, the mystery of both
Testaments was couched, but that St Paul himself hath told us so?
Gal. iv. 22. "For it is written (sayth he), that Abraham had two sons, the one

by a bondmaid, the other by a free-woman. But he who was of the bondwoman was born after the flesh, but he of the freewoman by promise. Which things are an allegorie; for these are the two covenants, the one from Mount Sinai, which gendereth to bondage, which is Agar; for this Agar is Mount Sinai in Arabia, and answereth to Jerusalem that now is, and is in bondage with her children; but the Jerusalem from above is free, which is the mother of us all." I could instance in many more such places, as that of the royall prophet, " that the dew of Hermon descends to Mount Sion, which is altogether impossible in the literall sense, for every geographer knows there is a vast distance between these two. But to return to my former discourse : some philosophers, who by the speciall mercy of God attained to the Ternarius, could never notwithstanding obtaine the perfect medecine, neither did they understand it. I never met in all my reading but with six authors who fully apprehended this mystery—the first an Arabian, a most profound but exceedingly obscure writer, and from him, I conceive, Artesius borrowed all his knowledge—The second a most ancient Christian Anonymous, the greatest that ever was in point of practice, for he ascended to that glorious metaphysicall height where the Archtype shadows the Intellectuall Sphæres. The other four are famously known in Christendom. To instruct thee then, this mystery is perfected when the Light in a suddain, miraculous coruscation strikes from the Center to the Circumference, and the Divine Spirit hath so swallowed up the body that it is " glorified like the Sun and Moon in their splendour. In this rotation it doth passe (and no sooner) from the naturall to a supernaturall state, for it is no more fed with visibles but with invisibles, and the eye of the Creator is perpetually upon it. After this the material parts are never more to be seen, and this is that sinless and oft-celebrated invisibility of the Magi." Verily, this is the way that the prophets and apostles went; this is the true primitive divinity, not that clamourous sophistrie of the schooles. I know the world will be ready to boy me out of countenance for this because my yeares are few and green. I want their two crutches, the prætended modern sanctitie, and that solemnitie of the beard which makes up a doctor. But, reader, let me advise thee if by what is here written thou attainest to any knowledge in this point (which I hold impossible without a divine assistance), let me advise thee, I say, not to attempt any thing rashly; for Agrippa tells me : " Whosoever doth approach unpurified, calls down judgment on himself, and is abandoned to the devouring of the evil spirit." There is in the Magicall Records a memorable story of a Jew, who having by permission rifled some spiritual treasures, was translated into the wilderness, and is kept there for an example to others. I will give thee the best counsel that can be given, and that out of a poet:

> " Entreat a sober mind in healthful frame."

Thou must prepare thy self till thou art conformable to Him whom thou wouldst entertain, and that "in every respect." Thou hast Three that are to receive, and there are three accordingly that give. Fitt thy roofe to thy God in what thou canst, and in what thou canst not he will help thee. When thou hast thus set thy house in order, do not think thy guest will come without invitation. Thou must tyre him out with pious importunities,

> Perpetuall knockings at his doore,
> Teares sullying his transparent roomes,
> Sighes upon sighes ; weep more and more,
>   He comes.

This is the way thou must walk in, which if thou doest, thou shalt perceive a sudden illustration, and then shall there abide in thee fire with light, wind with fire, power with wind, knowledge with power, and the integrity of a healthy mind with knowledge. This is the chain that qualifies a Magician, for sayth Agrippa " to inquire into things future, and into things present, and into other arcane matters, and into the things which are indicated to men by divine providence, veracious maxims, and to perform works which do exceed the common course of Nature, is not possible apart from a profound and perfect doctrine, an immaculate life, and faith, and is not to be performed by light-minded and unlearned men." And in another place : " No man can give that which he himself hath not. But no man hath save he who, having suspended the elementary forces, having overcome Nature, having compelled Heaven, having attained the angelical, doth exceed his own archetype, co-operating then with his works he can accomplish all things." This is the place where if thou canst but once ascend, and then descend,

> " Then oft the Archetype of the World attain
> And oft to him recur, and, face to face,
> Unhindered gaze upon the Father's grace "—

Then, I say, thou hast got that Spirit whom all portentous mathematicians, wonder - working magicians, invidious alchemisticall torturers of nature, and venomous necromancers more evil than demons, dare to promise, that Spirit who doth discern and perform, and that without any crime, without offence to God, and with no injury to Religion. Such is the power he shall receive, who from the clamourous tumults of this world ascends to the supernaturall still voice from this base earth and mud whereto his body is allyed to the spiritual, invisible elements of his soul.* "He shall receive the life of the gods; he shall behold the Heroes intermingled with the deities, and shall himself be beheld by them." This, reader, is the Christian Philosopher's Stone, a Stone so often inculcated in Scripture. This is the Rock in the wildernesse, because in great obscurity, and few there are that know the right way unto it. This is the Stone of Fire in Ezekiel; this is the Stone with Seven Eyes upon it in Zacharie, and this is the White Stone with the New Name in the Revelation. But in the Gospel, where Christ himself speakes, who was born to discover mysteries and communicate Heaven to Earth, it is more clearly described. This is the Salt which you ought to have in your selves; this is the Water and Spirit, whereof you must be born again, and is that Seed which falls to the ground and multiplies to an hundredfold. But, reader, be not deceived in me. I am not a man of any such faculties, neither do I expect this blessing in such a great measure in this life; God is no debtor of mine. I can affirm no more of myself, but what my author did formerly. "Hold me, I bid thee, as a finger post which, ever pointing forward, shews the way to those undertaking a journey." Behold! I will deal fairly with thee; shew me but one good Christian who is capable of and fit to receive such a secret, and I will show him the right, infallible way to come by it. Yet this I must tell thee; it would sink thee to the ground to hear this mystery related, for it cannot ascend to the heart of the naturall man how neer God is to him, and how to be found. But of this enough. I will now speak of a Naturall, Cœlestiall medecine, and this latter is common amongst some wise men, but few are they who attain to the former. The common chymist works with the common fire, and without any medium, wherefore he generates nothing, for he works not, as God doth, to preservation, but to destruction; hence it is that he ends alwayes in the ashes. Do thou use it *cum phlegmati medii*, so shall thy materialls rest in a third element, where the violence of this tyrant cannot reach, but his *Anima*. There is also a better way, for if thou canst temper him with the Spirit of Heaven, thou hast altered him from a corrupting to a generating fire. Sublime the Middle Nature Fire "by the Triad and the Circle," till thou comest to a breach of inferiors and superiors. Lastly,

* Note 12.

separate from the magicall compounded earth that principle which
is called "the Middle Earth," because it is middlemost between the
Unarius and the Binarius, for as it attaines not to the simplicity of
the first, so it is free from the impurities of the second. This is
"the True Chrystalline Stone, a bright virgin earth without spot or
darknesse." This is "the Magian earth within the luminous æther,"
for it carries in its belly winde and fire. Having got this funda-
mentall of a little new world, unite the heaven in a triple proportion
to the earth; then apply a generative heat to both, and they will
attract from above the Star-Fire of Nature. "So shalt thou possess
the glory of all the world, and all darkness shall flee away from
thee." Now because the law of Nature is infallible, and confined
to the creature by God's royall assent, think not therefore there is
any necessity upon God, but what he hath enacted in general, he
can repeal in any particular. Remember who translated the dew
from the earth to the fleece, and from the fleece to the earth. God
bestowes not his blessings where they are to turn to curses. He
cursed the Earth once for Adam's sake; take heed he doth not curse
it again in thy work for thy sake. It is in vaine to look a blessing
from Nature without the God of Nature, for, as the Scripture sayth,
"without controversie the lesser is blessed of the greater." He must
be a good steward that shall overlook the treasuries of God. Have,
therefore, a charitable, seraphick soul, charitable at home in being
not destructive to thy self, as most men are; charitable abroad, in a
diffusive goodnesse to the poor, as many are not. There is in every
true Christian a spice, I can not say a grain of faith, for then we could
work miracles. But know thou that as God is the Father, so charity
is the nurse of faith. For there springs from charitable works a
hope of Heaven, and who is he that will not gladly believe what he
hopes to receive? On the contrary, there springs no hope at all
from the works of darknesse, and, by consequence, no faith, but that
faith of devils, to "believe and tremble." Settle not then in the
lees and puddle of the world; have thy heart in Heaven and thy
hands on earth. Ascend in piety and descend in charity, for this is
the Nature of Light and the Way of the Children of it. Above all
things, avoyd the guilt of innocent blood, for it utterly separates
from God in this life, and requires a timely and serious repentance
if thou wouldst find him in the next. Now for thy study: in the
winter time thy chamber is thy best residence. Here thou mayst
use fumigations and spicie lamps, not for superstition, but because
such recreate the animal spirits and the braine. In the summer,
translate thy self to the fields, where all are green with the Breath of

God, and fresh with the Powers of Heaven. Learn to refer all naturals to their spirituals " by help of the secret analogy," for this is the way the magicians went and found out miracles. Many there are who bestow not their thoughts on God till the world failes them. He may say to such guests, " When it can be forced on no one else, it is brought to me." Do thou think on him first and he will speak to thy thoughts at last. Sometimes thou mayst walk in groves, which, being full of majestie, will much advance the Soule, sometimes by clear, active rivers, for by such (say the mystick poets) Apollo contemplated :—

> " All things by Phœbus in his musing spake
>   The bless'd Eurotas heard."

So have I spent on the banks of Ysca many a quiet hour.

> " 'Tis day, my chrystal Usk : now the sad night
>   Resignes her place as tenant to the light.
> See the amazed mists begin to flye,
> And the victorious sun hath got the skie.
> How shall I recompense thy streams, thát keep
> Me and my soul awak'd when others sleep?
> I watch my stars, I move on with the skies,
> And weary all the planets with mine eyes.
> Shall I seek thy forgotten birth, and see
> What dayes are spent since thy nativity?
> Didst run with ancient Kishon? Canst thou tell
> So many yeers as holy Hiddekel?
> Thou art not paid in this. I'll leavie more
> Such harmless contributions from thy store,
> And dresse my Soul by thee as thou do'st passe,
> As I would do my body by thy glasse.
> What a clear, running chrystall here I find !
> Sure I will strive to gain as clear a mind,
> And have my spirits, freed from dross, made light,
> That no base puddle may allay their flight.
> How I admire thy humble banks ! Nought's here
> But the same simple vesture all the yeer.
> I'll learn simplicity of thee, when
> I walk the streets I will not storme at men,
> Nor look as if I had a mind to crie—
> ' It is my valiant cloth of gold, and I.'
> Let me not live, but I'm amazed to see
> What a clear type thou art of pietie.
> Why should thy flouds enrich those shores, that sin
> Against thy liberty, and keep thee in?
> Thy waters nurse that rude land which enslaves
> And captivates thy free and spacious waves.

> Most blessed Tutors!   I will learn of those
> To show my charity unto my foes,
> And strive to do some good unto the poor,
> As thy streams do unto the barren shore.
>   All this from thee, my Ysca?   Yes, and more:
> I am for many vertues on thy score.
> Trust me thy waters yet : why, wilt not so?
> Let me but drink again and I will go.
> I see thy course anticipates my plea,
> I'll haste to God, as thou dost to the Sea.
> And when my eyes in waters drown their beams,
> The pious imitation of thy streames,
> May every holy, happy, hearty teare
> Help me to run to Heaven, as thou dost there."

This is the way I would have thee walk in, if thou doest intend to be a solid, Christian philosopher.   Thou must, as Agrippa sayth, "live only to God and the angels," reject all things "which are in opposition to Heaven," otherwise thou canst have no communion with superiors.   Lastly, "be single, not solitary."   Avoid the multitude, as well of passions as persons.   Now for authors, I wish thee to trust no moderns, but Michael Sendivow, and that other of *Physia Restituta*, especially his first aphoristicall part.   The rest whom I have seen suggest inventions of their own, such as may passe with the whymzies of des Chartes, or Borillus his "Mathematicall Roses."   To conclude, I would have thee know that every day is a yeer contracted, that every yeer is an extended day.   Anticipate the yeer in the day, and lose not a day in the yeer.   Make use of indeterminate agents till thou canst find a determinate one.   The many may wish well, but one onely loves.   Circumferences spread but centers contract ; so superiors dissolve and inferiors coagulate.   Stand not long in the sun, nor long in the shade.   Where extremes meet, there look for complexions.   Learn from thy errors to be infallible, from thy misfortunes to be constant.   There is nothing stronger then perseverance, for it ends in miracles.   I could tell thee more, but that were to puzzle thee.   Learn this first, and thou mayst teach me the last.

Thus, reader, have I published that knowledge which God gave me "to the fruit of a good conscience."   I have not busheld my light nor buried my talent in the ground.   I will now withdraw and leave the stage to the next actor—some Peripatetick perhaps, whose *sic probo* shall serve me for a comœdie.   I have seen scolds laughed at, but never admired, so he that multiplies discourse makes a serious cause ridiculous.   The onely antidote to a shrew is silence, and the best way to convince fools is to neglect them.

" O blessed Souls ! whose watchful care it was
These saving truths before all truths to know
And so the mansions of the blest attain.   .
How credible to hold that minds like these
Do equally transcend both human vice
And human folly ! "

" If thou, O Jehovah, my God, shalt enlighten me, my darkness shall be made light."

MAGIA ADAMICA:

OR

THE ANTIQUITIE OF MAGIC, AND THE DESCENT THEREOF FROM ADAM DOWNWARDS PROVED.

WHEREUNTO IS ADDED

A PERFECT AND TRUE DISCOVERIE OF THE TRUE *CŒLUM TERRÆ*, OR THE MAGICIAN'S HEAVENLY CHAOS, AND FIRST MATTER OF ALL THINGS.

BY

EUGENIUS PHILALETHES.

IR, It was the question of Solomon, and it argued the supremacie of his wisedom, "What was best for man to do all the dayes of his vanitie under the sun?" If I wish my selfe so wise as to know this great affaire of life, it is because you are fit to manage it. I will not advise you to pleasures, to build houses, and plant vineyards, to enlarge your private possessions, or to multiplie your gold and silver. These are old errors, like Vitriol to the Stone, so many false receipts which Solomon hath tried before you, "And behold all was vanitie, and vexation of spirit." I have some times seen actions as various as they were great, and my own sullen fate hath forced me to severall courses of life, but I finde not one hitherto which ends not in surfeits or satietie. Let us fansie a man as fortunate as this world can make him; what doth he doe but move from bed to board, and provide for the circumstances of those two scenes? To day hee eates and drinkes, then sleeps, that hee may doe the like to morrow. A great happinesse! to live by cloying repetitions, and such as have more of necessity than of a free pleasure. This is *idem per idem*, and what is held for absurditie in reason can not, by the same reason, be the true perfection of life. I deny not but temporall blessings conduce to a temporall life, and by consequence are pleasing to the body, but if we consider the Soule, shee is all this while upon the wing, like that dove sent out of the Ark, seeking a place to rest. Shee is busied in a restless inquisition, and though her thoughts, for want of true knowledge, differ not from desires, yet they sufficiently prove she hath not found her satisfaction. Shew me then but a practice wherein my Soule shall rest without any further disquisition, for this is it which Solomon calls vexation of spirit, and you shew mee "what is best for man to doe under the sun." Surely,

Eccle ii. 3.

Eccle. ii. 11.

sir, this is not the Philosophers' Stone, neither will I undertake to define it, but give me leave to speak to you in the language of Zoroaster:

" Seek thou the channel of the Soule."......

I have a better confidence in your opinion of mee than to tell you I love you, and for my present boldness you must thank yourself; you taught me this familiaritie. I here trouble you with a short discourse, the brokage and weake remembrances of my former and more entire studies. It is no laboured piece, and indeed no fitt present, but I beg your acceptance as of a *caveat*, that you may see what unprofitable affections you have purchased. I propose it not for your instruction; Nature hath already admitted you to her schoole, and I would make you my judge, not my pupill. If therefore amongst your serious and more deare retirements, you can allow this trifle but some few minutes, and think them not lost, you will perfect my ambition. You will place mee, sir, at my full height, and though it were like that of Statius, amongst gods and stars, I shall quickly find the earth again, and with the least opportunitie present my self,

Sir,

Your obedient Servant,

E. P.

TO THE READER.

ELL fare the Dodechedron! I have examined the nativity of this book by a cast of constellated bones, and *Deux Ace* tells me this parable. Truth (sayd the witty Aleman) was commanded into exile, and the Lady Lie was seated in her throne. To performe the tenor of this sentence, Truth went from amongst men, but she went all alone, poore and naked. She had not travailed very far when standing on a high mountain, she perceived a great train to passe by. In the middest of it was a chariot attended with kings, princes, and governors, and in that a stately Donna, who, like some queen-regent, commanded the rest of the company. Poor Truth, shee stood still whiles this pompous squadron past by, but when the chariot came over against her, the Lady Lie, who was there seated, took notice of her, and causing her pageants to stay, commanded her to come nearer. Here she was scornfully examined whence she came? whither she would goe? and what about? To these questions she answered, as the custome of Truth is, very simply and plainly. Whereupon the Lady Lie commands her to wait upon her, and that in the reare and taile of all her troop, for that was the known place of Truth. Thanks then not to the stars but to the configurations of the dice! They have acquainted mee with my future fortunes, and what praeferment my booke is likely to attain to. I am, for my part, contented, though the consideration of this durty reare be very nauseous, and able to spoile a stronger stomach than mine. It hath been said of old: *Non est Planta Veritatis super terram.* Truth is an herb that grows not here below, and can I expect that these few seeds which I scatter thus in the storm and tempest should thrive to their full eares and harvest? But, reader, let it not trouble thee to see the truth come thus behind; it may be there is more of a chase in it than of attendance, and her conditions not altogether so bad as her station. If thou art one of those who draw up to the

chariot, pause here a little in the reare, and before thou dost addresse
thy self to Aristotle and his Lady Lie, think not thy courtship lost if
thou doest kisse the lips of poor Truth.   It is not my intention to
jest with thee in what I shall write, wherefore read thou with a good
faith what I will tell thee with a good conscience.   God when Hee
first made man, planted in him a spirit of that capacitie that he
might know all, adding thereto a most fervent desire to know, lest
that capacitie should be useless.   This truth is evident to the posteritie of man, for little children, before ever they can speak, will
stare upon anything that is strange to them; they will cry, and are
restless, till they get it into their hands, that they may feel it and
look upon it, that is to say, that they may know what it is in some
degree, and according to their capacitie.   Now, some ignorant nurse
will think that they doe all this out of a desire to play with what they
see, but they themselves tell us the contrarie, for when they are past
infants, and begin to make use of language, if any new thing appeares
they will not desire to play with it, but they will ask you what it is,
for they desire to know.   And this is plain out of their actions, for
if you put any rattle into their hands, they will view it and studie it
for some short time, and when they can know no more, then they
will play with it.   It is well known that if you hold a candle near
to a little child, hee will (if you prævent him not) put his finger
into the flame, for hee desires to know what it is that shines so
bright.   But there is something more than all this, for even
these infants desire to improve their knowledge.   Thus, when they
look upon anything, if the sight informes them not sufficiently,
they will, if they can, get it into their hands, that they may feel
it, but if the touch also doth not satisfie, they will put it
into their mouthes to taste it, as if they would examine things by
more senses than one.   Now, this desire to know is born with them,
and it is the best and most mysterious part of their nature.   It is to
be observed that when men come to their full age, and are serious
in their disquisitions, they are ashamed to erre, because it is the
proprietie of their nature to know.   Thus we see that a philosopher
being taken at a fault in his discourse, will blush as if he had committed something unworthy of himself, and truly the very sense of
this disgrace prevailes so far with some, they had rather persist in
their error, and defend it against the truth, than acknowledge their
infirmities, in which respect I make no question but many Peripateticks are perversely ignorant.   It may bee they will scarcely hear
what I speak, or, if they hear, they will not understand.   Howsoever,
I advise them not wilfully to prevent and hinder that glorious end

and perfection for which the very Author and Father of Nature created them. It is a terrible thing to præfer Aristotle to Ælohim, and condemn the truth of God to justifie the opinioun of Man. Now, for my part, I dare not be so irreligious as to think God so vain and improvident in his workes that he should plant in man a desire to know, and yet deny him knowledge it self. This, in plain termes, were to give me eyes, and afterwards shut me up in darknesse, lest I should see with those eyes. This earnest longing and busie inquisition wherein men tyre themselves to attain to the truth, made a certain master of truth speak in this fashion. *Ergo liquido apparet in hac Mundi structurâ, quam cernimus, aliquam triumphare Veritatem ; quæ toties rationem nostram commovet, agitat, implicat, explicat ; toties inquietatem, toties insomnem miris modis sollicitat, non fortuitis, aut aliunde adventitiis, sed suis et propriis et originariis Naturæ illicibus ; quæ omnia cum non fiunt frustra, utique contingit, ut veritatem eorum quæ sunt, aliquo tandem opportuno tempore amplexemur.* "It is clear therefore (saith he) that in this fabric of the world, which we behold, there is some truth that works, which truth so often stirs up, puzzles, and helps our reason, so often sollicites her when shee is restless, so often when shee is watchfull, and this by strange meanes, not casual and adventitious, but by genuine provocations and pleasures of Nature ; all which motions being not to no purpose, it falls out at last that in some good time wee attain to the true knowledge of those things that are." But because I would not have you build your philosophie on coralls and whistles, which are the objects of little children, of whom we have spoken formerly, I will speak somewhat of those elements in whose contemplation a man ought to employ himself, and this discourse may serve as a preface to our whole philosophie. Man, according to Trismegistus, hath but two elements in his power, namely, earth and water, to which doctrine I adde this, and I have it from a greater than Hermes, that God hath made man absolute Lord of the First Matter, and from the First Matter, and the dispensation thereof, all the fortunes of man, both good and bad, doe proceed. According to the rule and measure of this substance, all the world are rich or poore, and hee that knows it truly, and withall the true use thereof, he can make his fortunes constant, but hee that knowes it not, though his estate be never so great, stands on a slipperie foundation. Look about thee then, and consider how thou art compassed with infinite treasures and miracles, but thou art so blind thou doest not see them ; nay, thou art so mad, thou doest think there is no use to be made of them, for thou doest believe that knowledge is a mere Peripateticall chat, and that the fruits of it are not works but words. If this were true, I would never advise thee to spend one minute of thy life upon learning. I would first be one of those should ruine all libraries and universities in the world, which God forbid any good Christian should desire. Look up then to Heaven, and when thou seest the cœlestiall fires move in their swift and glorious circles, think also there are here below some cold natures which they overlook, and about which they move incessantly to heat and concoct them. Consider, again, that the Middle Spirit, I mean the aire, is interposed as a refrigeratorie to temper and qualifie that heat, which otherwise might be too violent. If thou doest descend lower and fix thy thoughts where thy feet are, that thy wings may be like those of Mercurie at thy heeles, thou wilt find the earth surrounded with the water, and that water, heated and stirred by the sun and his starrs, abstracts from the earth the pure subtil and saltish parts, by which means the water is thickened and coagulated as with a rennet. Out of these two Nature generates all things. Gold and silver, pearles and diamonds, are nothing else but water and salt of the earth concocted. Behold! I have in a few words discovered unto thee the whole system of Nature, and her royal high-way of generation. It is thy duty now to improve the truth, and in my book thou may'st, if thou art wise, find thy advantages. The foure elements are the objects and, implicitly, the subjects of man, but the earth is invisible. I know the common man will stare at this, and judge me not very sober when I affirme the earth, which of all things is most gross and palpable, to be invisible. But, on my Soule, it is so, and, which is more, the eye of man never saw the earth, nor can it be seen without art. To make this element visible is the greatest secret in Magic, for it is a miraculous Nature, and of all others the most holy, according to that computation of Trismegistus—"the Heaven, the Æther, the Aire, and the most sacred Earth." As for this fæculent, gross body upon which we walk, it is a compost and no earth, but it hath earth in it, and even that also is not our Magicall Earth. In a word, all the elements are visible but one, namely the earth, and when thou hast attained to so much perfection as to know why God hath placed the Earth *in abscondito*, thou hast an excellent figure to know God himself, and how he is visible, how invisible. Hermes affirmeth that in the beginning the earth was a quakemire, or quivering kind of jelly, it being nothing else but water congealed by the incubation and heat of the Divine Spirit. *Cum adhuc* (sayth hee) *terra tremula esset, lucente sole compacta est.* "When as yet the earth was a quivering, shaking substance, the sun afterwards shining upon it, did compact it, or make it solid." The same author introduceth God speaking to the earth, and impregnating her with all sorts of seeds, in these words : *Cumque manus æquè validas implesset rebus, quæ in Naturâ, ambienteque erant, et pugnos valide constringens ; Sume (inquit) ô Sacra Terra, quæ Genetrix omnium es futura, nè ullâ re egena videaris ; et manus, quales oportet Deum habere, expandens, demisit omnia ad rerum constitutionem necessaria.* "When God (saith he) had filled his powerfull hands with those things which are in Nature, and in that which compasseth Nature, then, shutting them close again, hee said : Receive from me, O holy Earth! that art ordained to be the Mother of all, lest thou shouldst want any thing; when presently opening such hands as it becomes a God to have, hee poured down all that was necessary to the constitution of things." Now, the meaning of it is this : the Holy Spirit moving upon the Chaos, which action some divines compare to the incubation of a hen upon her eggs, did together with his heat communicate other manifold influences to the matter. For as wee know the sun doth not onely dispense heat but some other secret influx, so did God also in the Creation, and from him the sun and all the starrs received what they have, for God himself is a Supernaturall Sun, or fire, according to that oracle of Zoroaster :

> The Architect who by his power alone
> Built up the cosmos, manifests himself
> Another orb of flame.

He did therefore hatch the Matter and bring out the secret essences, as a chick is brought out of the shell, whence that position of the same Zoroaster—

> One single heat did all that is produce.

Neither did he only generate them then, but he also preserves them now, with a perpetuall efflux of heat and spirit. Hence hee is styled in the Oracles,

> Eternal Father both of Gods and Men
> Who doth the fire, the light, the starry air,
> And all the golden sequence of the worlds,
> Most copiously animate.

This is advertisement enough: and now, reader, I must tell thee I have met with some late attempts on my two former discourses,* but truth is proof, and I am so far from being overcome that I am

* Note 13.

no where understood.   When I first eyed the libell, and its addresse to Philalethes, I judged the author serious, and that his design was not to abuse mee but to informe himselfe.   This conceit quickly vanished, for, perusing his forepart, his eares shot out of his skin, and presented him a perfect asse.   His observations are one continued "asse's skin," and the oyster-whores read the same philosophie every day.   'Tis a scurril, senselesse piece, and, as he well stiles him self, a chip of a block-head.

His qualities indeed are transcendent abroad, but they are peers at home ; his malice is equall to his ignorance.   I laughed to see the foole's disease—a flux of Gale which made him still at the chops, whiles another held the presse for him like Porphyry's bason to Aristotle's well.   There is something in him prodigious ; his excrements run the wrong way, for his mouth stools, and hee is so 'far from man that hee is the aggravation of a beast.   These are his parts, and for his person, I turn him over to the dog-whippers, that hee may be well lashed, *a posteriori*, and bear the *errata* of his front imprinted in his rere.   I cannot yet find a fitter punishment, for since his head could learn nothing but nonsense, by sequel of parts, his tayle should be taught some sense.

This is all, at this time, and for my present discourse, I wish it the common fortune of truth and honestie, to deserve well and hear ill.   As for applause, I fish not so much in the aire as to catch it. It is a kind of popularity, which makes mee scorn it, for I defie the noyse of the rout, because they observe not the truth, but the success of it.   I do, therefore, commit this piece to the world without any protection but its own worth, and the æstimate of that Soule that understands it.   For the rest, as I cannot force, so I will not beg their approbation.   I would not bee great by imposts, nor rich by briefes.   They may be what they will, and I shall be what I am.

EUGENIUS PHILALETHES.

MAGIA ADAMICA;

OR,

THE ANTIQUITIE OF MAGIC.

HAT I should profess Magic in this discourse, and justifie the professors of it withall, is impietie with many but religion with mee. It is a conscience I have learnt from authors greater than my self, and Scriptures greater than both. Magic is nothing else but the wisdom of The Creator revealed and planted in the creature. It is a name (as Agrippa saith) *ipsi Evangelio non ingratum*, not distastefull to the very Gospel it self. Magicians were the first attendants our Saviour met withall in this world, and the onely philosophers who acknowledged him in the flesh before that hee himself discovered it. I find God conversant with them, as he was formerly with the patriarchs; he directs them in their travels with a star, as hee did the Israelites with a pillar of fire; hee informs them of future dangers in their dreams, that having first seen his Son, they might in the next place see his salvation. This makes me believe they were Sons of the Prophets as well as Sons of Art, men that were acquainted with the very same Mysteries by which the prophets acted before them. To reconcile this science, and the masters of it, to the world is an attempt more plausible than possible, the prejudice being so great that neither reason nor authority can ballance it. If I were to persuade a Jew to my principles, I could do it with two words אמרו הכמים, the Hachamim, or Wisemen, have spoken it. Give him but the authoritie of his fathers, and presently hee submits to the seale. Verily, our primitive Galileans (I mean those Christians whose lamps burnt near the cross and funerall) were most compendious in their initiations. A Proselyte in those dayes was con-

firmed with a simple "Believe," and no more.   Nay, the solemnitie
of this short induction was such that Julian made it the topic of his
apostasie : " You have (sayd he) nothing more than your *Crede* to
establish your religion."   Such was the simplicitie of those first times,
" Whilst as yet shone the blood of Christ," whiles his wounds were
as yet in their eyes, and his bloud warm at their hearts.   But, alas !
those holy drops are frozen, our salvation is translated from the
crosse to the rack, and dismembered in the inquisition-house of
Aristotle.   Bee not angry, O Peripatetick ! for what else shall I call
thy schooles, where by severall sects and factions Scripture is so
seriously murdered *pro et con !*   A spleen first bred and afterwards
promoted by disputes, whose damnable divisions and distinctions
have minced one truth into a thousand hereticall whimzies.   But
the breach is not considered ; divinitie is still but chaff, if it be not
sifted by the engine, if it acts not by the demonstrative hobby-
horse.   Thus, zeale, poysoned with logic, breathes out contentious
calentures, and faith, quitting her wings and perspective, leans on
the reed of a syllogism.   Certainly I cannot yet conceive how reason
may judge those principles, *Quorum veritas pendet á solâ Revelantis
authoritate*, " whose certaintie wholly depends on God," and, by
consequence, is indemonstrable without the Spirit of God.   But if
I should grant that, which I will ever deny, verily, a true faith consists not in reason, but in love, for I receive my principles, and
believe them being received, *solo erga Revelantem amore*, " onely out
of affection to Him that reveales them."

Thus our Saviour would have the Jewes to believe him first for
his own sake, and when that failed for his worke's sake.   But some
divines believe onely for Aristotle's sake ; if logic renders the tenet
probable, then it is Creed, if not 'tis Alcoran.   Nevertheless,
Aristotle himself, who was first pedlar to this ware, and may for
sophistrie take place of Ignatius in his own conclave, hath left us
this concession : " That reason is subject to error as well as opinion."
And Philoponus expounding these words of his, *Non solùm scientiam,
sed et principium scientiæ esse aliquod dicimus, quo cognoscimus terminus,*
that is, " We say not onely science but the principle also of science
to be something whereby we understand the termes," hath this
excellent and Christian observation : " Taking indeed (saith hee)
the mind to bee the principle or first cause of knowledge, not our
own, but that of God which is above us ; but taking the Termes to
be Intellectuall and Divine Formes."   Thus, according to Aristotle
(if you trust the comment), the Divine Mind is the first cause of
knowledge, for if this Mind once unfolds himself, and sheds his light

upon us, wee shall apprehend the Intellectuall Formes, or Types of
all things that are within him.   These Formes hee very properly
calls ὅρους, because they terminate or end all things, for by them the
creature is defined and hath his individuation, or, to speak with
Scotus, his *Hæcceitie*, by which he is this and not that.   This, now,
is the demonstration we should look after, namely, the expansion or
opening of the Divine Mind, not a syllogism that runs perhaps on
all fours.   If once wee be admitted to this Communion of Light,
wee shall be able, with the Apostle, to give a reason for our faith,
but never without it.   Now, you are to understand that God unfolds
not himself, *nisi magno cœlo priùs patefacto*, "unlesse the Heaven of
Man bee first unfolded."   *Amovete ergo velamen intellectus vestri,*   Cornelius
"Cast off the Veile that is before your faces," and you shall bee no   Agrippa.
more blind.   God is not God a far off, but God at hand.   "Behold
(saith he) I stand at the doore and knock."   Open your selves then,
for it is written, "If any man opens, I will come in and sup with
him."   This is the Inward, Mysticall, not the Outward, Typicall
Supper, and this is the Spirituall Baptism with Fire, not that
elemental one with water.   Truely, I am much comforted when I
consider two things—first, that Magic did afford the first professors
of Christianity, whose knowledge and devotion brought them from
the East to Jerusalem; secondly, that this art should suffer as
religion doth, and for the very same reason.   The main motives
which have occasioned the present rents and divisions of the Church
are the ceremonies and the types used in it, for, without controversie,
the Apostles instituted, and left behind them, certaine elements or
signes, as water, oill, salt, and lights, by which they signified
unto us some great and revered Mysteries.   But our Reformers,
mistaking these things for superstitions, turned them all out of
doores.   But, verily, it was ill done, for if the shadow of St Peter
healed, shall not these shadowes of Christ doe much more?   The
Papist, on the contrary, knowing not the signification of these types,
did place a certain inhærent holiness in them, and so fell into
a very dangerous idolatrie.   I omit many things which he invented
of his own, as images, holy lambes, and reliques, adding these dead
bones to the primitive and beauteous bodie of the Church.   Now
to draw the parallel : the Magicians, they also instituted certain
signes, as the Key to their Art, and these were the same with the
former, namely, water, oile, salt, and light, by which they tacitly
discovered unto us their three Principles, and the Light of Nature,
which fills and actuates all things.   The common man perusing
their books, but not their sense, took candles, common water,

oile, and salt, and began to consecrate and exorcize them, to make up his damnable and devilish magic.   The magicians had a maxim amongst themselves, *Quod nulla vox operatur in Magiâ, nisi prius Dei voce formetur*, " That no word is efficacious in Magic, unless it be first animated with the word of God."   Hence in their books there was frequent mention made of *Verbum* and *Sermo*, which the common man interpreting to his own fansie, invented his charmes and *vocabula*, by which he promised to do wonders.   The magicians in their writings did talk much of triangles and circles, by which they intimated unto us their more secret Triplicitie, with the rotation of Nature from the beginning of her Week to her Sabaoth. By this circle also, or rotation, they affirmed that Spirits might be bound, meaning that the Soul might be united to the body. Presently upon this the common man fansied his triangles and characters, with many strange cobwebs or figures, and a circle to conjure in; but knowing not what spirit that was which the magicians did bind, he laboured and studied to bind the devill.*
Now, if thou wilt question mee who these magicians were, I must tell thee they were Kings, they were Priests, they were Prophets— men that were acquainted with the Substantial, Spirituall Mysteries of Religion, and did deal or dispense the outward, typicall part of it to the people.   Here then wee may see how Magic came to be out of request, for the lawyers and common divines, who knew not these secrets, perusing the ceremonial, superstitious trash of some scribblers, who prætended to Magic, præscribed against the Art itself as impious and antichristian, so that it was a capital sin to professe it, and the punishment no lesse than death.   In the interim, those few who were the first masters of the science, observing the first monitories of it, buried all in a deep silence.   But God having suffered his truth to be obscured for a great time, did at last stirr up some resolute and active spirits, who, putting the pen to paper, expelled this cloud, and in some measure discovered the light.   The leaders of this brave body were Cornelius Agrippa, Libanius Gallius, the philosopher, Johannes Trithemius, Georgius Venetus, Johannes Reuchlin, called in the Greek Capnion, with severall others in their severall dayes, and after all these, as an usher to the train, and one born out of due time, Eugenius Philalethes.
Seeing then I have publickly undertaken a promise, which I might have governed privately with much more content and advan- tage, I think it not enough to have discovered the abuses and mis- fortunes this science hath suffered, unless I endeavour withall to

* Note 14.

demonstrate the antiquitie of it. For certainly it is with arts as it is with men, their age and continuance are good arguments of their strength and integritie. Most apposite then was that check of the Ægyptian to Solon : *O Solon, Solon ! Vos Græci semper pueri estis, nullam antiquam habendes Opinionem, nullam disciplinam tempore canam.* " You Græcians (said hee) are ever childish, having no ancient opinion, no discipline of any long standing." But as I confesse my self no antiquarie, so I wish some Selden would stand in this breach, and make it up with those fragments which are so neer dust that time may put them in his glass. I know, for my own part, it is an enterprise I cannot sufficiently performe, but since my hand is already in the bag, I will draw out those few pebbles I have, and thus I fling them at the mark.

This Art, or rather this Mysterie, is to bee considered severall wayes, and that because of its severall subjects. The primitive, original existence of it is God himself, for it is nothing else but the practice or operation of the Divine Spirit working in the matter, uniting principles into compounds, and resolving those compounds into their principles. In this sense wee seeke not the antiquity of it, for it is æternall, being a Notion of the Divine Wisdome and existent before all time, or the creation of it. Secondly, we are to consider it in a derivative sense, as it was imparted and communicated to man, and this properly was no birth or beginning, but a discovery or revelation of the Art. From this time of its revelation wee are to measure the antiquitie of it, where it shall be our task to demonstrate upon what motives God did reveale it, as also to whom and when.

The eye discovers not beyond that stage wherein it is conversant, but the eare receives the sound a great way off. To give an experienced testimonie of actions more ancient than our selves is a thing impossible for us, unless wee could look into that Glass where all occurrences may bee seen, past, present, and to come. I must therefore build my discourse on the traditions of those men to whom the Word, both written and mysticall, was intrusted, and these were the Jewes in generall, but more particularly their Cabalists. It is not my intention to rest on these Rabbins as fundamentals, but I will justifie their assertions out of Scripture, and entertain my reader with proofes both divine and humane. Finally, I will passe out of Judæa into Ægypt and Græce, where againe I shall meet with these Mysteries, and prove that this Science did stream (as the Chimists say their Salt Fountain doth) out of Jurie and watered the whole Earth.

It is the constant opinion of the Hebrewes that before the Fall of

Adam there was a more plentifull and large communion between Heaven and Earth, God and the Elements, than there is now in our days. But upon the transgression of the first man, Malchuth (say the Cabalists) was cut off from the Ilan,* so that a breach was made between both worlds, and their channel of influences discontinued. Now Malchuth is the Invisible, Archetypall Moone, by which our visible, cœlestiall moone is governed and imprægnated. And truly it may be that upon this retreate of the Divine Light from inferiors, those spots and darkness which we now see succeeded in the body of this planet, and not in her alone but about the sun also, as it hath been discovered by the telescope. Thus (say they), God to punish the sin of Adam withdrew himself from the creatures, so that they were not feasted with the same measure of influences as formerly. For the Archetypall Moone which is placed in the השמים *Hascha-maim*, to receive and convey downe the influx of the six superior Invisible Planets, was (as the Jewes affirme) either separated from the Ilan, or her breasts were so sealed up that she could not dispense her milk to inferiors in that happy and primitive abundance. But because I would not dwell long on this point, let us heare the *Porta Lucis.* Cabalist himself state it in a clear and apposite phrase. *Initia Creationis Mundi Divina Cohabitatio erat descendens in Inferiora, et cum esset Divina cohabitatio inferiùs reperti sunt Coeli et Terra uniti, et erant Fontes, et Canales activi in perfectione, et trahebantur à Superiore ad Inferius, et inveniebatur Deus complens supernè et infernè. Venit Adam primus, et peccavit, et diruti sunt Descensus, et compacti sunt Canales, et desiit Aquæ ductus, et cessavit Divina Cohabitatio, et divisa est Societas.* That is: "In the Beginning of the Creation of the world God did descend and cohabitate with things here below, and when the Divine Habitation was here below, the Heavens and the Earth were found to be united, and the vital springs and channels were in their perfection, and did flow from the Superior to the Inferior World, and God was found to fill all things both Above and Beneath. Adam, the first man, came, and sinned, where upon the descents from above were restrained, and their Channels were broken, and the Water-Course was no more, and the Divine Cohabitation ceased, and the Societie was divided." Thus far my Rabbi. Now because I have promised Scripture to my Cabalism, I will submit the tradition to Moses, and truly that Rabbi also is of my side, for thus I read in Genesis, "And to Adam he said, Because thou hast eaten of the tree, whereof I commanded thee, saying, Thou shalt not eate of it. Cursed is the ground for

* Note 15.

thy sake, in sorrow shalt thou eate of it all the dayes of thy life, thornes and thistles shall it bring forth unto thee, and thou shalt eate the herb of the field. In the sweate of thy face shalt thou eate bread, untill thou returne unto the ground, for out of it wast thou taken, for dust thou art, and to dust shalt thou returne." This is the curse, and Adam was so sensible of it that he acquainted his posterity with it. For Lamech, prophesying of his son Noah, hath these words. "This same shall comfort us, concerning our worke and toyle of our hands, because of the ground which the Lord hath cursed." And this indeed was accomplished in some sense after the Floud, as the same Scripture tells us. "And the Lord said in his heart, I will not again curse the ground any more for man's sake." Here now we are to consider two things: first, the curse itself, and next the latitude of it. To manifest the nature of the curse, and what it was, you must know that good essentially is light, and evill is darkness. The evill, properly, is a corruption that immediately takes place upon the removall of that which is good. Thus, God having removed his candlestick and light from the elements, presently the darkness and cold of the matter prævailed, so that the earth was nearer her first deformitie, and, by consequence less fruitfull and vitall. Heaven and Hell, that is, light and darkness, are the two extremes which consummate good and evill. But there are some meane blessings which are but *in ordine*, or disposing to Heaven, which is their last perfection, and such were these blessings which God recalled upon the transgression of the first man. Againe, there are some evills which are but degrees conducing to their last extremitie, or Hell, and such was this curse, or evill, which succeeded the transgression. Thus our Saviour under these notions of blessed and cursed comprehends the inhabitants of light and darkness: Come you blessed, and goe you cursed. In a word then, the curse was nothing else but an act repealed, or a restraint of those blessings which God of his mere goodness had formerly communicated to his creatures. And thus I conceive there is a very fair and full harmonie between Moses and the Cabalists. But to omit their depositions, though great and high, we are not to seek in this point for the testimonie of an angel. For the tutor of Esdras, amongst his other mysterious instructions, hath also this doctrine. "When Adam transgressed my statutes, then was that decreed which now is done. Then were the entrances of this world made narrow, full of sorrow and travell: they are but few and evill, full of perils, and very painfull. But the entrances of the elder world were wide and sure, and brought forth immortall fruit." Thus much for the

Genesis c. iii. v. 17.

Gen v. 29.

Gen. viii. 25.

Es. vii. 11-13.

curse it self; now for the latitude of it. It is true that it was intended chiefely for man, who was the only cause of it, but extended to the elements in order to him, and for his sake. For if God had excluded him from Eden, and continued the earth in her primitive glories, he had but turned him out of one Paradise into another, wherefore he fits the dungeon to the slave, and sends a corruptible man into a corruptible world. But in truth it was not man, nor the earth alone, that suffered this Curse, but all other creatures also; for saith God to the serpent: "Thou art cursed above all cattle, and above every beast of the field," so that cattle and beasts also were cursed in some measure, but this serpent above them all. To this also refers the apostle in his Epistle to the Romans, where he hath
C. viii. v. 20. these words: "For the creature was made subject to vanitie, not willingly, but by reason of him who hath subjected the same in hope. Because the creature it self also shall be delivered from the bondage of corruption into the glorious liberty of the Children of God." Here by the creature he understands not man but the inferior species, which he distinguisheth from the Children of God, though he allows them both the same liberty. But this is more plaine out of the subsequent texts, where he makes a clear difference between man and the whole creation. "For we know (saith he) that the whole creation groaneth and travaileth together in paine untill now. And not only they but ourselves also, which have the first fruits of the Spirit, even we our selves groane within our selves, waiting for the adoption, to wit, the redemption of our body. Here we see the first fruits of the Spirit referred to man, and why not some second subordinate fruits of it to the creatures in general? For as they were cursed in the fall of man, for man's sake, so it seems in his restitution they shall be also blessed for his sake. But of this enough. Let us now summe up, and consider the severall inconveniences our first parent was subject to, for they will be of some use with us hereafter. First of all, he was ejected from the presence of God, and exposed to the malice and temptations of the devill. He was altered from good to bad, from incorruptible to corruptible. "In the daye (saith the Scripture) thou eatest thereof thou shalt dye the death." He was excluded from a glorious paradyse, and confined to a base world, whose sickly, infected elements, conspiring with his own nature, did assist and hasten that death which already began to reign in his body. Heaven did mourn over him, the earth, and all her generations, about him. He looked upon himself as a felon and a murderer, being guilty of that curse and corruption which succeeded in the world because of his fall, as we have sufficiently proved out of

the Mosaicall and Cabalisticall traditions.   He was ignorant, and
therefore hopeless, of Life Æternall, and for this temporall present
life, he was not acquainted with the provisions of it.   The elements
of husbandrie were not as yet known; there was neither house
nor plow, nor any of those manuall arts which make up a worldly
providence.   He was exposed to the violence of rains and winds,
frosts and snows, and, in a word, deprived of all comforts, spiritual
and natural.   What should I say more?   He was a mere stranger
in this world, could not distinguish medecines from poysons, neither
was he skilled in the ordinarie præparations of meate and drink.
He had no victuals ready to his hands but the crude, unseasoned
herbage of the earth, so that he must either starve or feed, as
Nebuchadnezar did, with the beasts of the field.   He heard indeed
sometimes of a tree of life in Eden, but the vegetables of this world,
for ought he knew, might be so many trees of death.   I conclude,
therefore, that he had some instructor to initiate him in the wayes
of life, and to shew him the intricate and narrow paths of that
wilderness.   For, without question, his outward miseries and his
inward despaire were motives whereupon God did reveall a certaine
art unto him by which he might relieve his present necessities, and
embrace a firme hope of a future and glorious restitution.   For God
having ordained a second, æternal Adam, did by some mysterious
experience manifest the possibility of his coming to the first, who
being now full of despaire, and overcharged with the guilt of his own
sin, was a very fit patient for so divine and mercifull a physician.
But, omitting our own reasons, which we might produce to this
purpose, let us repayre to the Cabalists, who indeed are very high in
the point, and thus they deliver themselves.   God (say they) having
made fast the doores of his Paradyse, and turned out Adam, sometimes the dearest of his creatures, did notwithstanding the present
punishment retaine his former affection for him still.   For God is
said to love his creatures, not that there is anything lovely in them
without their creator, but in that hee desires their perfection.   That
is to say, he would have them conformable to himself, and fitt to
receive his image or similitude, which is a spiritual impress of his
beauty.   Now, to restore this similitude in Adam was impossible,
unlesse God should reassume that to himself which was now fallen
from him.   So transcendent and almost incredible a mercy had God
treasured up in his secret will, being resolved to unite the nature of
man to his own, and so vindicate him from death by taking him into
the Deitie, which is the true fountain and centre of life.   This will
(say the Cabalists) was first revealed to the angels, and that by God

Gen. iii. 22. himself, in these words : *Ecce Adam sicut unus ex nobis* : " Behold an
Adam like one of us, knowing good and evill ! "   This speech they
call *Orationem occultissimam à Creatore mundi cum beatis angelis
in suæ Divinitatis penetralibus habitam*, " a most secret conference
which God had with the blessed angels in the inner chambers of
Heaven."   Now that the same Scripture should speak one thing in
the letter and another in the mysterie is not strange to mee, how
difficult soever it may seem to another.   For, verily, this text may
not concern the first Adam, who knowing evill by committing it,
could not be like God in respect of that knowledge, which made
him sinfull and altogether unlike him.   For God (if I may so expresse
it) knows the evill onely speculatively, inasmuch as nothing can
escape his knowledge, and therefore is not guilty of evill, for, as
Trithemius hath well observed, *scientia mali non est malum sed usus*—
" The knowledge of evill is not evill, but the practice of it."   It
remains then that this speech concerned the second Adam, Christ
Jesus, who knew the evill but did not commit it, and therefore was
" like one of us," that is like one of the Trinitie, knowing good and
evill, and yet no way guiltie of the evill.   This primitive and compendious gospell was no sooner imparted to the angels but they
became ministers of it, the Law (as St Paul saith) " being ordained
into their hands," till Christ should take it into his own, and their
administration to man took beginning with this oracle.   Thus (say
the Cabalists), Raziel the angel was presently dispatched to communicate the intelligence to Adam, and to acquaint him with the
mysteries of both worlds, æternall and temporall.   For as he could
not obtain the blessings of the æternall world unless by a true faith
hee apprehended the Three Æternall Principles of it, so neither
could he fully enjoy the benefits of this temporall world unless hee
truly understood the Three Visible Substances whereof it consists.
For there are Three above and Three beneath, Three (as St John
saith) in Heaven and Three on earth.   The inferior bear witness of
the superior, and are their only proper receptacles.   They are sig-
natures and created books where wee may reade the mysteries of
the supernaturall Trinitie.   But to proceed in our former discourse.
The Cabalists doe not onely attribute a guardian to Adam, but to
every one of the patriarchs, allowing them their præsidents and
tutors both to assist and instruct them in their wearisome and
worldly peregrinations—a doctrine in my opinion not more religious
than necessary, how prodigious soever it may seem to some phan-
tastic insipid theologians.   For certainly it is impossible for us to
find out mysteries of our selves ; wee must either have the Spirit of

God or the instruction of his ministers, whether they bee men or angels. And thus we see out of the traditions and doctrine of the Jewes how their Cabala and our Magic came first into the world. I shall now examine the Scriptures and consult with them, where (if I am not much mistaken) I shall find some consequences which must needs depend on these principles, and thus I apply myself to the task.

The first harvest I read of was that of Cain, and the first flocks those of Abel. A shepheard's life, in those early dayes, was no difficult profession, it being an employment of more care than art, but how the earth was plowed up before the sound of Tubal's hammers is a piece of husbandrie unknown in these dayes. Howsoever, it was a labour performed, and not without retribution. Cain hath his sheaves as well as Abel his lambs; both of them receive and both acknowledge the benefit. I find established in these two a certain priesthood; they attend both to the altar, and the first bloud was shed by sacrifice, the second by murder.

Now so dull am I, and so short of syllogismes, those strange pumps and hydragogues which lave the truth *ex puteo*, like water, that all my reason cannot make these men Levites without Revelation. For I desire to know how came they first to sacrifice, and by whom were they initiated? If you will say by Adam, the question indeed is deferred but not satisfied, for, I would know further, in what schoole was Adam instructed? Now, that it was impossible for him to invent these shadowes and sacraments of himself, I will undertake to demonstrate, and that by invincible reason, which no adversarie dare to contradict.

It is most certain that the hope and expectation of man in matters of sacrifices, consist in the thing signified, and not in the signe it self. For the material, corruptible shadow is not the object of faith, but the spiritual, æternall prototype which answers to it, and makes the dead figure effectual. The sacrifices of the Old Testament, and the Elements of the New, can be no way acceptable with God but inasmuch as they have a relation to Christ Jesus, who is the great, perfect sacrifice offered up once for all. It is plain then that sacrifices were first instituted upon supernatural grounds, for in Nature there is no reason to be found why God should be pleased with the death of his creatures. Nay, the very contrary is written in that book, for death, both natural and violent, proceeds not from the pleasure but from the displeasure of the Creator. I know the learned Alkind builds the efficacie of sacrifices on a sympathie of parts with the great world, for there is in every animal a portion of the Star-Fire, which Fire, upon the dissolution of the compound, is united to the general Fire from whence it first came, and produceth a sense, or motion, in the Limbus to which it is united. This indeed is true, but that motion causeth no joy there, and, by consequence, no reward to the sacrifices; for I shall make it to appeare elsewhere that the Astral Mother doth mourn and not rejoyce at the death of her children. Now, if wee look back on these two first Sacrifices, we shall find Abel and his oblation accepted, which could not be, had he not offered it up as a symbol, or figure, of his Saviour. To drive home my argument, then, I say that this knowledge of the type, in whom all offerings were acceptable, could not bee obtained by any humane industrie but by sole revelation. For the Passion of Christ Jesus was an ordinance wrapt up in the secret will of God, and he that would know it must of necessitie bee of his council. Hence it is called in Scripture the Hidden Mysterie, for the truth and certaintie of it was not to bee received from any, but onely from him who had both the will and the power to ordain it. And if you will tell mee (like the author of the Prædicables) that men sacrificed at first by the instinct of Nature, and without any respect to the type, I shall indeed thank you for my mirth whensoever you give mee so just a reason to laugh. It remaines then a most firme, infallible foundation that Adam was first instructed concerning the Passion, and, in order to that, he was taught further to sacrifice and offer up the bloud of beasts as types and prodroms of the Bloud of Christ Jesus, the altars of the Law being but steps to the Cross of the Gospell. Now, if it be objected that severall nations have sacrificed who did not know God at all, much less the Son of God, who is the prototype and perfection of all oblations, to this I answer that the custome of sacrificing was communicated to heathens by tradition from the first man, who having instructed his own children, they also delivered it to their posteritie, so that this vizard of religion remained, though the substance and true doctrine of it was lost. And thus, in my opinion, it sufficiently appears that the first men did sacrifice, not by Nature, as Porphyrius, that enemie of our Religion, would have it, but some by revelation, others by custome and tradition. But, now I think upon it, I have Scripture to confirme me concerning this Primitive Revelation, for Solomon, numbering those severall blessings which the Divine Wisdome imparted to the Ancient Fathers, amongst the rest specifies her indulgence to Adam. "Shee præserved (saith hee) the first-found father of the world, that was created alone, and brought him out of his Fall." Here I find Adam in some measure restored,

Porph. *De Sacrif.*

and how could that bee but by discovering unto him the Great Restorative, Christ Jesus, the second Adam, in whom he was to believe? for without faith he could not have been brought out of his Fall, and without Christ revealed and preached unto him, hee could have no faith, for hee knew not what to believe. It remaines then that hee was instructed, for as in these last dayes wee are taught by the Son of God and his apostles, so in those first times they were taught by the Spirit of God and his ministering angels. These were their tutors, for of them they heard the Word, and verily wee are told that faith comes by hearing.

It is now (as I think) sufficiently proved that Adam had his metaphysics from above. Our next service (and perhaps somewhat difficult) is to give some probable, if not demonstrative, reasons that they came not alone, but had their physics also to attend them. I know the Scriptures are not positive in this point, and hence the sects will lug their "consequence of reprobation." Truly, for my part, I desire not their ruin, but their patience. I have, though against the præcept, for many years attended their Philosophie, and if they spend a few hours on my Spermalogie it may cost them some part of their justice but none of their favours. But that we may come to the thing in hand : I hold it very necessary to distinguish arts, for I have not yet seen any author who hath fully considered their difference. The Art I speak of is truly physicall in subject, method, and effect, but as for arts publickly professed, and to the disadvantage of truth allowed, not one of them is so qualified, for they are mere knacks and baubles of the hand or braine, having no fundamentals in Nature. These, in my opinion, Solomon numbers amongst his vanities, when hee speakes in a certaine place, "That God had made man upright but hee had sought out many inventions." Of these inventions we have a short catalogue in Genesis, where Moses separates the corn from the chaff, the works of God from the whymzies of man. Thus wee read that Jubal was the father of such as dwell in tents, his brother Tubal the father of all such as handle the harp and organ, and Tubal-Cain an instructer of every artificer in brasse and iron. What mischiefs have succeeded this brasse-and-iron Cyclops, I need not tell you. If you know not the fates of former times, you may studie the actions of your owne ; you live in an age that can instruct you. Verily, it is worth our observation that these arts, and their tooles, proceeded not from the posterity of Seth, in whose line our Saviour stands, for, as wee shall make it appeare hereafter, questionlesse they had a better knowledge, but they proceeded from the seed of Cain, who in action was a murderer, and in the circumstances of it a fratricide.

Acts xvii. 18.

Eccles. vii. 29.

To be short, there is no vanity to the vanity of sciences, I mean those inventions, and their professors, which produce nothing true and natural, but effects either false or in their ends corrupt and violent. But 'tis no conquest to tread on ruines. Cornelius Agrippa hath already laid these rhodomontados in the dirt, and that so handsomely they were never since of a general reputation. Give me an Art then that is a perfect, entire map of the creation, that can lead me directly to the knowledge of the true God, by which I can discover those Universal, Invisible Essences which are subordinate to him—an Art that is no way subject to evill, and by which I can attain to all the secrets and mysteries in Nature. This is the Art wherein the physics of Adam and the patriarchs consisted, and that this Art was revealed to him, I will undertake to demonstrate by Scriptures, and the practice of his posteritie.

De Vanit. Scient.

This truth, I am certain, will seem difficult, if not incredible to most men, the providence of God being prejudiced in this point, for they will not allow him to instruct us in naturall things, but onely in supernaturals, such as may concern our soules and their salvation. As for our bodies, he must not præscribe for their necessities by teaching us the true physic and discovering the lawes of his creation, for though he made Nature, yet he may not tutor us in natural sciences. By no means! Aristotle and his syllogism can doe it much better. Certainly this opinion is nothing different from that of the Epicure, *Deum ad Cœli cardines obambulare, et nulla tangi mortalium cura*, "That God takes the aire, I know not in what walks and quarters of his Heaven, but thinks not of us mortals who are here under his feet." Questionlesse, a most eminent impietie to make God, as Tertullian said of old, *Otiosum et inexercitum neminem in rebus humanis*, "An idle, unprofitable nobody, having nothing to doe with our affaires as they are natural and humane." Sure, these men are afraid lest his mercy should diminish his majestie: they suffer him to trade onely with our immortal parts, not with corruptible bodies that have most need of his assistance; they are base subjects which he hath turned over to Galen and the Apothecaries. Not so, my friend, he hath created physic, and brings it out of the earth, but the Galenist knowes it not. Hee it is that pities our afflictions, he is the good Samaritane that doth not passe by us in our miseries, but poures oile and wine into our wounds. This I know very well and will prove it out of his own mouth. Did not hee instruct Noah to build an Ark, to pitch it within and without, and this to save life in a time when hee himselfe was resolved to destroy it? In a time when the world was acquainted with no mechanics but a little hus-

Apolog. Adversus Gent. c. 24.

bandrie, and a few knacks of Tubal-Cain and his brethren? But even those inventions also proceeded from that light which hee planted in man, an essence perpetually busie, and whose ambition it is to performe wonders, yet hee seldome produceth any thing of his owne but what is fantastic and monstrous. Did he not put his Spirit in Bezaleel, the son of Uri, and in Aholiab, the son of Ahisamach? Exod. xxxi Did hee not teach them to devise cunning workes, to work in gold, in silver, in brasse, in cutting of stones, in setting of them, in carving of timber, and in all manner of workmanship? But to come nearer to our purpose : did hee not informe Moses in the composition of the oile and the perfume? Did hee not teach him the symptoms of the leprosie, and the cure thereof? Did he not præscribe a plaster of figs for Hezekiah, and, to use your owne term, an opthalmic for Tobit? Did not Jesus Christ himself in the dayes of his flesh work most of his miracles on our bodies, though his great cure was that of our Soules? Is hee not the same then to day as yesterday? Nay, was hee not the same from the beginning? Did he care for our bodies then, and doth he neglect them now? Or, being seated on the right hand of the Majesty on high, is hee become less good because more glorious? God forbid! To think so were a sin in superlatives. Let us then take him for our præsident, "for he is not (saith S. Paul) such an one which cannot be touched with the feeling Heb. iv. 15. of our infirmities," but hee is indeed one that looks to our present estate as well as to our future and is as sensible of our infirmitie as hee is carefull of our immortalitie. When hee was on earth, with the dust of that earth hee made the blind to see, and of mere water he made wine. These were the visible elements of his physic, or rather (so the notion doth not offend you) of his magic. But shall I shew you his librarie, and in that his three-fold philosophie? Observe then first and censure afterwards. "Have salt in your selves," and again, "you are the salt of the earth," and, in a third place, "Salt is good." This is his mineral doctrine; will you know his vegetable? It is in two little books—Mustard-seed and a Lillie. Lastly, he hath his animal magic, and truly that's a scroll sealed up, I know not who may open it. "Hee needed not that any should bear witnesse of man, for he Jo. ii. 25. knew what was in man." And what of all this blasphemie? sayes some splenetick sophister? Behold, I will instruct thee! First of all, have salt in thy self, for it will season thy soule that is infected, and præserve thy braines, that are putrified with the dirt of Aristotle. In the second place, learn what the salt of the earth is, to which the disciples are compared, and that by a regular, solid speculation. Thirdly, come up to experience, and by a physicall, legitimate practice know in what sense "salt is most good." Fourthly, examine the lilies by fire, and the water of fire, that thou mayst see their miraculous, invisible treasures, and wherein that speech of Truth is verified, "That Solomon in all his royaltie was not cloathed like one of them." If thou wilt attempt a higher Magic, thou mayst, being first seasoned, but in this place it is not my designe to lead thee to it. Animal and vegetable mysteries thou canst never perfectly obtain without the knowledge of the first mineral secret, namely, the salt of the earth, which is salt and no salt, and the præparation thereof. This discourse, I confesse, is somewhat remote from what I first intended, namely, that philosophie was first revealed to Adam, as well as Divinitie, but some pates are blocks in their own wayes, and, as I told you formerly, will not believe that God dispenseth with any naturall secrets. This made mee produce these few instances out of Scripture, as præparatives to the proposition it self, and, if hee be anything ingenious to the reader. His compliance to my principles I expect not, nay, I am so far from it, hee may suspend his charitie. Let him bee as rigid as justice can make him, for I wish not to prævaile in any thing but the truth, and, in the name of truth, thus I begin.

You have been told formerly that Cain and Abel were instructed in matters of sacrifice by their father Adam, but Cain having murdered his brother Abel, his priesthood descended to Seth, and this is confirmed by those faculties which attended his posteritie, for Enoch, Lamech, and Noah, were (all of them) prophets. It troubles you perhaps that I attribute a priesthood to Abel, but I have, besides his own practice, Christ's testimonie for it, who accounts the bloud of Abel amongst that of the persecuted prophets and wise men. Now, to conclude that these men had no knowledge in philosophie because the Scripture doth not mention any use they made of it, is an argument that denies something but proves nothing. To shew the vanitie of this inference, I will give you an example out of Moses himself. Wee know very well there are no prophecies of Abraham extant, neither doe wee read any where that ever hee did prophesie, but notwithstanding he was a prophet. For God reproving Abimelech, King of Gerar, who had taken Sarah from him, supposing she had been his sister, hath these words: "Now, therefore restore the man his wife, for hee is a prophet, and hee shall pray for thee, and thou shalt live." Hence wee may learn that the Holy Ghost doth not alwayes mention the secret perfections of the Soul in the public character of the person. Truly, I should not be so impudent as to expect your

Luke xi. 15, and Matt. xxiii. 35.

Gen xx. 7.

assent to this doctrine if the Scriptures were silent in every text, if I did not find there some infallible steps of Magick, such as may lead me without a lanthorn to the archives of the Art it self. I know the troupe and tumult of other affaires are both the many and the maine in the historie of Moses.   But in the whole current I meet with some arts which may not be numbered amongst the fortunes of the patriarchs, but are performances extraordinarie, and speak their causes not common.   I have ever admired that discipline of Eliezer, the steward of Abraham, who when he prayed at the well in Mesopotamia could make his camels also kneele.   I must not believe there was any hocus in this, or that the spirit of Banks may be the spirit of prayer.   Jacob makes a covenant with Laban, that all the spotted and brown cattle in his flocks should be assigned to him for his wages.   The bargain is no sooner made but he finds an art to multiplie his own colours, and sends his father-in-law almost a wool-gathering.   "And Jacob took him rods of green ^{Gen. xxx. 37.} poplar, and of the hasel and chesnut-tree, and pilled white strakes in them, and made the white appear which was in the rods ; and hee set the rods which he had pilled before the flocks in the gutters, in the watering troughs when the flocks came to drink, that they should conceive when they came to drink.   And the flocks conceived before the rods, and brought forth cattle ring-straked, speckled, and spotted."   As for that which the Scripture tells us elsewhere, namely, that "Jacob saw in a dream, and behold the rams that leaped on ^{Gen. xxxi. 10.} the cattle were ring-straked, speckled, and grisled," this doth no way impair our assertion, or prove this generation miraculous and supernatural, for no man, I believe, is so mad as to think those appearances, or rams of the dream did leap, and supplie the natural males of the flock, God using this apparition onely to signifie the truth of that art Jacob acted by, and to tell him that his hopes were effected.   But I shall not insist long on any particular, and therefore I will passe from this dream to another.   Joseph being seventeen years old, an age of some discretion, propounds a vision to his father, not loosely and to no purpose, as wee tell one another of our dreams, but expecting, I believe, an interpretation, as knowing that his father had the skill to expound it.   The wise patriarch being not ignorant of the secrets of the two Luminaries, attributes males to the sun and females to the moon, then allowes a third signification to the minor stars, and lastly answers his son with a question : "What is this dream that thou hast dreamed ?   Shall I and thy mother and thy brethren indeed come to bow down our selves to thee to the earth ?"

Now, I think no man will deny but the interpretation of dreams belongs to magic, and hath been ever sought after as a piece of secret learning. True it is, when the interpreter receives his knowledge immediately from God, as Daniel did, then it falls not within the limits of a naturall science, but I speak of a physicall exposition, as this was, which depends on certain abstruse similitudes, for hee that knowes the analogie of parts to parts in this great body, which wee call the world, may know what every signe signifies, and, by consequence, may prove a good interpreter of dreames. As for Jacob's first practice, which wee have formerly mentioned, namely, the propagation of his speckled flocks, it is an effect so purely magicall that our most obstinate adversaries dare not question it. I could cite one place more which refers to this patriarch and points at the fundamentals of Magic, but being annexed to this discourse, it would discover too much; I shall, therefore, leave it to the search of those who are considerable proficients, if not masters, in the Art. The summ of all is this: Man of himself could not attain to true knowledge; it was God in mere mercie did instruct him. To confirm this, I shall desire the reader to consider his own experience. Wee have in these our dayes many magicall books extant, wherein the Art is discovered both truly and plainly. Wee have also an infinite number of men who studie those books, but after the endeavours of a long life not one in ten thousand understands them. Now, if wee, with all these advantages, cannot attain to the secrets of Nature, shall we think those first fathers did who had none of our libraries to assist them, nor any learned man upon earth to instruct them? Could they doe that without means which we cannot doe with means, and those too very considerable? The Peripatetics perhaps will tell me their syllogism is the engine that will perform all this. Let them then in *Barbara* or *Baroco* demonstrate the First Matter of the Philosophers' Stone. But they will tell mee there is no such thing. Behold, I tell them again, and assure them too on my salvation there is, but, in truth, their logic will never find it out. It is clear, then, that God at first instructed Adam, from him his children received it, and by their tradition it descended to the patriarchs, every father bequeathing these secrets to his child, as his best and most lasting legacie. I have now attended Jacob, the Israel of God, both in his pilgrimage at Padan-Aram and in his typicall inheritance, the earnest of the land of Canaan. But two removalls perfect not the wanderings of a patriarch; God calls him from the habitation of his fathers to the prison of his posteritie, and provides him a place of freedom in the house of bondage. I must follow him where his fortune leads, from Isaac's Hebron to the

Goshen of Pharaoh, then back again to the cave and dust of Mach-pelah. As for his sons and their traine, who attended his motion thither, I find not any particular remembrance of them, onely Moses tells one of a generall exit: "Joseph died, and all his brethren, and all that generation." I must now then, to prove the continuance of and succession of this Art, address my self to the court, where I shall find the son of Levi newly translated from his ark and bulrushes. Yet there is something may be said of Joseph, and, verily, it proves how common Magic was in those dayes, for having conveyed his cup into the sack of Benjamin, and by that policie detained his brethren, hee asks them: "What deed is this that you have done? Knew yee not that such a man as I can certainly divine?" *Exod. i. 6.* *Gen. xliv. 15*

In this speech he makes his brethren no strangers to the performances of Art, but rather makes their familiarity therewith an argument against them: "Knew you not?" But the following words are very effectuall, and tell us what qualified persons the ancient Magi were. They were indeed (as hee speaks of himself) such as Joseph was, princes and rulers of the people, not beggarly gipsies and mountebanks, as our doctors are now. It was the ambition of the great in those days to bee good, and as these secrets proceeded from God, so were they also entertained by the Gods, I mean by Kings, for saith the Scripture, "I have said yee are Gods," a name communicated to them because they had the power to doe wonders, for in this magicall sense the true God speaks to Moses: "See, I have made thee a God to Pharaoh, and thy brother Aaron shall bee thy prophet." And, verily, this true knowledge, and this title that belongs to it, did that false serpent prætend to our first parents: *Eritis sicut Dii, scientes bonum et malum,* "You shall be as gods, knowing good and evill." But 'tis not this subtill dragon, but *bonus ille Serpens,* that good, crucified serpent, that can give us both this knowledge and this title, "for by him all things were made, and without him not anything was made that is made." If hee made them, then hee can teach us also how they were made. I must now refer my self to Moses, who, at his first acquaintance with God, saw many transmutations—one on his own flesh, another of the rod in his hand, with a third promised and afterwards performed upon water. It is written of him that he was skilled in all the learning of the Egyptians, but, for my part, I doe much question what kind of learning that was, the Scripture assuring mee, and that by the pen of Moses, these wonders were effected by enchantments. This is certain, their learning was ancient, for I find magicians in Ægypt *Exod. vii. 1.* *Gen. iii. 5.* *John i. 3.* *Exod. vii. 11, 12.*

four hundred and thirty years, and upwards, before Jamnes and Jambres. This is confirmed by Pharaoh's dream, which his own sorcerers and wizards could not interpret, but Joseph alone ex-

Gen. ix. 41. pounded it. Verily, it cannot bee denied but some branches of this art, though extremely corrupted, were dispersed among all nations by tradition from the first man, and this appeares by more testimonies than one. For in the land of Canaan, before ever Israel possessed it, Debir, which Athniel, the son of Kenaz, conquered, was an universitie, at least had in it a famous librarie, wherefore the Jewes called it Kiriath-Sepharim. I might speak in this place of the universalitie of religion, for never yet was there a people but had some confused notion of a Deitie, though accompanied with lamentable ceremonies and superstitions. Besides, the religions of all nations have alwaies prætended to powers extraordinarie, even to the performance of miracles, and the healing of all diseases, and this by some secret meanes not known to the common man : and, verily, if wee examine all religions, whether false or true, wee shall not find one but it prætends to something that is mysticall. Certainly, if men be not resolved against reason, they must grant these obliquities in the matters of faith proceeded from the corruption of some principles received (as we see that heretics are but so many false interpreters), but notwithstanding in those very errors there remained some marks and imitations of the first truth. Hence comes it to passe that all parties agree in the action but not in the object. For example, Israel did sacrifice, and the heathen did sacrifice, but the one to God, the other to his idol. Neither were they onely conformable in some rites and solemnities of divinitie, but the heathen also had some hints left of the Secret Learning and philosophie of the patriarchs, as wee may see in their false Magic, which consisted, for the most part, in astrologicall observations, images, charmes, and characters. But it is my designe to keep in the road, not to follow these deviations and misfortunes of the Art, which, notwithstanding, want not the weight of argument, the existence of things being proved as well by their miscarriage as by their successe. To proceed then, I say that during the pilgrimage of the patriarchs, this knowledge was delivered by tradition from the father to his child, and indeed it could be no otherwise, for what was Israel in those dayes but a private familie ? Notwithstanding, when God appointed them their possession, and that this private house was multiplied to a nation, then these secrets remained with the elders of the tribes, as they did formerly with the father of the familie. These elders, no doubt, were the Mosaicall Septuagint, who made up the

Sanhedrim, God having selected some from the rest to be the stewards and dispensers of his mysteries.   Now, that Moses was acquainted with all the abstruse operations and principles of Nature, is a truth, I suppose, which no man will resist.   That the Sanhedrim also participated of the same instruction and knowledge with him is plain out of Scripture, where wee read that " God took of the spirit that was in Moses, and gave it to the seventy." Numb. xi. 25.

But, lest any man should deny that which wee take for granted, namely, the philosophie of Moses, I shall demonstrate out of his own books, both by reason as also by his practice, that hee was a Natural Magician.

First of all then, it is most absurd, and therefore improbable, that hee should write of the creation who was no way skilled in the secrets of God and Nature, both which must of necessitie be known before wee should undertake to write of the creation.   But Moses did write of it, *ergo*—.   Now, I desire to know what hee hath written—truth or lie.   If truth, how dare you denie his knowledge?   If a lie (which God forbid), why will you believe him?   You will tell mee perhaps he hath done it onely in generall termes, and I could tell you that Aristotle hath done no otherwise ; but think you in good earnest that he knew no more than what hee did write?   There is nothing you can say in this point but wee can disprove it, for in Genesis he hath discovered many and especially those secrets which have most relation to this Art.   For instance, hee hath discovered the *minera* of man, or that substance out of which man and all his fellow-creatures were made.   This is the First Matter of the Philosophers' Stone ; Moses calls it sometimes water, sometimes Earth, for, in a certain place, I read thus : " And God said, Let the waters Gen. i. 20. bring forth abundantly the moving creature that hath life, and fowle that may fly above the earth in the open firmament."   But elsewhere wee read otherwise : " And out of the ground the Lord God formed Gen. ii. 19. every beast of the field and every fowle of the aire."   In this later text hee tells us that God made every fowle of the aire out of the ground, but in the former it is written hee made them out of the water.   Certainly, Aristotle and his organ can never reconcile these two places, but a little skill in Magic will make them kisse and be friends without a philtre.   This substance then is both earth and water, yet neither of them in their common complexions, but it is a thick water and a subtle earth.   In plain termes it is a slimie, spermatic, viscous masse, impregnated with all powers coelestiall and terrestriall.   The philosophers call it water and no water, earth and no earth, and why may not Moses speak as they doe? or why may

they not write as Moses did ?   This is the true Damascene Earth, out
of which God made man ; you then that would be chimists, seem not
to be wiser than God, but use that subject in your Art which God himself makes use of in Nature.   He is the best workman, and knowes what
matter is most fit for his work ; hee that will imitate him in the effect
must first imitate him in the subject.   Talk not then of flint stones
and antimonie ; they are the poet's pin-dust and egg-shells ; seek this
earth, this water.   But this is not all that Moses hath written to
this purpose ; I could cite many more magicall and mysticall places,
but in so doing I should be too open, wherefore I must forbeare.
I shall now speak of his practice, and, truly, this is it which no
distinction, nor any other logicall quibble, can waive, nothing but
experience can repell this argument, and thus it runs : " And Moses
took the calf which they had made, and grinded it to powder, and
strewed it upon the water, and made the children of Israel drink of
it." ·Certainly, here was a strange kind of spice, and an art as
strange as the spice it self.   This calf was pure gold, the Israelites
having contributed their eare-rings to the fabric.   Now would I
gladly know by what meanes so solid and heavy a body as gold may
be brought to such a light powder that it may be sprinkled on the
face of the water and afterwards drunk up.   I am sure here was
Aurum potabile, and Moses could never have brought the calf to this
passe had he not plowed with an heifer.   But of this enough ; if
any man think hee did it by common fire, let him also doe the like,
and when he hath performed he may sell his powder to the
apothecaries.   If I should insist in this place on the Mosaicall
ceremoniall law, with its severall reverend shadows and their signi-
fications, I might lose my self in a wilderness of mysteries both
divine and naturall, for, verily, that whole system is but one vast
skreen, or a certain majestic umbrage drawne over two worlds,
visible and invisible.   But these are things of a higher speculation
than the scope of our present discourse will admit of.   I onely
informe the reader that the Law hath both a shell and a kernell ; it
is the letter speaks, but the spirit interprets.   To this agrees Gregorie
Nazianzen, who makes a two-fold Law, του γραμματος and του
*De Statu
Episcop.* πνευματος—one literall, another spirituall.   And elsewhere hee mentions τὸ φαινόμενον του νόμου, και του χρυπτόμενον, the hidden and the
manifest part of the Law, the manifest part (saith he) being
appointed τοῖς πολλοῖς και χάτωμινουοι, for many men, and such
whose thoughts were fixed here below, but the hidden τοῖς ὀλίγοις και
τά ανω φρονουοι, for few onely, whose mindes aspired upwards to
heavenly things.   Now that the Law, being given, might benefit the

people in both parts, spiritual and literal, therefore did the Lawgiver institute the Sanhedrim, a councell of seventy elders, upon whom hee had poured his spirit, that they might discerne (as Esdras did) the "deep things of the night," in plain termes, the hidden things of his Law.   From these elders the Cabala (I believe) had its originall, for they imparted their knowledge by word of mouth to their successors, and hence it came to passe that the Science it self was styled Cabala, that is, a Reception.   This continued so long as Israel held together, but when their frame began to discompose, and the dilapidations of that house proved desperate, then Esdras, a prophet incomparable (notwithstanding the brand of Apocrypha) writ that Law in tables of box which God himself had sometimes written in tables of stone.   As for the more secret and mysterious part thereof, it was written at the same time in seventy secret bookes, according to the number of Elders in whose hearts it had been sometimes written.

And this was the very first time the Spirit married the Letter, for these sacraments were not trusted formerly to corruptible volumes, but to the æternall tables of the Soul.   But it may bee there is a blind generation who will believe nothing but what they see at hand, and therefore will deny that Esdras composed any such bookes.   To these owles (though an unæqual match) I shall oppose the honour of Picus, who himself affirmes that in his time hee met with the Secret Bookes of Esdras, and bought them with a great price.   Nor was this all, for Eugenius, Bishop of Rome, ordered their translation, but hee dying, the translators also fell asleep.   It is true indeed some thing may be objected to me in this place concerning the Cabala, an art which I no way approve of, neither doe I condemn it, as our adversaries condemne Magic, before I understand it, for I have spent some yeares in the search and contemplation thereof.   But why then should I propose that for a truth to others which I account for an error my self?   To this I answer, that I condemne not the true Cabala, but the inventions of some dispersed, wandering rabbis, whose braines had more of distraction than their fortunes.   Of this thirteenth tribe I understand the satirist when hee promiseth so largely—

"What dreames soe'er thou wilt, the Jews will sell."

These, I say, have produced a certain upstart, bastard Cabala, which consists altogether in alphabeticall knacks, ends alwayes in the letter where it begins, and the vanities of it are grown voluminous. As for the more ancient and physicall traditions of the Cabala, I embrace them for so many sacred truths, but, verily, those truths were unknown to most of those rabbis whom I have seen, even to Rambam himself, I mean Rabbi Moses Ægyptius, whom the Jewes have so magnified with their famous hyperbola, "From Moses until Moses there hath not arisen one who is like unto Moses."

But, to deale ingenuously with my readers, I say the Cabala I admit of consists of two parts, the Name and the Thing. The former part is merely typicall in reference to the latter, serving only as the shadow to the substance. I will give you some instances. The literal Cabala, which is but a veile cast over the secrets of the physicall, hath Three Principles, commonly styled *Tres Matres*, or the Three Mothers. In the masculine complexion the Jewes call them אמש, *Emes*, in the fœminine אשם, *Asam*, and they are א, *aleph*, מ, *mem*, ש, *schin*. Now I will shew you how the physical Cabala expounds the literall. *Tres Matres* אמש, *Emes* (saith the great Abraham, or as some think Rabbi Akiba), *id est, Aer, Aqua, et Ignis; Aqua quieta, Ignis sibilans, Aer spiritus medius.* That is, "the Three Mothers, *Emes*, or Aleph, Mem, and *Schin*, are Aire, Water, and Fire; a still Water (mark that), a hissing Fire, and Aire, the middle spirit. Again, sayth the same rabbi; *Tres Matres* אמש, *Emes in Mundo, Aer, Aqua, et Ignis. Coeli ex Igne creati sunt, Terra ex Aquis, Aer egressus est ex spiritu qui stat medius.* "The Three Mother Emes in this world are Ayre, Water, and Fire. The Heavens were made of the Fire, the Earth was made of the Water (mark well this Cabalism) and the Ayre proceeded from a middle spirit. Now, when the Cabalist speaks of the generation of the Three Mothers, he brings in Ten Secret Principles, which, I think, ten men have not understood since the Sanhedrim, such nonsense doe I find in most authors when they undertake to discourse of them. The First Principle is a Spirit which sits *in retrocesso suo fontano*, " in his primitive, incomprehensible retreats," like water in its subterraneous channel before it springs. The Second Principle is the Voice of that First Spirit; this breaks forth like a well-spring, where the water flowes out of the earth and is discovered to the eye. They call it "Spirit from Spirit." The Third Principle is "Spirit from Spirits," a Spirit which proceeds both from the First Spirit, and from his Voice. The Fourth Principle is "Water from Spirit," a certain Water which proceeded from the Third Spirit, and out of that Water went Aire and Fire. But God forbid that I should speak any more of them publickly; it is enough that wee know the original of the creature, and to whom wee ought to ascribe it. The Cabalist when hee would tell us what God did with the Three Mothers useth no other phrase than this, *Ponderavit Aleph cum omnibus, et omnia cum Aleph, et sic de singulis.* "He weighed (saith he) Aleph with all, and all with Aleph, and so he did with the other Mothers." This is very plain, if you consider the various mixtures of the elements, and their secret proportions. And so much for the physicall part of the Cabala; I will now shew you the metaphysicall. It is strange to consider what unitie of spirit and doctrine there is amongst all the Children of Wisdom. This proves infallibly that there is an Universall Schoole-master, who is present with all flesh, and whose principles are ever uniforme, namely, the Spirit of God. The Cabalists agree with all the world of Magicians that man in spirituall mysteries is both agent and patient. This is plain, for Jacob's ladder is the greatest mysterie in the Cabala. Here wee find two extremes—Jacob is one, at the foot of the ladder, and God is the other, who stands above it, *emittens* (saith the Jew) *Formas et Influxus in Jacob, sive Subjectum Hominem*—"shedding some secret influx of Spirit upon Jacob, who, in this place, typifies man in general." The rounds or steps in the ladder signifie the Middle Nature, by which Jacob is united to God, inferiors united to superiors. As for the angels, of whom it is said they ascended and descended by the ladder, their motion proves they were not of the superior hierarchie, but some other secret essences, for they ascended first and descended afterwards, but if they had been from above, they had descended first, which is contrarie to the text. And here, reader, I would have thee studie. Now to return to Jacob; it is written of him that he was asleep, but this is a mysticall speech, for it signifies death, namely, that death which the Cabalist calls *Mors Osculi*, or the Death of the Kisse, of which I must not speake one syllable. To bee short, they agree with us "in the arcanum of theology,"—that no word is efficacious in Magic unlesse it be first quickened by the Word of God. This appears out of their Semhamphores, for they hold not the names of the angels effectuall unlesse some name of God, as יה, or אל, be united to them; then (say they) in the power and vertue of those names they may worke. An example hereof wee have in all extracted names, as Vehu-Jah, Elem-Jah, Jeli-El, Sita-El. Now, this practice in the letter was a most subtle administration of the conjunction of the Substantiall Word, or Spirit with the Water. See that you understand me rightly, for I meane with the elements, and so much for the truth. To conclude, I would have the reader observe that the false, grammaticall Cabala consists onely in rotations of the alphabet and a metathesis of letters in the text, by which means the Scrip-

ture hath suffered many racks and excoriations.   As for the true
Cabala, it useth the letter onely for artifice, whereby to obscure and
hide her physicall secrets, as the Egyptians heretofore did use their
hieroglyphics.   In this sense the primitive professors of this Art had
a literall Cabala, as it appeares by that wonderfull and most ancient
inscription in the rock in Mount Horeb.   It containes a prophecie
of the Virgin Mother, and her Son, Christ Jesus, engraven in Hieroglyphics, framed by combination of the Hebrew letters, but by whom
God onely knows ; it may be by Moses or Elijah.   This is most
certain ; it is to be seen there this day, and wee have for it the
testimonie of Thomas Obecinus, a most learned Franciscan, and
Petrus a Valle, a gentleman, who travailed both of them into those
parts.   Now, that the learning of the Jewes, I mean their Cabala,
was chimicall, and ended in true physicall performances, cannot be
better proved than by the Booke of Abraham the Jew, wherein he
layd down the secrets of this Art in indifferent plaine termes and
figures, and that for the benefit of his unhappy country-men, when
by the wrath of God they were scattered all over the world.   This
book was accidentally found by Nicholas Flammel, a French-man,
and with the help of it hee attained at last to that miraculous
Medecine which men call the Philosophers' Stone.   But let us hear
the *Monsieur* himself describe it.

" There fell into my hands (saith he), for the summ of two florins,
a gilded Book, very old and large.   It was not of paper nor parch-
ment, as other books bee, but it was made of delicate rindes (as it
seemed to mee) of tender young trees.   The cover of it was of
brasse, well bound, all ingraven with letters or strange figures, and
for my part, I think they might well bee Greek characters, or some
such ancient language.   Sure I am, I could not read them, and I
know well they were not notes, nor letters of the Latine, nor of the
Gaule, for of them I understood a little.   As for that which was
within it, the bark leaves were ingraven, and with admirable diligence
written, with a point of iron, in faire and neat Latin letters, coloured.
It contained thrice seven leaves, for so were the leaves counted at
the top, and alwayes every seventh leaf was without any writing, but
instead thereof, upon the first seventh leafe, there was painted a
Virgin, and serpents swallowing her up ; in the second seventh a
Crosse, where a Serpent was crucified ; and in the last seventh there
were painted Deserts, or Wildernesses, in the middest whereof ran
many faire fountains, from whence there issued forth a number
of Serpents, which ran up and down here and there. Upon the
first of the leaves was written in great capitall letters of gold—

ABRAHAM THE JEW, PRINCE, PRIEST, LEVITE, ASTRO-
LOGER, AND PHILOSOPHER, TO THE NATION OF THE
JEWES, BY THE WRATH OF GOD DISPERSED AMONG
THE GAULES, SENDETH HEALTH.

After this it was filled with great execrations and curses (with this
word Maranatha, which was often repeated there) against every
person that should cast his eyes upon it, if hee were not sacrificer
or scribe. Hee that sold me this booke knew not what it was worth,
no more than I when I bought it. I believe it had been stolen, or
taken by violence, from the miserable Jewes, or found hid in some
part of the ancient place of their habitation. Within the booke, in the
second leaf, he comforted his nation, counselling them to fly vices,
and above all idolatrie, attending with sweet patience the comming
of the Messiah, who should vanquish all the kings of the earth, and
should reigne with his people in glorie æternally. Without doubt,
this had been some wise and understanding man. In the third
leafe, and in all the other writings that followed, to help his captive
nation to pay their tributes to the Roman Emperors, and to doe other
things which I will not speak of, hee taught them in common words
the transmutation of mettals; hee painted the vessels by the sides, and
hee informed them of the colours, and of all the rest, except the
First Agent, of the which he spake not a word, but onely (as he said)
on the fourth and fifth leaves he had entirely painted it, and figured
it with very great cunning and workmanship, for though it was well
and intelligibly figured and painted, yet no man could ever have
been able to understand it without being well skilled in their Cabala,
which goeth by tradition, and without having well studied their
bookes. The fourth and fifth leafe, therefore, was without any
writing, all full of faire figures shining, or, as it were, inlightened,
for the worke was very exquisite. First hee painted a young man,
with wings at his ancles, having in his hand a caducean rod, writhen
about with two serpents, wherewith hee strooke upon a helmet
which covered his head; hee seemed, to my small judgment, to be
Mercurie, the pagan God. Against him there came running, and
flying with open wings, a great old man, who upon his head had an
houre-glass fastened, and in his hands a hooke or sithe, like Death,
with the which, in terrible and furious manner, he would have cut
off the feet of Mercurie. On the other side of the fourth leafe, hee
painted a faire flower, on the top of a very high mountaine, which
was sore shaken with the North winds; it had the root blue, the
flowers white and red, the leaves shining like fine gold; and round
about the dragons and griffons of the North made their nests. On

H

the fifth leafe there was a faire Rose tree flowered in the middest of a Sweet Garden, climbing up against a hollow oake, at the foot whereof boiled a fountain of most white water, which ran headlong down into the depths, notwithstanding it passed first among the hands of infinite people, who digged in the earth, seeking for it; but because they were blind none of them knew it, except here and there one, which considered the weight. On the last side of the fifth leafe was painted a king with a great faulchion, who caused to bee killed in his presence by some souldiours a great multitude of little infants, whose mothers wept at the feet of the mercilesse souldiours. The bloud of these infants was afterwards gathered up by other souldiours, and put in a great vessell, whereto the Sun and the Moone came to bathe themselves. And thus you see that which was in the first five leaves. I will not represent unto you that which was written in good and intelligible Latin on all the other written leaves, for God would punish mee because I should commit a greater wickednesse than he who (as it is sayd) wished that all the men of the world had but one head, that hee might cut it off at one blow."

Thus farre Nicholas Flammel.

I could now pass from Moses to Christ, from the old testament to the new: not that I would interpret there, but request the sense of the illuminated. I desire to know what my Saviour means by Luc. xi. 52. the key of knowledge, which the lawyers (as he tells mee and them too) had taken away. Questionlesse it cannot signifie the Law itself, for that was not taken away, being read in the synagogue every Sabaoth. But to let go this: I am certain, and I could prove it all along from his birth to his passion, that the doctrine of Christ Jesus is not only agreeable to the Laws of Nature, but is verified and established thereby. When I speak of the laws of Nature, I mind not her excessive irregular appetites and inclinations, to which shee hath bin subject since her corruption, for even Galen looked on those obliquities as diseases, but studied Nature herself, as their cure. We know by experience that too much of any thing weakens, and destroyes our Nature, but if wee live temperately, and according to law, wee are well, because our life accords with Nature. Hence diet is a prime rule in physic, far better indeed than the pharmacopœa, for those sluttish recepts doe but oppresse the stomach, being no fit fuel for a cœlestiall fire. Believe it then, these excessive bestiall appetites proceeded from our fall, for Nature of her self is no lavish insatiable glut, but a most nice delicat essence. This appears by those fits and pangs she is subject to whenever she is overcharged. In common, customarie excesses there is not any, but knows this truth by experience, indeed in spiritual sins, the body is not immediately troubled but the conscience is terrified, and surely the body cannot be very well, when the soul itself is sick. We see then that corruption, and sin do not so much agree with us, as they do disturb us, for in what sense can our enemies be our friends, or those things which destroy Nature, be agreeable to Nature? How then shall we judge of the Gospel? Shall we say that the præservation of man is contrarie to man, and that the doctrine of life agrees not with life itself? God forbid: The laws of the resurrection are founded upon those of the Creation, and those of regeneration upon those of Generation, for in all these God works upon one and the same matter, by one and the same spirit. Now that it is so, I meane that there is a Harmonie between Nature and the Gospel, I will prove out of the Sinic monument of Kim Cim, priest of Judæa.* In the yeare of redemption 1625, there was digg'd up in a village of China call'd Sanxuen, a square stone, being neer ten measures of an hand-breadth long and five broad. In the uppermost part of this stone was figur'd a Crosse, and underneath it an inscription in Sinic characters, being the title to the monument, which I find thus render'd in the Latine.

> Lapis in Laudem et memoriam æternam
> Legis Lucis, et veritatis portatæ
> de Judæa, et in China
> promulgatæ,
> Erectus.

That is: A stone erected to the praise, and eternal remembrance of the Law of Light, and Truth, brought out of Judæa, and published in China. After this followed the body of the monument, being a relation how the Gospel of Christ Jesus was brought by one Olo puen out of Judæa, and afterwards by the assistance of God planted in China. This happened in the yeare of our Lord six hundred and thirtie six. Kim Cim, the Author of this historie, in the very beginning of it, speaks mysteriously of the Creation. Then he mentions three hundred sixty five sorts of Sectaries, who succeeded one another, all of them striving who should get most proselyts. Some of their vaine Opinions he recites, which indeed are very suitable with the rudiments, and vagaries of the heathen philosophers. Lastly he describes the professors of Christianitie, with their habit of life, and the excellence of their law. *Difficile* (saith he) *est ei Nomen Con-*

* Note 16.

gruum reperire, cum ejus effectus sit Illuminare, omnia Claritate per-
fundere ; unde Necessarium fuit eam appellare; Kim ki ao, h.e. Legem
claram et magnam.   That is : " It is a hard matter to find a fit name
for their law, seeing the effect of it is to illuminate, and fill all with
knowledge ; It was necessarie therefore to call it Kim ki ao, that is,
the great Law of Light."   To be short, Ole puen was admitted to
the court by Tai cum veu huamti, king of China ; here his doctrine
was thoroughly searched, examined, and sifted by the king himself,
who having found it most true and solid, caused it to be proclaim'd
through his dominions, Now upon what this doctrine was founded,
and what æstimat the king had both of it and it's professors, we may
easily gather from the words of his proclamation.   First then where
he mentions Olo puen, he calls him *Magnæ virtutis Hominem,* " a
man of great virtue or power ; " it seems he did something more than
prate and preach, could confirm his doctrine, as the Apostles did
theirs, not with words only, but with works.   Secondly the proclamation speaking of his doctrine runs thus ; *Cujus intentum docendi nos*
a fundamentis examinantes, invenimus doctrinam ejus admodum excel-
lentum, et sine strepitu exteriori, fundatam principaliter in creatione
mundi : That is, " the drift of whose teaching, we have examin'd
from the very fundamentals, we find his doctrine very excellent,
without any worldly noyse, and principally grounded on the Creation
of the world."   And again in the same place.   *Doctrina ejus non est*
multorum verborum, nec superficie tenus suam fundat veritatem : " His
doctrine is but of few words, not full of noyse and notions, neither
doth he build his truth on superficial probabilities."   Thus we see
the Incarnation, and birth of Christ Jesus (which to the common
philosopher are fables and impossibilities, but in the Booke of Nature
plaine evident truths) were proved, and demonstrated by the primitive Apostles and teachers out of the creation of the world.   But
instead of such teachers, we have in these our days two epidemical
goblins, a schoole-man, and a saint forsooth.   The one swells with a
syllogistial pride, the other wears a broad face of revelation.   The
first cannot tell me why grasse is green : The second with all his
devotion knows not A. B. C., yet prætends he to that infinite Spirit
which knows all in all ; and truly of them both this last is the worst.
Surely the Devill hath been very busie, to put out the candle, for
had all written truths been extant, this false learning and hypocrisie
could never have prevailed.   Kim Cim mentions seven and twenty
books which Christ Jesus left on earth to further the conversion of
the world.   It may be we have not one of them ; for though the
books of the new Testament are just so many, yet being all written,

at least some of them a long time after Christ, they may not well passe for those Scriptures which this author attributes to our Saviour, even at the time of his ascension. What should I speak of those many books cited in the old testament, but no where to be found, which if they were now extant, no doubt but they would prove so many reverend, invincible patrons of magic. But ink and paper will perish, for the hand of man hath made nothing æternall. The Truth only is incorruptible, and when the letter fails, she shifts that body and lives in the spirit.

I have not without some labour, now traced this science from the very fall of man to the day of his redemption—a long, and solitary pilgrimage, the paths being unfrequented because of the briars and scruples of antiquitie, and in some places overgrown with the poppie of Oblivion. I will not deny but in the shades and ivie of this wildernesse, there are some birds of night, owles and bats, of a different feather from our phœnix; I meane some conjurers whose dark indirect affection to the name of magic, made them invent traditions more prodigious than their practices. These I have purposely avoyded, lest they should wormwood my stream, and I seduce the reader through all these groves and solitudes to the waters of Marah. The next stage I must move to, is that whence I came out at first with the Israelites, namely Ægypt; here if bookes faile me, the stones will cry out; Magic having been so enthron'd in this place, it seems shee would bee buried here also; so many monuments did shee hide in this earth, which have been since digged up; and serve now to prove that shee was sometimes above ground. To begin then, I will first speak of the Ægyptian Theologie, that you may see how far they have advanc'd, having no leader, but the light of Nature. Trismegistus is so orthodox and plain in the Mysterie of the Trinitie, the Scripture it self exceeds him not; but hee being a particular Author, and one perhaps that knew more than those of his order in generall, I shall at this time dispense with his authoritie. Their Catholic Doctrine, and wherein I find them all to agree, is this. Emepht, whereby they expresse their supreme God, and verily they mind the true one, signifies properly an intelligence, or spirit converting all things into himself, and himself into all things. This is very sound divinitie and philosophie, if it be rightly understood. Now (say they) Emepht produc'd an egg out of his mouth, which tradition Kircher expounds imperfectly, and withall erroneously. In the production of this egg was manifested another Deitie, which they call Phtha, and out of some other

natures and substances inclos'd in the egg, this Phtha formed all
things. But to deale a little more openly, wee will describe unto
you their hieroglyphic, wherein they have very handsomely, but
obscurely discovered most of their mysteries. First of all then,
they draw a circle, in the circle a serpent, not folded, but diameter-
wise, and at length; her head resembles that of a hawke, the tayle
is tyed in a small knot, and a little below the Head her wings are
volant. The circle points at Emepht, or God the Father being
infinite, without beginning, without end. Moreover it comprehends,
or conteines in it self the second Deitie Phtha, and the egg or chaos,
out of which all things were made. The hawke in the Ægyptian
symbols signifies light, and spirit; his head annexed here to the
serpent represents Phtha, or the Second Person, who is the first
light, as wee have told you in our Anthroposophia. Hee is said to
forme all things out of the egg, because in him, as it were in a glasse,
are types or images, namely, the distinct conceptions of the Paternall
Deitie, according to which, by cooperation of the Spirit, namely, the
Holy Ghost, the creatures are formed. The inferiour part of this
figure signifies the matter or chaos, which they call the egg of
Emepht. That you may the better know it, wee will teach you
something not common. The body of the serpent tells you it is a
fierie substance, for a serpent is full of heat and fire, which made
the Egyptians esteem him Divine: This appears by his quick
motion without feet or finns, much like that of the pulse, for his
impetuous hot spirit shootes him on like a squib. There is also
another analogie, for the serpent renews his youth, so strong is his
natural heat, and casts off his old skin. Truely the matter is a very
serpent, for shee renews herself a thousand wayes, and is never a
perpetuall tenant to the same forme. The wings tell you this subject or chaos is volatile, and in the outward complexion ayrie, and
waterie. But to teach you the most secret resemblance of this
hieroglyphic, the chaos is a certain creeping substance, for it
moves like a serpent *sine pedibus*, and truly Moses calls it not
water, but *serpitura aquæ*, "The creeping of water," or a water that
creepes. Lastly, the knott on the tayle, tells you this matter is of a
most strong composition, and that the elements are fast bound in it,
all which the philosophers know to be true by experience. As for
the affinitie of inferiors with superiors, and their private active love,
which conflicts in certain secret mixtures of Heaven with the matter,
their opinion stands thus. In the vital fire of all things here below,
the sun (they say) is King. In their secret water the moon is
Queen. In their pure aire the five lesser planets rule; and in their

central, hypostaticall earth, the fixed starrs. For these inferiors, according to their doctrine, are provinces, or thrones of those superiors, where they sit regent, and paramount. To speak plainly, Heaven it self was originally extracted from inferiors, yet not so intirely, but some portion of the Heavenly natures remained still below, and are the very same in essence and substance with the separated starrs and skies. Heaven here below differs not from that above but in her captivitie, and that above differs not from this below but in her libertie. The one is imprisoned in the matter, the other is freed from the grossness and impurities of it, but they are both of one and the same Nature so that they easily unite ; and hence it is that the superior descends to the inferior to visit and comfort her in this sickly infectious habitation. I could speak much more, but I am in haste, and though I were at leisure, you cannot in reason expect I should tell you all. I will therefore decline these general principles to tell you something that makes for the Ægyptian practice, and proves them philosophers adepted. The first monument I reade of to this purpose is that of Synesius, a very learned intelligent man. Hee found in the temple of Memphis πετρωας βιβλους, "bookes of stone," and in those hard leaves these difficult instructions

$$H' \; \phi\acute{u}\sigma\iota\varsigma \; \tau\hat{\eta} \; \phi\upsilon\sigma\epsilon\iota \; \tau\epsilon\rho\pi\epsilon\tau\alpha\iota$$
$$H' \; \phi\upsilon\sigma\iota\varsigma \; \tau\hat{\eta}\nu \; \phi\upsilon\sigma\iota\nu \; \nu\iota\kappa\alpha\tau\alpha$$
$$H' \; \phi\upsilon\sigma\iota\varsigma \; \tau\hat{\eta}\nu \; \phi\acute{u}\sigma\iota\nu \; \kappa\rho\alpha\tau\sigma\iota$$

That is, "One Nature delights in another ; One Nature overcomes another ; One Nature overrules another." These short lessons, but of no small consequence, are fathered on the great Hostanes. The second monument is that admirable, and most magical one mentioned by Barachias Abenesi, the Arabian. This also was a stone erected neare Memphis, and on it this profound scripture.

ΟΥΡΑΝΟ ΑΝΩ, ΟΥΡΑΝΟ ΚΑΤΩ,
ΑΣΤΡΑ ΑΝΩ, ΑΣΤΡΑ ΚΑΤΩ,
ΠΑΝ Ο ΑΝΩ, ΠΑΝ ΤΟΥΤΟ ΚΑΤΩ,
ΤΑΥΤΑ ΛΑΒΕ, ΚΑΙ ΕΥΥΥΚΕ.

That is,

Heaven above, Heaven beneath ;
Starres above, Starres beneath ;
All that is above, is also beneath ;
Understand this, and be happy.

Under this were figur'd certain apposite hieroglyphics, and for a close to all this dedicatorie subscription (I find it onely in the Coptic character, but our founts wanting that letter, I must give it you in the Greeke).

ΣΤΝΘΡΟΝΟΙΣ ΤΟΙΣ ΕΝ ΑΙΓΥΠΤΟΥ
ΘΕΟΙΣ ΙΣΙΑΣ ΑΡΧΙΕΡΕΤΣ ΑΝΕΣΤΗΣΕΝ

"Isias the High Priest erected this, to resident Gods in Ægypt."

And now, though I formerly suspended the authoritie of Trismegistus, I might, like the Italian, produce his weapons *Sfodrato;* but I love no velitations, and truth is so brave, it needs no feather. *Quod est Superiùs* (sayd Hermes) *est sicut id quod est inferiùs, et quod est inferiùs est sicut id quod est superius.* "That which is above is in proportion with that which is below, and that which is below is in proportion with that which is above." This is his mysterie, and 'tis great : The benefit that attends the purchase is no lesse; *habebis gloriam totius Mundi,* "All the pomp, and splendor of the world shall be thine." To this language, the dialect of Isias doth so echo, these two, like Euphorbus and Pythagoras, might pass for one.

> Cœlum sursùm, (sayd he) Cœlum deorsum ;
> Astra sursùm, Astra deorsùm :
> Omne quod sursùm, omne id deorsùm.

And then follows a reward for the intelligent, Hæc cape, et fælicitare, "*understand this, and thou art fortunate.*" Thou hast made thy self very happy. This is enough to prove that magic sometimes flourished in Egypt, and no doubt but they received the truth of it from the Hebrewes, who lived amongst them to the terme of four hundred and thirtie years. This is plain; for their own native learning was mere sorcerie and witchcraft, and this appears by the testimonie of Moses, who tells us their magicians produced their miracles by enchantments. And why I beseech you, should this instruction seem impossible? For Joseph, being married to Asenath, daughter of Potipherah, Priest of On, some of the Ægyptian priests, and those likely of his own alliance, might for that very relation receive a better doctrine from him. But this is not all I could say of this nation, and their secret learning, if I were dispos'd to bee their Mercurie. There is not any I believe, who prætend to antiquitie or philosophie, but have seen that famous monument, which Paul the Third bestow'd on his Cardinal Petrus Bembus, and was ever since called the Bembine Table. No doubt but the hieroglyphics therein contained, were they all reduced into letters, would make a volume as ample as mysterious. But 'tis not my designe to comment on Memphis, that were to make brick, and look out the straw withall, Ægypt having no compleat table but the world, over which her monuments are scatter'd. This place then was the pitcher to the fountain, for they received their mysteries immediately from the Hebrewes, but their doctrine, like their Nilus, swelling above its private channel, did at last over-run the universe. Jamblicus the divine, in that excellent discourse of his *De Mysteriis*, tells us that Pythagoras and Plato had all their learning *ex Columnis Mercurii*, "out of the pillars or hieroglyphical monuments of Trismegistus." But the ancient Orpheus in his poem *De Verbo Sacro*, where hee speaks of God, hath these words.

Nemo Illum, nisi Chaldæo de sanguine quidam progenitus vidit.

"None (saith he) hath ever seen God, but a certain man descended of the Chaldæan blood." Now this was Moses, of whom it is written, that he spake with God face to face, as one man speaks with another. After this he gives us a short character or description of the Deitie, not in the recesse, and abstract, but in reference to the incubation of his spirit upon Nature. Lastly he acquaints us with the originall of his doctrine, from whence it first came, and verily he derives it from the well-head.

Priscorum nos hæc docuerent Omnia Vates,
Quæ binis tabulis Deus olim tradidit Illis.

"The priests (saith he) (or prophets) of the ancient fathers taught us all these things, which God delivered to them here-tofore in two tables." Thanks be to that God, who made a heathen speak so plainly. I need not tell you to whom these tables were delivered, Cavellero D'epistola can informe you. I cited this place that it might appeare though the philosophie of Greece came generally out of Ægypt, yet some Græcians have been disciplined by the Jews, and this is proved by no contemptible testimonies. Aristobulus, who lived in the dayes of the Machabies, and was himself a Jew, writes to Ptolomie Philometor, King of Ægypt, and affirmes that the Pentateuch, or five books of Moses, were translated into Greek before the time of Alexander the Great, and that they came to the hands of Pythagoras and Plato. Indeed Numenius the Pythagorean calls Plato, *Mosem Atticâ linguâ loquentûm*, "Moses speaking in the Greek dialect"; by which he minded not a similitude of style, but a conformitie of principles. There is a storie of Clearcus the Peripatetic in his first *De Somno*, how true I know not, but the substance of it is this, He brings in his Master Aristotle relating how he met with a very reverend and learned Jew, with whom he had much discourse about things natural and divine, but his special confession is, That he was much rectified by him in his opinion of the Deitie. This perhaps might be, but certainly it was after he writ the Organon, and his other lame discourses, that move by the logical crutch. Now if you will ask me, what Greek did ever professe any magicall principles? To this I answer that if you bate Aristotle and his Ushers, who are born like the *insecta, ex putredine,* "out of their master's corruptions," Greece yeelded not a philosopher who was not in some positions magicall. If any man will challenge my demonstration herein, I doe now promise him my performance. To give you some particular instances, Hippocrates was altogether chemicall, and this I could prove out of his owne mouth, but at this time his works are not by me. Democritus who lived in the same age with him, writ his φυσικὰ καὶ μυστικά, that is, "Physical and Mysticall Things," in plaine English, "Natural Secrets." To this mystical piece Synesius added the light of his Comments, and dedicated them to Dioscorus, priest of Serapis. Of this Democritus, Seneca reports in his Epistles, That he knew a secret coition of pebbles, by which he turned them into emeralds. Theophrastus, a most ancient Greek author, in his Book *De Lapidibus,* mentions another mineral work of his own, wherein he had written something of Metals. True indeed, that discourse of his is lost, but notwithstanding his opinion is upon record, namely that he referred the originall of metalls to water. This is confirmed by his own words, (ὕδατος μέν τα μεταλλευόμενα κατά περ ἄργυρος καὶ χρύσος) as I find them cited by Picus in his Book *De Auro.* But that the Art of transmutation was in request in his dayes, and no late invention or imposture, as some think, appears by the attempts and practice of that Age of the same Theophrastus; for he mentions one Callias, an Athenian, who endeavouring to make gold, brought his materials into cinnabar. It were an endless labour for me to recite all the particulars, that Greece can affoord in order to my present designe. I will therefore close up all in this short summarie. There is no wisdome . in Nature but what proceeded from God, for he made Nature; he first found out, and afterwards ordained the very wayes, and method how to corrupt and how to generate. This, his own wisdome and knowledge, he communicated in some measure to the first man; from him his children received it, and they taught it their posteritie; but the Jewes having the spiritual birthright, this mysterie was their inheritance, and they possess it entirely, being the Annointed Nation, upon whom God had poured forth his Spirit. By tradition of the Jewes, The Ægyptians came to be instructed. From the Ægyptians these secrets descended to the Græcians, and from the Græcians (as we all know) the Romanes received their learning, and amongst other common arts, this magicall mysterious one. This is confirm'd by some proper, genuine effects and monuments thereof, namely that flexible malleable glasse, produced in the dayes of Tiberius, and the miraculous Olybian Lamp. But these times wherein I am now, and those through which I have past, are like some tempestuous day ; they have more clouds, than light. I will therefore enter Christendome, and here I shall find the Art in her infancie : True indeed, the cradle is but in some private hands, few know where, and many believe there is no such thing. The schoolemen are high in point of noyse, and condemne all but what themselves professe. It is Aristotle's Almodena ; they expose his Errors to the sale, and this continues for a long time. But every thing (as the Spaniard saith) hath its *Quando* ; many years are past over, and now the child begins to lisp, and peeps abroad in the fustian of Arnold and Lullie. I need not tell you how he hath thrived since ; doe but look upon his traine, for at this day who prætends not to magic, and that so magisterially, as if the regalos of the Art were in his powers? I know not any *refragans*, except some sickly Galenists, whose pale tallow faces speak more disease than physic. These indeed complaine their lives are too short, Philosophie too tedious, and so fill their mouths with *Ars longa, Vita brevis*. This is true (saith the Spanish Picaro) for they cure either late or never, which makes their Art long ; but they kill quickly, which makes life short, and so the Riddle is expounded.

CŒLUM TERRÆ;

OR,

THE MAGICIAN'S HEAVENLY CHAOS AND FIRST MATTER OF ALL THINGS.

HAVE now, reader, performed my promise, and according to my ability proved the antiquitie of Magic. I am not so much a foole as to expect a generall subscription to my endeavours, every man's *placet* is not the same with mine, but "the die is cast;" I have done this much, and he that will overthrow it must know, in the first place, it is his task to do more. There is one point I can justly bind an adversarie to, that he shall not oppose Man to God, heathen romances to Divine Scripture. He that would foyle me must use such weapons as I doe, for I have not fed my readers with straw, neither will I be confuted with stubble. In the next place, it is my designe to speake something of the Art it self, and this I shall doe in rationall termes, a form different from the ancients, for I will not stuffe my discourse like a wilderness with lions and dragons. To common philosophers that fault is very proper which Quintilian observed in some orators—*Operum fastigia spectantur, latent fundamenta*—"The spires of their Babel are in the clouds, its fundamentals no where; they talk indeed of fine things but tell us not upon what grounds." To avoid these flights in this my Olla (for I care not much what I shall call it) observe this composition; first, I shall speake of that One Only Thing, which is the Subject of this Art and the Mother of all things. Secondly, I will discourse of that most admirable and more than naturall Medecine which is generated out of this One Thing. Lastly, though with some disorder, I will discover the means how and by which this Art works upon the

Subject; but these being the keyes which lead to the very Estrado of Nature, where she sits in full solemnitie, and receives the visits of the Philosophers, I must scatter them in severall parts of the discourse. This is all, and here thou must not consider how long or short I shall be, but how full the discoverie; and truly it shall be such, and so much, that thou canst not in modestie expect more. Now then, you that would be what the ancient physicians were, "the health-imparting hands of the gods," not quacks and salvos of the pipkin; you that would performe what you publickly professe, and make your callings honest and conscionable, attend to the truth without spleen. Remember that præjudice is no religion, and, by consequence, hath no reward. If this Art were damnable, you might safely studie it notwithstanding, for you have a præcept to "prove all things," but to "hold fast that which is good." It is your duty not to be wanting to your selves, and, for my part, that I may be wanting to none, thus I begin.

Said the Cabalist, *Domus Sanctuarii quæ est hic inferiùs, disponitur secundum Domum Sanctuarii, quæ est superiùs*: "The Building of the Sanctuarie which is here below is framed according to that of the Sanctuarie which is above." Here wee have two worlds, visible and invisible, and two universall natures, visible and invisible, out of which both those worlds proceeded. The Passive Universall Nature was made in the image of the Active Universall One, and the conformitie of both worlds, or sanctuaries, consists in the originall conformitie of their principles. There are many Platonicks (and this last centurie hath afforded some apish disciples) who discourse very boldly of the similitude of inferiors and superiors, but if we thoroughly search their trash, it is a pack of small conspiracies, namely, of the heliotrope and the sun, iron and the loadstone, the wound and the weapon. It is excellent sport to hear how they crow, being roosted on these pitiful particulars, as if they knew the Universall Magnet which binds this great frame and moves all the members of it to a mutuall compassion. This is an humor much like that of Don Quixote, who knew Dulcinea but never saw her. ·Those students then who would be better instructed must first know there is an Universall Agent, who when Hee was disposed to create had no other patterne or exemplar whereby to frame and mould his creatures but himself, but having infinite inward ideas or conceptions in himself, as Hee conceived, so He created that is to say, Hee created an outward forme answerable to the inward conception or figure of his mind. In the second place, they ought to know there is an Universall Patient, and this Passive Nature was

created by the Universall Agent. This generall patient is the immediate Catholic character of God himself in his unitie and trinitie.
In plain termes, it is that substance which wee commonly call the
First Matter. But, verily, it is to no purpose to know this notion,
matter, unlesse we know the thing it self to which the notion relates;
wee must see it, handle it, and by experimentall ocular demon-
strations know the very centrall, invisible essences and properties
of it. But of these things heare the most excellent Capnion, who
informes his Jew and his Epicure of two Catholic natures, material
and spiritual. *Alteram* (saith he) *quæ videri oculis, et attingi manu
possit, prope ad omne momentum alterabilem. Detur enim venia (ut
ait Madaurensis) novitati Verborum, rerum obscuritatibus inservienti.
Hæc ipsa cum eadem et una persistere requeat, nihilominus à tali
virtute animi hospitio suscipitur, pro modo rectiùs quo est, quam quo
non est, qualis in veritate res est, id est, mutabilis. Alteram autem
substantiarum naturam incorruptam, immutabilem, constantem eandem-
que ac semper existentem.* The English of it speaks thus: "One
Nature is such it may be seen with the eyes, and felt with the hands,
and it is subject to alteration almost in every moment. You must
pardon (as Apuleius saith) this strange expression, because it makes
for the obscuritie of the thing. This very Nature, since shee may
not continue one and the same, is, notwithstanding, apprehended of
the mind under her such qualification, more rightly as shee is than
as shee is not, namely, as the Thing it self is in truth, that is to say,
changeable. The other Nature, or Principle of Substances, is incorruptible, immutable, constant, one and the same for ever, and
always existent." Thus hee; now, this changeable Nature whereof
he speaks is the first visible, tangible substance that ever God
made; it is white in appearance, and Paracelsus gives you
the reason why. *Omnia* (saith he) *in Dei manu alba sunt, is ea
tingit ut Vult*—"All things when they first proceed from God are
white, but hee colours them afterwards, according to his pleasure."
An example wee have in this very Matter, which the philosophers call
sometimes their Red Magnesia, sometimes their White, by which
descriptions they have deceived many men; for in the first præparation the Chaos is blood-red, because the Central Sulphur is stirred
up and discovered by the philosophicall fire. In the second, it is
exceeding white and transparent, like the Heavens. It is in truth
somewhat like common quicksilver, but of a cœlestiall transcendent
brightnesse, for there is nothing upon earth like it. This fine substance is the Child of the Elements, and it is a most pure, sweet
Virgin, for nothing as yet hath been generated out of her; but if at
any time she breeds, it is by the fire of Nature, for that is her hus-

band. Shee is no animal, no vegetable, no mineral; neither is shee extracted out of animals, vegetables, or minerals, but she is præexistent to them all, for shee is the mother of them. Yet one thing I must say, shee is not much short of life, for shee is almost animal. Her composition is miraculous, and different from all other compounds whatsoever. Gold is not so compact, but every sophister concludes it is no simple; but shee is so much one that no man believes she is more. Shee yields to nothing but love, for her end is generation, and that was never yet performed by violence. He that knows how to wanton and toy with her, the same shall receive all her treasures. First, shee sheds at her nipples a thick heavy water, but white as any snow—the philosophers call it Virgin-Milk. Secondly, she gives him blood from her very heart; it is a quick, heavenly fire, some improperly call it their sulphur. Thirdly, and lastly, shee presents him with a secret Chrystall, of more worth and lustre than the white rock and all her rosials. This is shee and these are her favours. Catch her if you can.

To this character and discoverie of my owne, I shall adde some more descriptions, as I find her limm'd, and drest by her other lovers. Some few (but such as know her very well) have written that shee is not onely one and three, but withall foure and five, and this truth is essentiall. The titles they have bestowed on her, are divers. They call her their Catholic or Magnesia, and the Sperme of the World, out of which all naturall things are generated. Her birth (say they) is singular, and not without a miracle; her complexion heavenly, and different from her parents. Her body also in some sense is incorruptible, and the common elements cannot destroy it, neither will shee mix with them essentially. In the outward shape or figure, shee resembles a stone, and yet is no stone, for they call her their white gum, and water of their sea, water of life, most pure, and most blessed water, and yet they minde not water of the clouds, or rain-water, nor water of the wel, nor dew: but a certain thick permanent, saltish water, a water that is drie, and wetts not the hand, a viscous, slimie water generated out of the saltish fatnesse of the earth. They call her also their twofold Mercurie, and Azoth begotten by the influences of two globes, Cœlestiall, and terrestriall. Moreover they affirme her to be of that nature, that no fire can destroy her, which of all other descriptions is most true, for shee is fire her self, having in her a portion of the universal fire of nature, and a secret cœlestiall spirit, which spirit is animated, and quickened by God himself, wherefore also they call her their most blessed stone. Lastly they say shee is a middle nature between thick and thin, neither altogether earthly, nor altogether firie, but a mean æreall substance to bee found every where, and every time of the year.

This is enough: but that I may speak something my self in plain termes, I say shee is a very salt, but extreme soft, and somewhat thin and fluid, not so hard, not so thick as common extracted salts, for shee is none of them, nor any kind of salt whatsoever that man can make. Shee is a sperme that Nature her self drawes out of the elements, without the help of art; man may find it, where Nature leaves it, it is not of his office to make the sperme, not to extract it, it is already made, and wants nothing but a matrix, and heat convenient for generation. Now should you consider with your selves where Nature leaves the seed, and yet many are so dull, they know not how to work, when they are told what they must doe. Wee see in animal generations, the sperme parts not from both the parents, for it remaines with the female, where it is perfected. In the great work though all the elements contribute to the composure of the sperme, yet the sperm parts not from all the elements, but remains with the earth, or with the water, though more immediately with the one, than with the other. Let not your thoughts feed now on the phlegmatic, indigested vomits of Aristotle, look on the green, youthfull, and flowerie bosome of the earth; consider what a vast universall receptacle this element is. The starrs and planets overlook her, and though they may not descend hither themselves, they shed down their golden locks, like so many bracelets, and tokens of their love. The sun is perpetually busie, brings his fire round about her, as if he would sublime something from her bosom, and rob her of some secret, inclosed jewell. Is there anything lost since the creation? Would'st thou know his very bed and pillow? It is the earth. How many cities dost thou think have perished by the sword? how many by earthquakes? and how many by the deluge? Thou doest perhaps desire to know where they are at this present: believe it they have one common sepulcher, what was once their mother, is now their tombe. All things return to that place from whence they came, and that very place is earth. If thou hast but leisure, run over the alphabet of Nature, examine every letter, I mean every particular creature in her booke—what becomes of her grasse, her corne, her herbs, her flowers? True it is both man and beast doe use them, but this only by the way, for they rest not till they come to earth again. In this element they had their first, and in this will they have their last station. Think (if other vanities will give thee leave) on all those generations that were before thee, and anticipate all those that shall come after thee. Where are all those beauties, the times past have produc'd, and what will become of those that shall appear in future ages? They will all to the same dust, they have one common house, and there is no familie so numerous as that of the grave. Doe but look on the daily sports of Nature, her clouds and mists, the scæne and pageanterie of the aire. Even these momentary things retreat to the closet of the earth. If the sun makes her drie, shee can drink as fast, what gets upon cloudes, comes down in water, the earth swallows up all, and like that philosophicall dragon eats her own tayle. The wise poets saw this, and in their mystical language call'd the earth Saturne, telling us withal shee did feed on her own children. Verily there is more truth in their stately verse, than in Aristotle's dull prose, for he was a blinde beast, and malice made him so. But to proceed a little further with you, I wish you to concoct what you reade, to dwell a little upon earth, not to fly up presently, and admire the meteors of your own braines. The earth you know in the winter time is a dull, dark, dead thing, a contemptible frozen phlegmatic lump. But towards the Spring, and fomentations of the sun, what rare pearls are there in this dung-hill? what glorious colours, and tinctures doth she discover? a pure eternall green overspreads her, and this attended with innumerable other beauties; roses red and white, golden lilies, azure violets, the bleeding hyacinths, with their severall cœlestiall odours and spices. If you will be advised by me, learn from whence the earth hath these invisible treasures, this annuall flora, which appears not without the complements of the sun. Behold I will tell you as plainly as I may. There are in the world two extremes, matter and spirit; one of these I can assure you is earth. The influences of the spirit animate and quicken the matter, and in the material extreme the seed of the spirit is to be found. In middle natures, as fire, aire, and water, this seed stays not, for they are but dispenseros, or media, which convey it from one extreme to the other, from the spirit to the matter, that is to the earth. But stay my friend, this intelligence hath somewhat stirr'd you, and now you come on so furiously, as if you would rifle the cabinet. Give me leave to put you back. I mind not this common, fæculent, impure earth, that falls not within my discourse, but as it makes for your manuduction. That which I speak of is a mysterie, it is a cœlum terræ, and terra cœli, not this dirt, and dust, but a most secret, cœlestiall, invisible earth. Raymund Lullie in his compendium of Alchimie calls the principles of art magic—*spiritus* c. 1. *fugitivos in aere condensatos, in formâ monstrorum diversorum, et animalium etiam hominum, qui vadunt sicut nubes, modo hùc, modo*

I

illùc. "Certain fugitive spirits condensed in the aire, in the shape of divers monsters, beasts and men, which move like cloudes hither and thither." As for the sense of our Spaniard, I refer it to his readers, let them make the most of it.

This is true; As the ayre, and all the volatile substances in it, are restlesse, even so it is with the first matter. The eye of man never saw her twice under one and the same shape, but as clouds driven by the winde are forced to this and that figure, but cannot possibly retain one constant forme, so is shee persecuted by the fire of Nature; for this fire, and this water are like two lovers, they no sooner meet, but presently they play and toy, and this game will not over till some new babee is generated. I have oftentimes admired their subtil perpetual motion, for at all times, and in all places these two are busie, which occasioned that notable sentence of Trismegistus, that action was the life of God. But most excellent, and magisterial is that oracle of Marcus Antoninus, who in his Discourse to himself, speaks indeed things worthy of himself. The Nature (saith he) of the universe delights not in any thing so much, as to alter all things and then to make the like again. This is her tick tack, shee plays one game, to begin another. The matter is placed before her like a piece of wax, and shee shapes it to all formes, and figures. Now shee makes a bird, now a beast, now a flowere, then a frog, and shee is pleas'd with her own magicall performances, as men are with their own fancies. Hence she is call'd of Orpheus, "the mother that makes many things, and ordaines strange shapes, or figures." Neither doth she, as some sinfull parents doe, who having their pleasure, care not for their child; she loves them still after shee hath made them, hath an eye over them all, and provides even for her sparrowes. 'Tis strange to consider that shee workes so well privately as publicly, not only in gardens where ladies may smell her perfumes, but in remote solitudes and deserts. The truth is, shee seeks not to please others so much as her self, wherefore many of her works, and those the choysest, never come to light. Wee see little children, who are newly come under her hand, will be dabling in dirt and water, and other idle sports affected by none but themselves. The reason is, they are not as yet captivated, which makes them seek their own pleasures; but when they come to age, then love or profit makes them square their actions according to other men's desires. Some cockney claps his revenues on his backe, but his galanterie is spoil'd, if his mistress doth not observe it. Another fights, but his victory is lost, if it be not printed, it is the world must heare of his valour. Now Nature is a free spirit, that seeks no applause, shee observes none more than her self, but is pleased with her own magic, as philosophers are with their secret philosophie. Hence it is that we find her busie, not only in the potts of the balconies, but in wildernesses, and ruinous places, where no eyes observe her but the starrs and planets. In a word, whersoever the fire of nature finds the Virgin Mercurie, there hath he found his love, and there they will both fall to their husbandrie, a pleasure not subject to surfets, for it still presents new varieties. It is reported of Marc Antonie, a famous, but unfortunate Romane, how he sent his agent over the world to copie all the handsome faces, that amongst so many excellent features, hee might select for himself the most pleasing face. Truly Nature is much of this straine, for shee hath infinite beautous patternes in her self, and all these shee would gladly see beyond her self, which she cannot doe without the matter, for that is her glasse. This makes her generate perpetually, and imprint her conception in the matter, communicating life to it, and figuring it according to her imagination. By this practice shee placeth her fancie, or idea, beyond her self, or as the peripatetics say, extra intellectum, beyond the divine mind, namely in the matter; but the ideas being innumerable, and withall different, the pleasures of the agent are maintain'd by their variety, or to speak more properly by his own fruitfulness, for amongst all the beauties the world affords, there are not two that are altogether the same. Much might be spoken in this place concerning beautie, what it is, from whence it came, and how it may be defaced, not onely in the outward figure, but in the inward idea, and lost for ever in both worlds. But these pretty shuttles I am no way acquainted with, I have no mysteries but Nature, wherefore I shall leave the fine ladies to fine lads, and speak of my simple Ælia Lœlia.

It was scarce day, when all alone
I saw Hyanthe and her throne.
In fresh, green damascs she was drest,
And o'er a sapphire globe did rest.
This slipperie sphære when I did see,
Fortune, I thought it had been thee.
But when I saw shee did present
A majestie more permanent,
I thought my cares not lost, if I
Should finish my discoverie.
   Sleepie shee look'd to my first sight,
As if she had watched all the night,
And underneath her hand was spread,
The white supporter of her head.

But at my second studied view,
I could perceive a silent dew
Steale down her cheeks; lest it should stayne
Those cheeks where only smiles should reigne.
The tears stream'd down for haste, and all
In chaines of liquid pearle did fall.
Faire sorrows; and more dear than joyes,
Which are but emptie ayres and noyse,
Your drops present a richer prize,
For they are something like her eyes.
    Pretty white foole! why hast thou been
Sulli'd with teares, and not with sin?
'Tis true; thy tears, like polish'd skies,
Are the bright rosials of thy eyes,
But such strange fates doe them attend,
As if thy woes would never end.
From drops to sighes they turn, and then
Those sighs return to drops agen:
But while the silver torrent seeks
Those flowers that watch it in thy cheeks,
The white and red Hyanthe weares,
Turn to rose-water all her teares.
    Have you beheld a flame that springs
From incense, when sweet, curled rings
Of smoke attend her last weak fires,
And shee all in perfumes expires?
So dy'd Hyanthe.   Here (said shee)
Let not this vial part from thee.
It holds my heart, though now 'tis spill'd,
And into waters all distill'd.
'Tis constant still; trust not false smiles,
Who smiles, and weeps not, shee beguiles.
Nay, trust not teares; false are the few,
Those teares are many that are true.
Trust mee, and take the better choyce,
Who hath my teares can want no joyes.

I know some sophisters of the Heptarchie, I mean those whose learning is all noyse, in which sense even py-annets and paraquitoes are philosophicall, will conclude this all bayt and poetrie, that wee are pleasing, not positive, and cheat even the reader's discretion. To prevent such impotent calumnies, and to spend a little more of our secret Light upon the well-disposed student, I shall in this place produce the testimonies of some able philosophers concerning the First Matter it self, as it is naturally found, before any alteration by art.   And here, verily, the reader may discover the mark; it is most easily done, if he will but eye the flights of my verse, or follow the more grave pace of their prose.   The first I shall cite is Arnoldus de Villa Nova, an absolute perfect master of the Art; hee describes the philosophicall Chaos in these plain termes. *Lapis est et non lapis,*

Spiritus, Anima, et Corpus ; Quem si dissolvis, dissolvitur, et si coagules coagulatur, et si volare facis, volat ; est enim volatilis, albus ut lacryma oculi : postea efficitur citrinus, salsus, pilis carens : quem nemo suâ linguâ tangere potest. Ecce ipsum jam sua demonstravi descriptione non tamen nominavi. Modo volo ipsum nominare, et dico, quod si dixeris eum Aquam esse, verum dicis; et si dixeris eum Aquam non esse, mentiris. Ne igitur decipiaris pluribus descriptionibus et operationibus, unum enim quid est, cui nihil alieni infertur. "It is (saith hee) a stone and no stone, Spirit, Soule, and Body ; which if thou dissolvest, it will bee dissolved, and if thou doest coagulate it, it will bee coagulated, and if thou doest make it fly, it will fly, for it is volatile, or flying, and clear as a teare; afterwards it is made citrine, then saltish, but without shoots or chrystals, and no man may touch it with his tongue. Behold, I have described it truly to thee, but I have not named it ! Now, I will name it, and I say that if thou sayest it is Water, thou doest say the truth, and if thou sayest it is not Water, thou doest lie. Bee not, therefore, deceived with manifold descriptions and operations, for it is but one thing, to which nothing extraneous may be added." Thus Arnoldus, and he borrowed this from the *Turba*. Let us now heare his disciple, Raymund Lullie, who speaking very enviously and obscurely of seven metallic principles, describes the third, wherein foure of the seven are included, in these words. *Tertium* (saith hee) *est Aqua clara composita, et illa est res Argento vivo magis propinqua, quæ quidem reperitur supra terram currens et fluens. Et istud argentum vivum in omni Corpore Elementato à materiâ æris est proprie generatum, et ideo ipsius humiditas est valde ponderosa.* That is : "the third Principle is a cleare compounded water, and it is the next substance in complexion to Quick-Silver, it is found running and flowing upon the earth. This Quick-Silver is generated in every compound out of the substance of the aire, and, therefore, the moysture of it is extreme heavy." To these I will add Albertus Magnus, whose suffrage in this kind of learning is like the stylanx to gold, for hee had thoroughly searched it, and knew very well what part of it would abide the test. *Mercurius Sapientum* (saith hee) *est Elementum Aquam frigidum, et humidum, Aqua permanens, spiritus Corporis, vapor unctuosus, Aqua Benedicta, Aqua virtuosa, Aqua Sapientum, Acetum Philosophorum, Aqua Mineralis, Ros cœlestis gratiæ, Lac Virginis, Mercurius Corporalis, et aliis infinitis nominibus in Philosophorum libris nominatur, quæ quidem nomina quamvis varia sunt, semper tamen unam et eandem rem significant, utpote Solum Mercurium Sapientum. Ex ipso toto elicitur omnis virtus Artis Alchimiæ, et suo modo Tinctura alba et rubea.* In plain English thus: "The Mercurie of the Wisemen is a waterie element, cold and moyst. This is their permanent water, the spirit of the Bodie, the unctuous vapour, the Blessed Water, the virtuous water, the water of the Wisemen, the Philosopher's Vinegar, the Mineral Water, the Dew of Heavenly Grace, the Virgin's Milk, the Bodily Mercurie, and with other numberlesse names is it named in the bookes of the Philosophers, which names, though they are divers, notwithstanding, always signifie one and the same thing, namely, the Mercurie of the Wisemen. Out of this Mercurie alone all the Virtue of the Art is extracted, and, according to its Nature, the Tincture, both red and white." To this agrees Rachaidibi the Persian: *Sperma Lapidis* (saith hee) *est frigidum et humidum in Manifesto, et in Occulto calidum et siccum.* "The Sperme, or first matter, of the Stone, is outwardly cold and moyst, but inwardly hot and drie," all which is confirmed by Rhodian, another instructor (it seemes) of Kalid, King of Persia. His words are these: *Sperma est album et liquidum, postea rubeum. Sperma istud est lapis fugitivus, et est aereum et volatile, et est frigidum et humidum, et calidum et siccum.* "The Sperm (saith hee) is white and liquid, afterwards red. This Sperm is the flying stone, and it is æreal and volatile, cold and moyst, hot and drie." To these subscribes the author of that excellent tract intituled *Liber Trium Verborum. Hic est Liber* (saith hee) *Trium Verborum, Liber Lapidis preciosi, qui est Corpus æreum et volatile, frigidum et humidum, aquosum et adustivum, et in eo est caliditas et siccitas, frigiditas et humiditas, alia virtus in occulto alia in manifesto.* "This is the Book of Three Words," meaning thereby Three Principles, "the Book of the Precious Stone, which is a body æreal and volatile, cold and moyst, waterie and adustive, and in it is heat and drought, coldnesse and moysture, one virtue inwardly, the other outwardly." Belus, the philosopher, in that famous and most classic Synod of Arisleus, inverts the order, to conceale the practice, but if rightly understood, he speaks to the purpose. *Excelsum* (sayth hee) *est hoc apud Philosophos magnos Lapidem non esse lapidem, apud idiotas vile et incredibile. Quis enim credet Lapidem aquam, et aquam lapidem fieri, cum nihil sit diversius? Attamen revera ita est. Lapis enim est hæc ipsa per manens aqua, et dum aqua est lapis non est.* "Amongst all great philosophers it is magisterial, that our stone is no stone, but amongst ignorants it is ridiculous and incredible. For who will believe that water can be made a stone, and a stone water, nothing being more different than these two? And yet in very truth it is so. For this very permanent water is the stone, but whiles it is water, it is no stone." But in this sense the ancient Hermes abounds, and almost discovers too much. *Scitote filii sapientum, quod priscorum philosophorum aquæ est divisio, quæ dividit ipsam in alia quatuor.* "Know (saith he), you that are the children of the wise, the separation of the ancient philosophers was performed upon water, which separation divides the water into other foure substances." There is extant a very learned author, who hath written something to this purpose, and that more openly than any, whom we have formerly cited. *Sicuti mundus originem debet aquæ, cui Spiritus Domini incubabat, rebus tàm cœlestibus, quàm terrestribus omnibus indè prodeuntibus; ita Limbus hic emergit ex aquâ non vulgari, neque ex Rore Cœlesti, aut ex aere condensato in cavernis terræ, vel in recipiente ipso, non ex abysso maris, fontibus, puteis, fluminibusquè hausta, sed ex aquà quadam perpessâ, omnibus obviâ, paucissimis cognitâ, quæ in se habet, quæ cunque ad totius operis complementum sunt necessaria, omni amoto extrinseco.* "As the world (saith he) was generated out of that water, upon which the Spirit of God did move, all things proceeding thence, both cœlestiall and terrestriall, so this chaos is generated out of a certain water that is not common, not out of dew, nor ayre condensed in the caverns of the earth, or artificially in the receiver; not out of water drawn out of the sea, fountains, pitts, or rivers, but out of a certain tortured water, that hath suffered some alteration, obvious it is to all, but known to very few. This water hath all in it, that is necessarie to the perfection of the work, without any extrinsecal addition." I could produce a thousand authors more, but that were tedious; I shall conclude with one of the Rose Brothers, whose testimonie is æquivalent to the best of these, but his instruction far more excellent. His discourse of the first matter is somewhat large, and to avoyd prolixitie, I shall forbeare the Latin, but I will give thee his sense in punctuall, plaine English.

" I am a Goddesse (saith hee, speaking in the person of Nature) for beauty and extraction famous, born out of our own proper Sea, which compasseth the whole Earth, and is ever restlesse. Out of my breasts I poure forth milk and blood; boyle these two, till they are turned into silver and gold. O most excellent subject! out of which all things in this world are generated, though at the first sight thou art poyson, adorn'd with the name of the flying eagle. Thou art the first matter, the seed of Divine benediction, in whose body there is heat and rain, which, notwithstanding, are hidden from the wicked because of thy habit, and virgin vestures which is scatter'd over all the world. Thy parents are the Sun and Moon, in thee there is Water and Wine, gold also and silver upon earth, that mortall man may rejoyce. After this manner, God sends us his blessing and wisdome with raine, and the Beams of the Sun, to the eternal glory of his name. But consider, O man, what things God bestows upon thee by this means. Torture the eagle till shee weeps, and the lion bee weakened and bleed to death. The blood of this lion, incorporated with the teares of the eagle, is the treasure of the earth. These creatures use to devoure and kill one another, but, notwithstanding, their love is mutuall, and they put on the proprietie, and nature of a salamander, which if it remains in the fire without any detriment, it cures all the diseases of men, beasts and metals. After that the ancient philosophers had perfectly understood this subject, they diligently sought in this mysterie for the center of the middlemost tree in the terrestrial paradyse, entering in by five litigious gates. The first gate was the knowledge of the true matter, and here arose the first, and that a most bitter, conflict. The second was the præparation by which this matter was to bee præpared, that they might obtain the Embers of the eagle, and the Blood of the Lion. At this gate there is a most sharp fight, for it produceth water and blood, and a spirituall bright body. The third gate is the Fire, which conduceth to the maturitie of the Medicine. The fourth gate is that of multiplication and augmentation, in which proportions and weights are necessarie. The fifth and last gate is Projection. But most glorious, full rich and high, is he who attains to the fourth gate, for hee hath got an Universall Medicine for all diseases. This is that great character of the book of Nature, out of which her whole alphabet doth arise. The fifth gate serves only for metals.* This mysterie, existing from the foundation of the world, and the Creation of Adam, is of all others the most ancient, a knowledge which God Almighty, by his word, breathed into Nature, a miraculous power, the blessed fire of life, the transparent carbuncle, and red gold of the wise men, and the divine benediction of this life. But this mysterie, because of the malice and wickedness of men, is given only to few, notwithstanding, it lives and moves every day in the sight of the whole world, as it appears by the following parable. I am a poysonous dragon, present every where, and to bee had for nothing. My water and my fire dissolve and compound; out of my body thou shalt draw the Green, and the Red Lion: but if thou doest not exactly know mee, thou wilt with my fire destroy thy five senses. A most pernicious quick poyson comes out of my nostrils, which hath been the destruction of many. Separate therefore the thick from the thin artificially, unlesse thou dost delight in extreme povertie. I give thee faculties both male and female and

* Note 17.

the powers both of Heaven and earth. The mysteries of my art are to bee performed magnanimously, and with great courage, if thou wouldest have mee overcome the violence of the fire, in which attempt many have lost both their labour and their substance. I am the Egg of Nature known only to the wise, such as are pious and modest, who make of mee a little world. Ordain'd I was by the All-Mighty God for men, but (though many desire mee) I am given only to few, that they may relieve the poore with my treasures, and not set their minds on gold that perisheth. I am call'd of the philosophers, Mercurie: my husband is gold (philosophicall.) I am the old dragon that is present every where on the face of the earth; I am father and mother; youthfull and ancient; weak and yet most strong; life and death; visible and invisible; hard and soft, descending to the earth, and ascending to the heavens; most high and most low; light and heavy; in mee the order of Nature is oftentimes inverted, in colour, number, weights and measure. I have in mee the light of Nature; I am dark and bright; I spring from the earth, and I come out of Heaven; I am well known, and yet a meer nothing; all colours shine in mee, and all metals by the beams of the sun. I am the Carbuncle of the Sun, a most noble clarified earth, by which thou mayest turn copper, iron, tin, and lead into most pure gold." *

Now, gentlemen, you may see which way the philosophers move; they commend their secret water, and I admire the teares of Hyanthe. There is something in the fansie besides poetrie, for my mistriss is very philosophicall, and in her love a pure platonic. But now I think upon't, how many rivals shall I procure by this discourse? Every reader will fall to, and some fine thing may break her heart with non-sense. This love indeed were meer luck, but for my part I dare trust her, and lest any man should mistake her for some things formerly named, I will tell you truly what shee is; She is not any known water whatsoever, but a secret, spermatic moysture, or, rather, the Venus that yeelds that moysture. Therefore do not you imagine that shee is any crude, phlegmatic, thin water, for shee is a fatt, thick, heavie, slimie humiditie; But lest you should think I am grown jealous, and would not trust you with my mistriss, Arnoldus de Villa Nova shall speak for me; hear him. *Amplius tibi dico, quod nullo modo invenire potuimus, nec similiter invenire potuerunt philosophi, aliquam rem perseverantem in igne, nisi solam unctuosam humiditatem. Aqueam humiditatem videmus de facili evaporare, arida remanet, et ideo separantur, quia non sunt naturales. Si autem eas humiditates consyderemus, quæ difficulter separantur ab his quæ sunt naturales, non*

* *Aureliæ Occultæ Philosoph.*, Pt. II. *Theat. Chem.*, IV. p. 499.

invenimus aliquas nisi unctuosas, et viscosas. "I tell thee furthur (saith hee) that wee could not possibly find, neither could the philosophers find before us, any thing that would persist in the fire, but only the unctuous humiditie. A waterie humiditie, we see will easily vapour away, and the earth remains behind, and the parts thereof separated, because their composition is not natural. But if we consider those humidities which are hardly separated from those parts which are naturall to them, wee find not any such, but the unctuous, viscous humidities." It will be expected perhaps by some flint and antimonie-doctors, who make their philosophicall contrition with a hammer, that I should discover this thing out-right, and not suffer this strange bird-lime to hold their pride by the plumes. To these, I say, it is water of silver, which some have called Water of the Moon, but 'tis Mercurie of the sun, and partly of Saturn, for it is extracted from these three metalls, and without them it can never bee made. Now they may unriddle, and tell me what it is, for it is truth, if they can understand it.

To the ingenious and modest reader, I have something else to replie, and I believe it will sufficiently excuse mee. Raimund Lullie, a man who had been in the center of Nature, and without all question understood a great part of the Divine will, gives mee a most terrible charge not to prostitute these principles. *Juro tibi* (saith hee) *supra animam meam, quod si ea reveles, damnatus es. Nam a Deo omne procedit bonum, et ei soli debetur. Quare servabis, et secretum tenebis illud, quod ei debetur revelandum, et affirmabis quam per rectam proprietatem subtrahis, quæ ejus honori debentur. Quia si revelares brevibus verbis illud quod longinquo tempore formavit, in die magni judicii condemnareris, tanquam qui perpetrator existens contra majestatem Dei læsam, nec tibi remitteretur casus læsæ majestatis. Talium enim revelatio ad Deum, et non ad alterum spectat.* That is; "I swear to thee upon my soule, that thou art damn'd, if thou shouldest reveale these things. For every good thing proceeds from God, and to him only it is due. Wherefore thou shalt reserve, and keep that secret, which God only should reveale, and thou shalt affirme thou doest justly keep back those things whose revelation belongs to his honour. For if thou shouldest reveale that in a few words, which God hath been forming a long time, thou shouldest be condemned in the great day of judgement as a traytor to the majestie of God, neither should thy treason be forgiven thee. For the revelation of such things belongs to God, and not to man." So sayd the wise Raymond.

Now, for my part, I have always honoured the magicians, their

Theor. cap. 6.

philosophie being both rational and majestic, dwelling not upon notions, but effects, and those such as confirme both the wisdome and power of the Creator. When I was a meer errant in their books, and understood them not, I did believe them. Time rewarded my faith, and payed my credulitie with knowledge. In the interim, I suffered many bitter calumnies, and this by some envious adversaries, who had nothing of a scholar, but their gownes, and a little language for vent to their non-sense, but these could not remove mee; with a Spartan patience I concocted my injuries, and found at last that Nature was magicall, not peripateticall. I have no reason then to distrust them in spirituall things, whom I have found so orthodox and faithfull even in naturall mysteries. I doe believe Raymund, and in order to that faith, I provide for my salvation. I will not discover, that I may not be condemn'd. But if this will not satisfie thee, who ever thou art, let me whisper thee a word in the ear, and afterwards doe thou proclaim it on the housetopps. Doest thou know from whom, and how that sperme or seed which men, for want of a better name, call the first matter, proceeded? A certain illuminatee, and in his daies a member of that societie, which some painted buzzards use to laugh at, writes thus; *Deus optimus maximus ex nihilo aliquid creavit, illud aliquid vero fiebat unum aliquod, in quo omnia, creaturæ cælestres et terestres.* "God (saith hee) incomparably good and great, out of nothing created something, but that something was made one thing, in which all things were contained, creatures both cœlestiall and terrestriall." This first something was a certain kind of cloud, or darknesse, which was condensed into water, and this water is that one thing in which all things were contained. But my question is, what was that Nothing, out of which the first cloudy chaos, or something was made? Canst thou tell mee? It may be thou doest think it is a meere nothing. It is indeed *nihil quo ad nos*, nothing that wee perfectly know. It is nothing as Dionysus saith, *Nihil eorum quæ sunt, et nihil eorum quæ non sunt.* "It is nothing that was created, or of those things that are : and nothing of that which thou doest call nothing, that is of those things which are not, in thy empty destructive sense." But, by your leave, it is the true thing, of whom we can affirme nothing; it is that transcendent essence, whose theologie is negative, and was known to the primitive church, but is lost in these our dayes. This is that Nothing of Cornelius Agrippa, and in this nothing, when hee was tyr'd with humane things, I mean humane sciences, hee did at last rest: *nihil scire* (sayd hee) *est vita felicissima*, "to know nothing is the happiest life;" true indeed, for to know this Nothing, is life eternall.

See Jacob Behmen in his most excellent and profound Discourse of the Three Principles.

See Dyonys: Ar. Th. Neg.

Learne then to understand that magicall axiom, *Ex invisible factum est visibile*, "the visible was formed from the non-visible," for all visibles came out of the invisible God, for hee is the Well-Spring from whence all things flow, and the creation was a certain stupendous metaphysicall birth, or deliverie. This fine virgin-matter, or chaos, was the second nature, from God himself, and, if I may say so, the child of the Blessed Trinitie. What doctor then is hee whose hands are fit to touch that subject upon which God himself, when he workes, lays his own spirit, for, verily, so we reade; The Spirit of God moved upon the face of the water? And can it bee expected then, that I should prostitute this mysterie to all hands whatsoever, that I should proclaim it, and crie it, as they cry oysters? Verily, these considerations, with some other which I will not for all the world put to paper, have made mee almost displease my dearest friends, to whom, notwithstanding, I owe a better satisfaction. Had it been my fortune barely to know this matter, as most men doe, I had perhaps been lesse carefull of it. But I have been instructed in all the secret circumstances thereof, which few upon earth understand. I speak not for any ostentation, but I speak a truth which my conscience knowes very well. Let me then, reader, request thy patience, for I shall leave this discoverie to God, who, if it bee his blessed will, can call unto thee, and say: "Here it is, and thus I worke it." I had not spoken all this in my own defence, had I not been assaulted (as it were) in this very point, and told to my face I was bound to discover all that I knew, for this age looks for dreams and revelations, as the traine to their invisible righteousnesse. I have now sufficiently discoursed of the matter, and if it be not thy fortune to find it by what is here written, yet thou canst not bee deceived by what I have sayd, for I have purposely avoyded all those termes, which might make thee mistake any common salts, stones, or minerals for it. I advise thee, withall, to beware of all vegetables, and animals, avoyd them and every part of them whatsoever. I speak this because some ignorant, sluttish broylers are of opinion, that man's bloud is the true subject. But alas! is man's bloud in the bowels of the earth, that metals should be generated out of it? or was the world, and all that is therein, made of man's bloud, as of their first matter? Surely no such thing. The first matter was existent before man, and all other creatures whatsoever, for shee is the mother of them all. They were made of the first matter, and not the first matter of them. Take heed then, Let not any man deceive thee. It is totally impossible to reduce any particular to the first matter, or to a sperm, without our Mercurie,

Gen. c. 1.

and being so reduced, it is not universall, but the particular sperm of its own species, and works not any effects but what are agreeable to the nature of that species, for God hath seal'd it with a particular idea.

Let them alone then who practise upon man's bloud in their chemicall stones, and athanors, or, as Sendivow hath it, *in fornaculis mirabilibus;* they will deplore their error at last, and sit without sack-cloth, in the ashes of their compositions. But I have done; I will now speak something of generation, and the wayes of it, that the process of the philosophers upon this matter, may be the better understood. You must know that Nature hath two extremes, and between them a middle substance, which elsewhere wee have call'd the middle *Anima* nature. Example enough wee have in the creation. The first *Magica.* extreme was that cloud, or darkness, whereof we have spoken formerly; some call it the remote matter, and the invisible chaos, but very improperly, for it was not invisible. This is the Jewish *Ensoph* outwardly, and it is the same with that Orphic Night—

"O Night! thou black nurse of the golden stars."

Out of this darkness all things that are in this world came, as out of their fountain or matrix: hence that position of all famous poets and philosophers, *omnia ex Nocte prodiisse,* "that all things were brought forth out of Night." The middle substance is the water, into which that night or darkness was condensed, and the creatures framed out of the water make up the other extreme. But the magicians when they speak strictly, will not allow of this last extreme, because Nature doth not stay here, wherefore their philosophie runs thus; Man (say they) in his natural state, is in the meane creation, from one of which hee must recede to one of two extremes; either to corruption, as commonly all men doe, for they die, and moulder away in their graves: or else to a spirituall glorified condition, like Enoch and Elijah, who were translated, and this (say they) is a true extreme, for after it there is no alteration.* Now the magicians reasoning with themselves, why the meane creation should be subject to corruption, concluded the cause and original of this disease to be in the chaos it self, for even that was corrupted, and cursed upon the Fall of Man. But examining things further, they found that Nature in her generations did onely concoct the chaos with a gentle heat; shee did not separate the parts, and purifie each of them by it self, but the purities and impurities of the sperme remained together in all her productions, and this domestic enemie

* Note 18.

prevayling at last, occasioned the death of the compound. Hence they wisely gathered, that to minister vegetables, animals, or minerals for physic, was a meer madness, for even these also had their own impurities and diseases, and required some medicine to cleanse them. Upon this adviso, they resolved (God without all question being their guide) to practise on the chaos it self; they opened it, purified it, united what they had formerly separated, and fed it with a twofold fire, thick and thin, till they brought it to the immortal extreme, and made it a spirituall Heavenly body.* This was their physic, this was their magic. In this performance they saw the image of that face, which Zoroaster calls *Triadis Vultus ante essentiam*, etc. They perfectly knew the *secundea*, which contains all things in her naturally, as God contains all things in himself spiritually. They saw that the life of all things here below was a thick fire, or fire imprisoned and incorporated in a certaine incombustible æreall moysture. They found, moreover, that this fire was originally derived from Heaven, and in this sense Heaven is styled in the oracles,

Ignis, Ignis derivatio, et ignis penu.

In a word, they saw with their eyes, that Nature was male and female; *Ignis ruber super dorsum ignis candidi*, as the cabalists expresse it: " A certain fire of a most deep red colour, working on a most white, heavy, salacious water, which water also is fire inwardly, but outwardly very cold." By this practice, it was manifested unto them, that God himself was Fire according to that of Eximidius in *Turba*: *Omnium rerum initium esse Naturam quandam eamque perpetuam infinitam, omnia foventem coquentemque.* " The beginning of all things (sayth he) is a certain nature, and that eternall, and infinite, cherishing and heating all things." The truth is, life, which is nothing else but light and heat, proceeded originally from God, and did apply to the chaos, which is elegantly called by Zoroaster, *fons fontium, et fontium cunctorum, matrix continens cuncta.* " The fountain of fountains, and of all fountains, the matrix containing all things." Wee see by experience that all individuals live not only by their own heat, but they are preserved by the outward universal heat, which is the life of the great world. Even so truly the great world it self lives not altogether by that heat which God hath inclosed in the parts thereof, but it is præserved by the circumfused influent heat of the Deitie; For above the heavens God is manifested like an infinite burning world of light and fire, so that hee

* Note 19.

overlooks all that he hath made, and the whole fabric stands in his heat and light, as a man stands here on earth in the Sun-shine. I say then that the God of Nature employes himself in a perpetuall coction, and this not onely to generate, but to preserve that which hath been generated; for his spirit and heat coagulate that which is thin, rarifie that which is too grosse, quicken the dead parts, and cherish the cold. There is indeed one operation of heat, whose method is vitall and far more mysterious than the rest; they that have use for it, must studie it. I have for my part spoken all that I intend to speak, and though my book may prove fruitless to many, because not understood, yet some few may be of that spirit as to comprehend it: *amplæ mentis ampla flamma*, sayd the great Chaldæan. But because I will not leave thee without some satisfaction, I advise thee to take the Moone of the Firmament, which is a middle nature, place her so that every part of her may be in two elements at one and the same time, these elements also must equally attend her body, not one furthur off, not one nearer than the other. In the regulating of these two, there is a twofold geometrie to be observed, natural and artificial. But I may speak no more. The true furnace is a little simple shell, thou mayst easily carry it in one of thy hands. The glasse is one, and no more, but some philosophers have used two, and so mayst thou. As for the work it self, it is no way troublesome; a lady may reade the " Arcadia," and at the same time attend this philosophie without disturbing her fancie. For my part I think women are fitter for it than men, for in such things they are more neat and patient, being used to a small chemistrie of sack-possets, and other finicall sugar-sops. Concerning the effects of this medecine, I shall not speak anything at this time; hee that desires to know them, let him read the Revelation of Paracelsus, a discourse altogether incomparable, and in very truth miraculous. And here without any partialitie, I shall give my judgement of honest Hohenheim. I find in the rest of his works, and especially where he falls on the stone, a great many false processes, but his doctrine of it in general is very sound. The truth is, hee had some pride to the justice of his spleen, and in many places hee hath erred of purpose, not caring what bones he threw before the schoole-men : for he was a pilot of Guadalcana, and sayled sometimes in his *Rio de la recriation*. But I had almost forgot to tell thee that, which is all in all, and it is the greatest difficultie in all the art, namely the Fire. It is a close, ayrie, circular, bright fire; the philosophers call it their sun, and the glasse must stand in the shade. It makes not the matter to vapour, no not so much as to sweat; it digests only with a still, piercing, vitall heat. It is continuall, and therefore at last alters the chaos, and corrupts it : The proportion and regiment of it is very scrupulous, but the best rule to know it by, is that of the synod : *facite nè fasianus volet ante insequentem*. "Let not the bird fly before the fowler;" make it Sit while you give fire, and then you are sure of your prey. For a cloze, I must tell thee the philosophers call'd this fire their balneum, but it is *balneum naturæ*, "a natural bath," not an artificial one, for it is not any kind of water, but a certain subtill temperate moysture which compasseth the glasse, and feeds their Sun, or Fire. In a word, without this bath nothing in the world is generated. Now that thou mayst the better understand what degree of fire is requisit for the work, consider the generation of man, or any other creature whatsoever. It is not kitchen fire, nor feaver that works upon the sperm in the womb, but a most temperate moyst, natural heat, which proceeds from the very life of the mother. It is just so here ; Our matter is a most delicate substance, and tender like the animal sperme, for it is almost a living thing, nay in very truth it hath some small portion of life, for Nature doth produce some animals out of it. For this very reason the least violence destroyes it, and prevents all generation, for if it be over-heated but for some few minutes, the white, and red sulphurs will never essentially unite, and coagulate. On the contrary, if it takes cold but for half an hour, the work being once well begun, it will never sort to any good purpose. I speak out of my own experience, for I have (as they phrase it) given my self a box on the eare, and that twice or thrice, out of a certain confident negligence, expecting that, which I knew well enough could never bee. Nature moves not by the theorie of men, but by their practice, and surely wit and reason can perform no miracles, unlesse the hands supplie them. Bee sure then to know this Fire in the first place, and accordingly bee sure to make use of it. But for thy better securitie, I will describe it to thee once more. It is a drie, vaporous humid fire ; it goes round about the glasse, and is both equall and continuall. It is restlesse, and some have call'd it the white philosophicall coale. It is in it self naturall, but the præparation of it is artificiall: it is a heat of the dead, wherefore some call it their unnatural, necromantic fire. It is no part of the matter, neither is it taken out of it, but it is an external fire, and serves only to stirr up, and strengthen the inward oppressed fire of the chaos. But let us hear Nature her self, for thus shee speaks in the serious romance of Mehung. *Post putrefactionem sit ipsa generatio, id que per internum incomburibilem calorem, ad argenti vivi frigiditatem calefaciendam, quod tantum equidem patitur, ut tandem cum sulphure suo uniatur. Omne illud uno in vase complexum est, ignis, aer, et aqua videlicit, quæ in terreno suo vase accipio, eademque uno in alembico relinquo; et tum coquo, dissolvo, et sublimo, absque malleo, forcipe, vel lima, sine carbonibus, vapore, igne aut máriæ-balneo, et sophistarum alembicis; cælestem, namque meum ignem habeo, qui elementatem, prout materia idoneam decentemque formam habere desyderat, excitat.* That is: "After putrefaction succeeds generation, and that because of the inward incombustible sulphur, that heats or thickens the coldness and crudities of the quicksilver, which suffers so much thereby, that at last it is united to the sulphur, and made one body therewith. All this (namely fire, ayre, and water) is contained in one vessell; in their earthly vessel, that is, in their grosse body, or composition, I take them, and then I leave them in one alembic, where I concoct, dissolve, and sublime them without the help of hammer, tongs or file; without coals, smoake, fire, or bath, or the alembics of the sophisters. For I have my heavenly fire, which excites, or stirs up the elementall one, according as the matter desires a becomming, agreeable forme." Now Nature every where is one and the same, wherefore shee reads the same lesson to Madathan, who thinking in his ignorance to make the stone without dissolution, receives from her this check. *An tu nunc cochleas, vel cancros cum testis devorare niteris? An non prius à veiustissimo planetarum coquo maturari, et præparari illos oportet?* "Doest thou think (says hee) to eat oysters, shells and all? Ought they not first to bee opened, and prepar'd by the most ancient cooke of the planets?" With these agrees the excellent Flammel, who speaking of the Solar, and Lunar Mercurie, and the plantation of the one in the other, hath these words. *Sumantur itaque, et noctu, interdiuque assidué supra ignem in alembico foveantur. Non autem ignis carbonarius, vel è ligno confectus, sed clarus pellucidusque ignis sit, non secus ac Sol ipse, qui nunquam plus justo calidus ardensque sed omni tempore ejusdem caloris esse debet.* "Take them therefore (sayth hee) and cherish them over a fire in thy Alembic. But it must not be a fire of coales, nor of any wood, but a bright shining fire, like the sun it self, whose heat must never be excessive, but alwayes of one and the same degree." This is enough, and too much, for the secret in it self is not great, but the consequences of it are so, which made the philosophers hide it. Thus, reader, thou hast the outward agent most fully and faithfully described. It is, in truth, a very simple mysterie, and if I should tell it openly, ridiculous. Howsoever by this, and not without it, did the magicians unlock the

K

chaos, and certainly it is no newes that an iron-key should open a treasurie of gold.   In this Universall Subject they found the natures of all particulars, and this is signified to us by that maxim : *Qui Proteum novit, adeat Pana.*   " He who is familiar with Proteus is on the threshold of the knowledge of Pan."   This Pan is their chaos, or Mercurie, which expounds Proteus, namely the particular creatures, commonly call'd individuals ; for Pan transformes himself into a Proteus, that is, into all varieties of species, into animals, vegetables, and minerals ; for out of the universall Nature, or first matter, all these are made, and Pan hath their proprieties in himself.   Hence it is that Mercurie is call'd the interpreter, or expositor of inferiors and superiors, under which notion the ancient Orpheus invokes him. " Hear me ô Mercurie, thou messenger of Jove, and son of Maia, the expositor of all things."   Now, for the birth of this Mercurie, and the place of it, I find but few philosophers that mention it. Zoroaster points at it, and that very obscurely, where he speaks of his Jynges or the Ideas in these words :

Multæ quidem hæ scandunt lucidos mundos,
Insilentes: quarum summitates sunt tres.
Subjectum est ipsis principale pratum.

This *pratum,* or meadow of the ideas, a place well known to the philosophers (Flammel calls it their Garden, and the Mountain of the Seven Metals, see his Summarie, where hee describes it most learnedly, for he was instructed by a Jew) is a certain secret, but universall region : one calls it *regio lucis,* " the region of light," but to the cabalist it is *Nox Corporis,* a terme extremely opposite and significant.*   It is in few words the rendezvous of all spirits, for in this place the ideas when they descend from the bright world to the dark one, are incorporated.   For thy better intelligence thou must know, that spirits whiles they move in Heaven, which is the fire-world, contract no impurities at all, according to that of Stellatus ;

Omne quod est supra lunam, æternumque bonumque
Esse scias, nec triste aliquid cælestia tangit.

" All (sayth hee) that is above the moon, is eternall and good, and there is no corruption of Heavenly things."   On the contrary, when spirits descend to the elementall matrix, and reside in her kingdom, they are blurred with the original leprosie of the matter, for here the curse raves and rules, but in Heaven it is not prædominent.   To put an end to this point, let us hear the admirable Agrippa state it ; this is hee between whose lipps the truth did breathe, and knew no

* Note 20.

other oracle. *Cœlestium vires, dum in se existunt, et à Datore Lumi-* *num per sanctas intelligentias, et cœlos influuntur, quousque ad lunam pervenerint : earum influentia bona est, tanquam in primo gradu ; deinde autem quando in subjecto viliori suscipitur, ipsa etiam vilescit.* That is ; "the Heavenly powers or spirituall essences whiles they are in themselves, or before they are united to the matter, and are shower'd down from the Father of Lights through the holy Intelligences and the Heavens, untill they come to the moone : their influence is good, as in the first degree ; But when it is received in a corrupt subject, the influence also is corrupted." Thus he ; now the astronomers pretend to a strange familiaritie with the starrs, the natural philosophers talk as much : and truly an ignorant man might well think they had been in heaven, and conversed, like Lucian's Menippus, with Jove himself. But, in good earnest, these men are no more eagles than Sancho ; their fansies are like his flights in the blanket, and every way as short of the skies. Ask them but where the influences are received, and how ; bid them by faire experience prove they are present in the elements, and you have undone them ; if you will trust the foure corners of a figure, or the three legs of a syllogism, you may ; this is all their evidence. Well fare the magicians then, whose art can demonstrate these things, and put the very influences in our hands. Let it be thy studie to know their Region of Light, and to enter into the treasures thereof, for then thou mayst converse with spirits, and understand the nature of invisible things. Then will appear unto thee the Universal Subject, and the Two Mineral Spermes, white and red, of which I must speak somewhat, before I make an end.

In the Pythagoricall synod, which consisted of threescore and ten philosophers, all masters of the art, it is thus written. *Ignis spissum in aera cadit ; aeris vero spissum, et quod ex igne spisso congregatur, in aquam incidit ; aquæ quoque spissum, et quod ex ignis et aeris spisso coadunatur, in terrâ quiescit. Ista istorum Trium spissitudo in Terra quiescit, inque eâ conjuncta sunt. Ipsa ergo terra omnibus cæteris elementis spissior est, uti palàm apparet et videre est.* That is, "the thicknesse, or sperme of the fire falls into the ayre ; the thickness or spermatic part of the ayre, and in it the sperm of the fire, falls into the water ; the thickness or spermatic substance of the water, and in it the two spermes of fire and ayre, fall into the earth, and there they rest, and are conjoyned. Therefore the earth it self is thicker than the other elements, as it openly appears, and to the eye is manifest." Remember now what I have told thee formerly concerning the earth ; what a generall hospitall it is, how it receives all things, not only beasts and vegetables, but proud and glorious man : when death hath ruined him, his coarser parts stay here, and know no other home. This earth to earth, is just the doctrine of the Magi; metalls (say they) and all things may be reduc'd into that whereof they were made. They speak the very truth; it is God's own principle, and he first taught it Adam. "Dust thou art, and to dust shalt thou return." But lest any man should be deceived by us, I think it just to informe you, there are two reductions; one is violent and destructive, reducing bodies to their extremes, and properly it is death, or the calcination of the common chimist. The other is vital, and generative, resolving bodies into their sperm, or middle substance out of which Nature made them, for Nature makes not bodies immediately of the elements, but of a sperm which shee drawes out of the elements. I shall explain myself to you by example. An egg is the sperm, or middle substance out of which a chick is engendred, and the moysture of it is viscous and slimie, a water and no water, for such a sperme ought to bee. Suppose Dr Coale, I meane some broyler, had a minde to generate something out of this egg: questionlesse he would first distill it, and that with a fire able to roast the hen that layd it; then would he calcine the *caput mortuum*, and finally produce his nothing. Here you are to observe that bodies are nothing else but sperm coagulated, and he that destroyes the body, by consequence destroyes the sperm. Now to reduce bodies into elements of earth and water, as wee have instanc'd in the egg, is to reduce them into extremes beyond their sperm, for elements are not sperm, but the sperm is a compound made of the elements, and containing in it self all that is requisite to the frame of the body. Wherefore be well advis'd before you distill, and quarter any particular bodies, for having once separated their elements, you may never generate, unless you can make a sperm of those elements, but that is impossible for man to doe, it is the power of God, and Nature. Labour then you that would be accounted wise, to find out our Mercurie, so shall you reduce things to their mean spermaticall chaos, but avoyd the broyling destruction. This doctrine will spare you the vain task of distillations, if you will but remember this truth: that spermes are not made by separation, but by composition of elements, and to bring a body into sperm, is not to distill it, but to reduce the whole into one thick water, keeping all the parts thereof in their first natural union. But that I may return at last to my former citation of the Synod; all those influences of the elements being united in one mass, make our sperm or our earth, which is earth and no earth. Take it if thou doest know it,

Gen. c. 3, ver. 19.

and divide the essences thereof, not by violence, but by naturall putrefaction, such as may occasion a genuine dissolution of the compound. Here thou shalt find a miraculous white water, an influence of the Moone, which is the Mother of our Chaos ; it rules in two elements—earth and water.   After this appears the sperm or influx of the sun, which is the father of it.   It is a quick cœlestiall fire, incorporated in a thin, oleous æreall moysture.   It is incombustible, for it is fire it self, and feeds upon fire, and the longer it stays in the fire, the more glorious it growes.   These are the two mineral spermes, masculine and fœminine : if thou doest place them both on their crystalline basis, thou hast the philosopher's flying firedrake, which at the first sight of the sun breathes such a poyson, that nothing can stand before him.   I know not what to tell thee more, unlesse in the vogue of some authors, I should give thee a flegmatic description of the whole process and that I can dispatch in two words.   It is nothing els but a continual coction, the volatile essences ascending and descending, till at last they are fix'd according to that excellent prosopopœia of the stone.

Non ego continùo morior, dum spiritus exit,
Nam redit assidùe, quamvis et sæpe recedat,
Et mihi nunc magna est anima, nunc nulla facultus.

Plus ego sustinui, quam corpus debuit unum ;
Tres animas habui, quas omnes intus habebam,
Discessere duæ, sed tertia pænè secuta est.

I am not dead, although my spirit's gone,
For it returns, and is both off, and on,
Now I have life enough, now I have none.

I suffer'd more, than one could justly doe ;
Three soules I had, and all my own, but two
Are fled : the third had almost left mee too.

"I have written, what I have written."   And now give me leave Joh. 19, 22. to look about mee.   Is there no powder-plott, or practice ?   What's become of Aristotel, and Galen ?   Where is the scribe and pharisee, the disputers of this world ?   If they suffer all this and believe it too, I shall think the general conversion is come about, and I may sing,

Jam redit et virgo, redeunt Saturnia regna.

But come what will come, I have once more spoken for the truth, and shall for conclusion speak this much again.   I have elsewhere call'd this subject, *limus cœlestis,* " a cœlestial slime," and the middle nature : The philosophers call it the venerable nature, but amongst all the pretenders I have not yet found one, that could tell me why. Hear me then, that whensoever thou doest attempt this work, it may be with reverence, not like some proud, ignorant doctor but with lesse confidence and more care.   This chaos hath in it the foure elements, which of themselves are contrarie natures, but the wisdome of God hath so placed them that their very order reconciles them. For example, ayre and earth are adversaries, for one is hot and moyst, the other cold and drie.   Now to reconcile these two, God placed the water between them, which is a middle nature, or of a mean complexion between both extremes.   For she is cold and moyst, and as she is cold, she partakes of the nature of the earth, which is cold and drie, but as she is moyst, she partakes in the nature of the ayre, which is hot and moyst.   Hence it is, that ayre and earth, which are contraries in themselves, agree and embrace one another in the water, as in a middle nature which is proportionate to them both, and tempers their extremities.   But, verily, this salvo makes not up the breach, for though the water reconciles two elements like a friendly third, yet shee her self fights with a fourth, namely with the fire : For the fire is hot and drie, but the water is cold and moyst, which are clear contraries.   To prevent the distempers of these two, God placed the ayre between them, which is a substance hot and moyst; and as it is hot, it agrees with the fire, which is hot and drie ; but as it is moyst, it agrees with the water, which is cold and moyst ; so that by mediation of the ayre, the other two extremes, namely fire and water, are made friends and reconciled. Thus you see, as I told you at first, that contrarie elements are united by that order and texture wherein the wise God hath placed them. You must now give me leave to tell you that this agreement, or friendship, is but partial, a very weak love, cold and skittish : for whereas these principels agree in one qualitie, they differ in two, as your selves may easily compute.   Much need, therefore, have they of a more strong and able mediator to confirme and preserve their weak unitie, for upon it depends the very æternitie, and incorruption of the creature.   This blessed cæment, and balsam, is the Spirit of the living God, which some ignorant scriblers have call'd a quintessence, for this very Spirit is in the chaos, and, to speak plainly, the fire is his throne, for in the fire he is seated, as we have sufficiently told you else where.   This was the reason why the Magi call'd the First Matter their Venerable Nature, and their Blessed Stone, and, in good earnest, what think you ? is it not so ?   This blessed Spirit fortifies, and perfects that weak disposition which the elements

Anthropo-
sophia Theo-
magica.

already have to union and peace, (for God works with Nature, not against her,) and brings them at last to a beauteous specificall fabric. Now, if you will aske me, where is the Soul, or as the School-men abuse her, the form all this while? What doth she doe? To this I answer, that shee is, as all instrumentals ought to be, subject and obedient to the will of God, expecting the perfection of her body;* for it is God that unites her to the body, and the body to her. Soule and body are the work of God, the one as well as the other: the soul is not the artificer of her house, for that which can make a body, can also repayre it, and hinder death; but the soule cannot doe this, it is the power, and wisdom of God. In a word to say that the soule form'd the body, because she is in the body, is to say that the jewell made the cabinet, because the jewell is in the cabinet, or that the sun made the world, because the sun is in the world, and cherisheth every part thereof. Learn therefore to distinguish between agents and their instruments, for if you attribute that to the creature, which belongs to the Creator, you bring your selves in danger of hell-fire, for God is a jealous God, and will not give his glorie to another. I advise my doctors, therefore, both divines and physicians, not to bee too rash in their censures, nor so magisterial in their discourse, as I have known some professors of physic to be; who would correct and undervalue the rest of their brethren, when, in truth, they themselves were most shamefully ignorant. It is not ten or twelve years experience in druggs and sopps can acquaint a man with the mysteries of God's creation. "Take this and make a world:" "Take I know not what, and make a pill or clyster," are different receipts. Wee should, therefore, consult with our judgements, before wee venture our tongues, and never speake but when we are sure we understand. I knew a gentleman, who meeting with a philosopher adept, and receiving so much courtesie as to be admitted to discourse, attended his first instructions passing well. But when this magician quitted my friend's known roade, and began to touch, and drive round the great wheele of Nature, presently my gentleman takes up the cudgells, and urging all the authorities which his vain judgement made for him, opprest this noble philosopher with a most clamorous, insipid ribaldrie. A goodly sight it was, and worthy our imitation, to see with what an admirable patience the other received him. But this errant concluded at last, that lead or quicksilver must be the subject, and that Nature worked upon one of both. To this the adeptus replied, "Sir, it may be so at this time, but if here after I find Nature in those old elements, where

* Note 21.

I have sometimes seen her very busie, I shall at our next meeting confute your opinion." This was all hee said, and it was something more than hee did. Their next meeting was referr'd to the Greek Calends, for he could never be seen afterwards, notwithstanding a thousand sollicitations. Such talkative babbling people as this gentleman was, who run to every doctor for his opinion and follow like a spaniell every bird they spring, are not fit to receive these secrets ; they must be serious, silent men, faithful to the art, and most faithfull to their teachers. Wee should always remember that doctrine of Zeno : "Nature (said hee) gave us one tongue, but two eares, that we might heare much, and speak little." Let not any man, therefore, be ready to vomit forth his own shame and ignorance : let him first examine his knowledge, and especially his practice, lest upon the experience of a few violent knacks, hee presume to judge Nature in her very sobrieties. To make an end ; if thou doest know the First Matter, know also for certain, thou hast discovered the sanctuarie of Nature ; there is nothing between thee and her treasures, but the doore : that indeed must be opened. Now if thy desire leads thee on to the practice, consider well with thy self what manner of man thou art, and what is that thou would'st do, for it is no small matter. Thou hast resolved with thyself to be a co-operator with the Spirit of the living God, and to minister to him in his worke of generation. Have a care therefore that thou doest not hinder his work : for if thy heat exceeds the naturall proportion, thou hast stirr'd the wrath of the moyst Natures, and they will stand up against the central fire, and the central fire against them, and there will be a terrible division in the chaos ; but the sweet spirit of peace, the true eternal quintessence, will depart from the elements, leaving both them and thee to confusion ; neither will hee apply himself to that matter, as long as it is in thy violent destroying hands. Take heed, therefore, lest thou turn partner with the Devill, for it is the Devil's designe from the beginning of the world to set Nature at variance with her self, that he may totally corrupt, and destroy her. *Nè tu augeas fatum*, "doe not thou furthur his designs." I make no question but many men will laugh at this, but, on my soule, I speak nothing but what I have known by very good experience ; therefore, believe mee. For my own part, it was ever my desire to bury these things in silence, or to paint them out in shadowes, but I have spoken thus clearly, and openly out of the affection I beare to some, who have deserved much more at my hands. True it is, I intended sometime to expose a greater work to the world, which I promised in my

Anthroposophia, but I have been since aquainted with that world and I have found it base, and unworthie : wherefore I shall keep in my first happy solitudes, for noyse is nothing to me, I seek not any man's applause. If it be the will of my God to call me forth, and that it may make for the honour of his Name, in that respect I may write again, for I feare not the judgment of man, but in the interim here shall be an end.

FINIS.

And now my book, let it not stop thy flight,
That thy just Author is not lord or knight.
I can define myself ; and have the art
Still to present one face, and still one heart.
But for nine years some great ones cannot see
What they have been, nor know they what to bee.
What though I have no rattles to my name,
Do'st hold a simple honestie no fame ?
Or art thou such a stranger to the times,
Thou canst not know my fortunes from my crimes ?
Goe forth, and fear not : some will gladly bee
Thy learned friends whom I did never see,
Nor shouldst thou fear thy welcome : thy small price
Cannot undo 'em, though they pay excise ;
Thy bulk's not great : it will not much distresse
Their emptie pockets, but their studies lesse.
Th' art no Galeon, as books of burthen bee,
Which cannot ride but in a librarie ;
Th' art a fine thing and little : it may chance
Ladies will buy thee for a new romance.
Oh how I'll envy thee when thou art spread
In the bright sun-shine of their eyes, and read
With breath of amber, lips of rose that lend
Perfumes unto their leaves, shall never spend :
When from their white hands they shall let thee fall
Into their bosomes, which I may not call
Ought of misfortune, thou do'st drop to rest
In a more pleasing place, and art more blest.
There in some silken, soft fold thou shalt lye
Hid like their love, or thy own mysterie.
Nor shouldst thou grieve thy language is not fine,
For it is not my best, though it be thine.
I could have voyc'd thee forth in such a dresse,
The spring had been a slut to thy expresse ;
Such as might fill the rude unpolished age,
And fix the reader's soule to ev'ry page :
But I have used a coarse and homely strain,
Because it suits with truth, which should be plain.

Last, my dear book, if any looks on thee
As on three suns, or some great prodigie,
And swear to a full point, I do deride
All other sects, to publish my own pride;
Tell such they lie, and since they love not thee,
Bid them go learne some high-shoe heresie.
Nature is not so simple, but shee can
Procure a solid reverence from man;
Nor is my pen so lightly plum'd that I
Should serve ambition with her majestie.
'Tis truth makes me come forth, and having writ
This her short scaene, I would not stifle it:
For I have call'd it childe, and I had rather
See't torn by them, than strangl'd by the father.

SOLI DEO GLORIA.

Amen.

NOTES.

NOTE 1 (page 5).

THIS is an important and conspicuous instance of direct, though veiled, reference to the most exalted phenomena of the ecstatic trance, to which the common magnetic trance of modern psychology is scarcely the threshold or the stepping-stone. The ancient mystics would appear to have discovered an arcane process for the elevation of hypnotism by which the divine everlasting pneuma was joined for a period to the psyche, or sensitive soul, and the spiritual correspondences of the subject were extended in an upward direction, so as to establish an ineffable intercourse with superior forms of subsistence. This condition of lucidity is unapproached by the operations of mesmerism, which are formed by the intervention and influenced by the special characterization of another and human mind. Now, it must be established as a radical principle, from the true mystic standpoint, that the elaboration of the arch-natural faculties in man can never be accomplished by this process. The creation of the Magus is personal in the strictest sense. "Magnetism between two individuals," says Éliphas Lévi, "is undoubtedly a marvellous discovery, but to create in one's self the magnetic condition, to induce one's own lucidity, and to direct one's own clairvoyance, is the perfection of magical art." Those of impressional temperament, and especially women, who imagine by the subjection of their individuality to a stronger and positive mind to make progress in practical mysticism should learn on the authority of practical mystics that they will not attain their end. Possibly the dangers of ordinary mesmerism in its other than healing branches have been to some extent exaggerated, but it is not exaggeration to affirm that the many mansions of the mystic house of light are not to be discovered by the exploration of blind avenues.

NOTE 2 (page 10).

This passage, as will readily occur to the student, is equivalent to an informal statement of the evolutionary hypothesis, and can also be reconciled with the cosmical expirations and inspirations of Para-Brahma. The substantial identity of the first universal matter or chaos with the philosophical chaos which is the root of the universal medicine, and with the red Adamic earth, is a point of particular importance. This first matter is still the foundation or heart of things, and is said to be strangely secreted in the "very bosome" of Nature. Its application to man is one part of the "grand secret" of the mystics; its extraction from man is another part, and both branches of the art are among those *magnalia Dei et Naturæ* which were piously preserved by the adepts, but are now gradually transpiring.

NOTE 3 (page 13).

The phenomena of vegetable palingenesis, now generally rejected as fabulous, are described seriously by several writers of the past. Duchêne states that he was acquainted at Cracovia with a Polish doctor who had the ashes of numerous plants separately preserved in phials, and that the heat of an ordinary candle was sufficient to revive the perfect simulacrum of a rose. Palingenesis, however, was not confined to plants, and there are ghastly details in such writers as Van der Beck concerning the apparitions of moaning phantoms from the fumes of distilled blood.

NOTE 4 (page 18).

With this fourth essence—the chariot of Nature, the mask of the Almighty, the vestment of the Divine Majesty—may be profitably compared the hypothesis of the Astral Light as elaborated by Lévi. This light he describes in a number of symbolical terms, which are rigorously parallel with those I have just cited—*e.g.*, "the burning body of the Holy Ghost."

NOTE 5 (page 21).

Numerous true recipes for the universal medicine are given in mystic physics, and all in their literal sense have as much value as alchemical formulæ. Such mystifications were often resorted to by even the highest adepts, not excluding "the dark disciple of the more dark Libanius Gallius," the illustrious Trithemius, who has left us the following process :—

The Far-famed Medicinal Powder of Trithemius.

Calami Aromatici.
Gentianæ.
Cimini.
Sileris Montani.
Anisi. } 15 gram. 625 milligr. of each.
Carvi.
Ameos.
Sem. petroselini.
Spicæ nardi.
Coralli rub.
Unionum sive perlarum mes } 156 gr. 250 milligr. of each.
   perforatum.

Zingiberis albi.
Amari dulcis.
Foliorum senæ. } 19 gr. 331 milligr. of each.
Tartari adusti.

Macis.
Cubebarum. } 7 gr. 813 milligr. of each.
Cariophyllorum, 27 gram. 344 milligr.
Reduce into powder.

Dose :—5 gr. 859 milligr. taken morning and evening in brodium or wine, during the first month ; during the second month, in the morning only ; during the third month, thrice a week, and so thenceforward through life. It strengthens the stomach, clears the brain, preserves the sight, invigorates memory, and prevents epilepsy and apoplexy.

NOTE 6 (page 29).

The Great Arcanum, according to Eliphas Lévi, is concerned with the mystery of universal generation ; the " Doctrine and Ritual of Transcendental Magic " contain many important references to the mysticism of the Garden and Tree. Students will be aware that the Pentagram is the sign of the Microcosmos, or Man, and by considering the nature of the Terrestrial Paradise of Man, and the tree which is in the centre of that, the Hermetic Doctrine of Analogy will lead them upward by several singular speculations to the secrets of psychic generation.

NOTE 7 (page 33).

The original edition of *Anthroposophia Theomagica* is embellished with a portrait of Cornelius Agrippa, which it has been deemed unnecessary to reproduce.

NOTE 8 (page 36).

The hypothesis of the astral body, and the part which it plays in the phenomena of apparitions, is now so well known that it scarcely requires explanation, but a full and synthetic account will be found by those who desire it in the third division of " The Mysteries of Magic."

NOTE 9 (page 51).

This passage concerning a " certain chain " in Nature is of high mystical importance. It contains an explanatory theory of the intercommunion of the several worlds of spirits, and of the possibility of our establishing, even in this life, an ecstatic correspondence with other forms of subsistence. This "certain chain" is the Jacob's Ladder whose typology is explained elsewhere in the writings of Eugenius. The union of the individual spirit with the universal god-consciousness, if not actually declared in this passage is at least analogically implied, and a secret of spiritual procreation or multiplication is also hinted at darkly. Those who are resolved to attempt the practical application of mystic principles should apply themselves with particular devotion to the philosophical expositions of this ineffable union which are to be found in the writings of adepts. They will also do well to seek with due discrimination for side-lights in the works of orthodox Christian mystics, who were un-doubtedly in possession of the keys of the process, though they do not seem to have unlocked the most secret doors, and whose principles were developed with more perspicuity than the professed expositors of the mysteries. There is much to be learned from the treatise of S. Bona-ventura, entitled *Itinerarium Mentis ad Deum*, who borrowed from Trismegistus, and seems to have been on the track of the Great Arcana.

NOTE 10 (page 53).

There is one substantial ground for the hope that consistent and painstaking students of the mystics may yet penetrate the "luminous obscurities" of Hermetic allegory, and that ground is the great additional perspicuity which characterises the expositions of the highest pneumatic mysteries, as compared with those upon subjects which, however strange and marvellous, are of indefinitely minor importance to the true soul-seeker. The passages which occasion this remark, and to which this note has reference, are a practically direct explanation of the significance of the magical duad in the three intelligible worlds, and should be marked for particular investigation ; and the hypostatic union of the soul with God is controversially based on analogies alleged to exist in the occult principles of the natural world.

NOTE 11 (page 54).

The evolution of the whole physical cosmos out of a single homogeneous substance of infinite tenuity is a hypothesis which has found favour with the scientists of to-day ; but how motion and differentiation originated in this homogeneous substance has been a serious crux for the theorists. Here in mystic physics we find the same doctrine, that "the original of all things is one thing," that "there is but one matter out of which there are found so many different shapes and constitutions," while the difficulty which has baffled materialism is overcome by recourse to the postulate of "a discerning spirit," which actuates this substance, that divine, intellectual agent which is always ultimately inevitable in any intelligent solution of the great problem of existence. It is worth noting that the fundamental distinction between matter and mind which has serious philosophical obstacles is practically destroyed by this hypothesis in its mystical aspect, which may be briefly epitomized as follows : There is but one substance infinitely differentiated in the universe.

NOTE 12 (pages 56 and 71).

The passages which are considered in this note are devoid of apparent connection, but I have an object in thus combining them which is not at variance even with their obvious significance. With regard to the "pure white Virgin," "the Bride of God and of the Stars," I cannot do better than cite an important passage from the late Edward Vaughan Kenealey's "Book of God," a work which I personally consider to have been written in the interests of a fraudulent theory, but it constitutes, together with its numerous sequels, a mine of theosophy, mythology, and legend, which is scarcely surpassed by "Anacalypsis," or by Cudworth's "Intellectual System."

"God, though One, the ancients did not suppose, as modern ascetics do, to be alone in solitary and morose magnificence. . . . Albeit none could share with HIM, the glory and surpassing majesty of the supreme heaven, they declared nevertheless that He was perpetually surrounded by other gods of light, beauty, purity, and divineness : immortal in their essence, for it emanated from the Most High ; but all proceeding in fiery stream from Him ; and all alike dependent upon His laws, as they were encompassed by His love. Chief among these—pre-eminent in wisdom, loveliness, and all that is essentially celestial and most pure, they held one Divine Nature to be. . . . The golden fancy of the Past exhausted itself in describing the matchless glory of this exalted Being. She was the Virgin-Spirit of most ineffable liveliness ; the Logos, the Protogonos ; the *Mimra-Daya*, or Word of God, by whose intermediate agency the whole spiritual and material Universe was developed, fashioned, beautified, and preserved."

Now, there is an interior and spiritual Virgin in every man, through whom he can work upward to Divinity, and can ascend to the invisible elements of his own undying Pneuma. This Pneuma corresponds in the microcosmos to the uncaused God as the psychal Virgin corresponds to the "Virgin-Spirit." The Psyche is thus the very key and root of the divine mysteries, and through her, in the mystical doctrine of pneumatology, is accomplished the progress to those powers and capacities which are described on page 70.

NOTE 13 (page 85).

The attempts here referred to were from the pen of the illustrious Platonist, Henry More, who in the year 1650 published, under the name of Alazonomastix Philalethes, some "Observations upon *Anthroposophia Theomagica* and *Anima Magica Abscondita*." Two rejoinders were issued by Eugenius—"The Man-Mouse taken in a Trap and tortur'd to Death for gnawing the Margins of Eugenius Philalethes," 1650, 8vo, and "The Second Wash, or the Moore scour'd once more," 1651, 8vo. Both writers had recourse to the scurrility of the period, but in wealth of opprobrious epithets, Thomas Vaughan proved superior to his opponent. He has been termed an irascible alchemist using a Billingsgate phraseology ; but the controversy which obtained him this apposite description is without interest to the modern student of mysticism.

NOTE 14 (page 90).

Believers in the inherent magical virtues of certain signs should take note of this passage, which indiscriminately denounces all ceremonial magic as a gross and material misconception of Hermetic symbolism. Eugenius Philalethes had, however, transcended, at least intellectually, the common elevation of practical magic, which, as he probably never attempted, he may, quite possibly, have misjudged. No sequence of rites and ceremonies may possess an intrinsic virtue, but they educate and direct imagination as well as the will, and though not to be counted as factors in psychic progress are not to be denounced as useless in their own sphere.

NOTE 15 (page 92).

The reunion of Malchuth with the Ilan seems to have been accomplished by the mystics so far as they were individually concerned, and the true method of this re-union is one of the secrets which the modern mystic should set himself to recover.

NOTE 16 (page 115).

It is needless to say that this story, with that of the inscription on Mount Horeb, is in all probability fabulous. I have been personally unable to discover anything concerning it, and as no mystical interest attaches to either, the reservation of the reader's judgment will not involve much difficulty or disappointment.

NOTE 17 (page 136).

In the search for the true process of the spiritual *magnum opus*, the analogical lines of physical alchemy should be rigorously followed, as I have elsewhere stated. The intimate connection of both operations is shown in the passage to which this note is made, and by which it would appear that the process with metals is simply a digression from the process of the mystic medicine. But the medicine itself is pneumatic, and the search for the medicine in its highest sense is the search of the mind after Psyche, of the mind united to Psyche after its own Spirit, and of the hypostatized triplicity after the arch-hypostatic union of the whole man with God.

NOTE 18 (page 141).

If this spiritual and glorified condition be in any way possible for the individual, it is possible in some way for the race. If so, it is the end of evolution, and I hope in a forthcoming work—AZOTH, OR THE STAR IN THE EAST—to show how this end may be accomplished.

NOTE 19 (page 142).

At the beginning of *Anthroposophia Theomagica* this chaos is described as a substance secreted in the very bosom of Nature, and is identified with the Adamic earth. It is evident from the context that the purification of this chaos described in the passage to which these remarks attach, involved an experimental investigation into the substance of life. Of this life the chaos is the first envelope, a point which is sufficient to show the extent to which the philosophers claim to have carried their investigations.

NOTE 20 (page 146).

In this connection it should be marked that a certain *Nox Corporis* would be involved in the evolution of the mystic trance, and this night is apparently the entrance to the *Regio Lucis*.

NOTE 21 (page 151).

This expectation will be commonly identified with the " firm hope of a glorious resurrection," but it admits also of another interpretation. The unceasing yearning of the universal soul of humanity towards a more perfect environment survives the faith in resurrection and does not depend thereon, and her whole physical environment is, in a sense, the soul's body. This desire for a better life, which takes a thousand shapes, may be viewed as a consciousness of the tendency and end of evolution, and evolution, interpreted by mystics, promises that spiritualised perfection of the body which alone the soul expects.

INDEX.

ÆLIA LŒLIA, 131.

Agrippa, Cornelius, not a supreme adept, xxiv. ; his defence by Eugenius, 33 ; calumnies of his detractors, 43-46.

Air, not an element, 18.

Alchemy, the historical radix of modern physics, xxvii.

Alexandrian Philosophy, xxi.

Aleph, Dark and Bright, 12.

Aqua vitæ, a MS. treatise by Thomas Vaughan, viii.

Archetype, 13.

Aristotle and the Peripateticks, 5, 7, 15, 16, 18, 19, 27, 47-50, 54, 74, 82, 88, 107, 129, 149.

Astral Light, Note 4.

Astral Mother, 98.

Astrology, xxv., xxviii.

Aurum Potabile, 108.

Azoth, 127.

Azoth, or the Star in the East, forthcoming work on the Transfiguration of Humanity, Note 18.

BLACK Magic, xxv., xxvii.

Bonaventura, S., his mystical theology, Note 9.

CHAOS, the original darkness, and the philosophical, 10, 12, 14, 16, 17, 118, 132, 139, 149, 150, Note 11, Note 19.

Contemplation, key to the triadic process, xxvi.

DEATH, a recession into the unseen, 34.

EARTH, as a subsidence of the primitive chaos, 17 ; a three-fold earth, 19 ; man made of an arch-natural earth, 22 ; this the subject of the philosophical medicine, 22, Note 2. See also p. 147.

Elements, two in number, 17 ; all elements three-fold, 19 ; four elements in magic, 57 ; magical opera-

tions futile without them, 58 ; Trismegistus on elements, 83.

Empyreall Heaven, 15, 36.

Evolution, xxix., and Note 2.

FALL of man, 9, 24, 92.

Fire of Nature, &c., 16, 18, 57.

Fire of the Philosophers, 143.

Flamel, Nicholas, his Book of Abraham the Jew, 112-114.

Fludd, Robert, his apology for the Rosicrucian order, xxv.

GRAND Magisterium, 65.

Grand mysteries and secrets, Note 9.

HYPNOTISM, exaltation of, xxvii., Note 1.

Hypostatic union, xxvii., Notes 10 and 17.

IMAGINATION of Deity, 14.

JACOB's Ladder, 20, and Note 6.

KABBALAH, an esoteric and pneumatic philosophy, xxiv. ; its greatest mystery is the typology of Jacob's Ladder, 111 ; a true and false Kabbalah, 109.

Kether, 53.

Key of Magic, 56, 89.

Kiss of God and Nature, 60.

—— Death of the Kiss, 111.

LUCIFER, 24.

Lully, Raymond, his penetration to the centre of Nature, 130.

MAGIC, the wisdom of the Creator, 87 ; primevally derived from God, 91.

Magical Records, 69.

Magician's Fire, 57.

Magnesia, Red and White, 126 ; Catholic Magnesia, 127.

Marriage and its mysteries, 23.

Magnet, the Soul's Magnet, 31.

Man, sidereal man, 36 ; once a pure, intellectual being, 27

Matter—the First Matter—God its im-

TURNBULL AND SPEARS, PRINTERS, EDINBURGH.